Through the Door of Life

LIVING OUT

Gay and Lesbian Autobiographies

David Bergman, Joan Larkin, and Raphael Kadushin
SERIES EDITORS

Through the Door of Life

A *Jewish Journey between Genders*

Joy Ladin

The University of Wisconsin Press

The University of Wisconsin Press
1930 Monroe Street, 3rd Floor
Madison, Wisconsin 53711-2059
uwpress.wisc.edu

Printed in the United States of America

Library of Congress Cataloging-in-Publication Data

Ladin, Joy, 1961–
Through the door of life :
a Jewish journey between genders / Joy Ladin.
p.   cm. — (Living out)
ISBN 978-0-299-28730-6 (cloth: alk. paper)
ISBN 978-0-299-28733-7 (e-book)
1. Ladin, Joy, 1961–
2. Jewish transgender people—United States—Biography.
I. Title.   II. Series: Living out.
PS3612.A36Z46   2012
811'.6—dc23
[B]
2011040974

ISBN 978-0-299-28734-4 (pbk.: alk. paper)

For our children

who learn from us

to become themselves

Contents

Part Three
The Door of Life

Acknowledgments

Excerpts from this book have appeared, some in somewhat different form, in *Keep Your Wives from Them* (North Atlantic Books, ed. Miryam Kabakov), *Transgender Outlaws: The Next Generation* (Seal Press, ed. Kate Bornstein and S. Bear Bergman), and *Balancing on the Mechitza: Transgender in the Jewish Community* (North Atlantic Books, ed. Noach Dzmura), as well as in *Tikkun, Prairie Schooner, Moment, Lilith, Southwest Review, Parnassus, New Haven Review, Feminist Studies, The King's English,* and *American Journal of Nursing*. The writing of the book was partially supported by a research grant from Yeshiva University, to which I am grateful for welcoming me in both my gender presentations and which showed great courage in becoming the first Orthodox Jewish institution to employ an openly transsexual employee. I am proud to be associated with YU's act of *tikkun olam*, repairing the broken world. I am also grateful to Cole Thaler, Tom Ude and their Lambda Legal colleagues who generously donated their services to help Yeshiva University and me through this difficult process.

This book wouldn't have been written without the prompting of Susan Loud, my therapist, who urged me to write autobiographically despite my lack of either a life or a self to write about it. Nancy Mayer's encouragement, affection, and unerring ethical compass guided me throughout the writing and transition processes.

Nothing of the person I have become would have been possible without the wisdom and love of Annie Kantar Ben Hillel. I was mothered through the tough early stages of transition by Barbara Dana, and I will always be grateful for the friendship and writing fellowship of my colleague Ann Peters, as well as of others too numerous to mention who contributed to the events and perspectives described in the pages that follow. This book might never have seen the light of day (or narrative coherence) without the dedication of Kent Wolf of Global Literary Agency. Like its author, the book has benefited immeasurably from the loving attention of Elizabeth Campbell Denlinger.

Through the Door of Life

A Blessing

Every day I say a blessing in Hebrew over my medication: "Blessed are You, O Lord our God, who has kept us, preserved us, and brought us to this time." That blessing is traditionally said at the beginnings of holidays, on the eating of new kinds of fruit, and at any joyous occasion at which Jews want to heighten their sense of gratitude by becoming mindful of the singularity of the moment and the precariousness of the lives that have brought us to it. It is not said on the taking of medication; it is specifically *not* to be said over daily events, for which there are different blessings; and it is never said over a disease.

The medications I take—progesterone tablets, which I swallow whole, and sweet circles of estrogen that I dissolve under my tongue—are synthetic versions of the powerful hormones that naturally define and regulate many of the physiological characteristics of normal female bodies. I don't have a normal female body. Born without the capacity to produce more than trace amounts of female hormones, for decades my body instead has produced testosterone, masculinizing my face, bones, muscle, hair, and skin.

Though there are few aspects of my physical form unravaged by testosterone's effects, thanks to my medication, those effects are diminishing. For the first time in my life, when I look in the mirror, I see someone who has begun to resemble—me.

I never thought I would see myself in the mirror. I never thought I would hold the means to become myself in my hands, that I would taste it dissolving under my tongue. Every day that I take this medication brings me slowly—very slowly, for there is so much to change and my body is so reluctant after all these years—closer to being the person I have always paradoxically wished to become and known myself to be.

At a stage in life—middle age—when many face the facts of mortality, I am experiencing rebirth—or at least, re-adolescence. This perhaps is only fair, since I spent so much of my life as a ghost, haunting a body that didn't feel like mine. Rather than embodying my identity, my body erased me, proved that I didn't, couldn't, exist. Now, every day, my body and I move closer toward belonging to each other.

This transformation is more than physical. As my body learns to metabolize and distribute fat according to female rather than male patterns, I am learning to live and to be alive. The sophistications accumulated over four and a half decades, the blasé attitudes, the taken-for-granted mechanics of daily life have all fallen away. Consumed by the ravenous insecurities of adolescence, I am shy, awkward, always verging on the inappropriate, a maelstrom of feeling and need, fear and excitement. The first times such identity-forming growth spurts happened, I was an infant, then an adolescent, too young and too caught up in the painful processes of becoming to register them as miracles. I have watched these processes as a parent, but I never expected—I had given up hope and was perhaps too foolish to fear—that one day I would be watching myself learn to walk and talk again, to say hello to grown-ups, to order in restaurants, to shop for clothes, to make friends. All this has become new again. Going to work, riding a subway, making a business call—each experience has become an adventure, uncomfortable, unpredictable, brimming with emotion and discovery.

But this newness is only the beginning of the blessings my illness has brought me. While I hid in the shell of my pretreatment body—a body that, though monstrous to me, was accepted as normal by those around me—I felt I stood outside the human species, a species heartbreakingly beautiful and dauntingly strange, composed of creatures who belonged to and with each other. I loved humanity from afar, passionately but impotently, giving little of myself, because I had no real self to give. And, honestly, what *could* I know of love, when my every act and word presumed that I would be instantly rejected by anyone who saw through the shell of my maleness to the unrealized creature squirming within? My self was a tissue of terrors and lies, an automated, reflexive cowardice perfected as a child. If love is based on authenticity, I was incapable of it, for I had never lived a day, a moment, as my true self.

And so it has come as a profound shock to discover, at the time of my greatest vulnerability, that I am surrounded by love. As I have become known to those around me—people from whom I had always hidden—I have been met again and again with compassion, acceptance, tenderness, a generosity of spirit that seems to have no limits. A few have embodied my worst nightmares of rejection. But my overwhelming experience has been to find myself in relationship to the finest, most loving human beings I can imagine. And, because I am once again at that awkward age, when every discovery breeds a new insecurity, a new challenge, a new possibility of failure, I feel dwarfed among these grown-up souls for whom loving and giving are as inevitable as breathing. Is it too late for me to learn to follow their examples? It is far too late to be asking such a question, but it is still too soon to answer. All I know is I am filled with love, too much love, love straining the cramped circumference within which I have always lived. Perhaps this problem is the ultimate blessing. What, I wonder, will I ever *do* with all this love?

Every day brings me closer to becoming the person who not only can but must answer. And so, every day, when I take the medication that is making this possible, I say the blessing that registers the wonder and privilege of being, the awe and responsibility of becoming: *Baruch atah Adoshem, Elokeinu melech ha-olam, shehechiyanu, v'kiyemanu, v'higeyanu, la-zman ha-zeh.*

Introduction

A Funny Thing Happened
on the Way to Stern College

September 2008

If I am not for myself, who is for me? If I am for myself alone,
what am I? And if not now, when?

Rabbi Hillel, *Pirkei Avot* 1:14

It was a beautiful New York September day, sunny, warm but
not hot, with a sky so blue it seemed to laugh at the hard-
nosed realism of the skyscrapers thrusting into it. As I walked south
from Grand Central to begin the fall 2008 semester at Stern College
for Women of Yeshiva University, I smiled into every face I could,
eager to share the fact that miracles can happen. I was a miracle,
my walk was a miracle, and even the most dubious citizen of this
most skeptical of cities would have to admit that the job toward
which I was walking was a certifiable miracle.

I hadn't done much smiling since I began my transition from
living as a man to living as a woman, a process that had shaken
and shattered nearly every aspect of my life. Though my gender
had felt wrong as long as I can remember, I had grown up as a
more or less normal boy in upstate New York, graduated early
from high school, and went to Sarah Lawrence College in search
of people who were as obsessed with poetry and intellectual
conversation as I was. During freshman orientation, I met the
woman with whom I would spend the next quarter of a century.

7

After graduation and a few weeks on the cheap in Europe, we moved to San Francisco, got married, and shared a decade of bad apartments and young-writer angst while I worked at The State Bar of California. Eventually, I went back to school in search of a career as a poet. My MFA in creative writing led to a PhD in American literature and to the life of a wandering academic. I taught at Princeton, Tel Aviv University (on a Fulbright scholarship), Reed College, and the University of Massachusetts at Amherst before I finally landed a tenure-track job at Stern that enabled me to combine my love of writing and literature with my love of Judaism. As I struggled to write and publish enough to complete degrees, get jobs, and earn tenure, my wife and I had three children, a son and two daughters. Our third was born right before I started commuting from our home in Massachusetts to my new job at Stern in August 2003. My first book of poetry, *Alternatives to History*, appeared that fall; my second, *The Book of Anna*, came out three years later, in 2006, and added enough weight to my CV to enable me to apply for early tenure.

Early tenure had been my goal since I started my PhD; it was the only way I could imagine supporting a growing family and mortgage-size student loans. But by the time *Anna* was published, my anxiety about mounting debt was eclipsed by a different kind of fear. The transsexuality I had fought to hide since I was a child was slowly making life unlivable. Unable to eat, unable to sleep, unable to think about anything but gender, I knew that it was only a matter of time before I could no longer live as a man. If I didn't receive tenure—and the protection of lifetime employment—before my transsexuality became apparent, I would be out of a job and my family would be out on the street.

Stern is the women's college of Yeshiva University, modern Orthodox Judaism's premier institution of higher learning, and Orthodox Judaism, like most traditional forms of religion, considers the things transsexuals do to fit our bodies to our souls to be sins. In my case, those sins included wearing women's clothing and taking hormones that destroyed my fertility. I was also violating customs and conceptions of gender that, while not mandated by Jewish law, are held to with religious conviction by many Orthodox

Jews—and that, I was sure, would make it impossible for Yeshiva University to continue to employ me.

Tenure came just in time, in June 2007, after a semester during which I struggled to get through classes without either sobbing or passing out. Although tenure was the triumphant culmination of my fifteen-year fight to establish myself in academia, it didn't make me happy. My gender identity crisis had destroyed my marriage, shattered my family, and turned me into an unwelcome stranger in my own home. Within weeks, I had moved into the first of a series of rented bedrooms. My children were grief stricken, angry, and baffled by the double blow of losing their happy family and the strange transformation of the father they loved.

A couple of weeks after receiving tenure, I wrote to the dean, explaining my transition. Stern's response informed me that although the school would keep me on the payroll, I was not allowed to set foot on campus. My "involuntary research leave," as the university called it, was the best-funded and most courteous form of discrimination imaginable, but it was still discrimination. Cut off from students I loved, expelled from the vocation I had worked so hard to master, I felt wounded in a way that was hard to explain; I couldn't shake the sense that my expulsion was my fault, that I was too repulsive to be seen on campus.

As so many transsexuals have found, the world exacts a steep price—home, family, friends, job—for the dream-come-true of becoming ourselves.

But, just as I'd begun to accept that my exile from Stern was permanent, a miracle happened. When my attorneys demanded that I be allowed to return to teaching for the fall 2008 semester—a demand they expected to be rebuffed—the university said "yes." We spent the summer negotiating conditions, including which bathrooms (single-stall unisex only) I would be permitted to use. Finally, September arrived, and, with it, my first happy day in a long time. After years of hiding and pretending, I was finally going to stand before my students and colleagues as the person—the woman—I knew myself to be. More important, after centuries of intolerance, an institution representing Orthodox Judaism was about to welcome an openly transgender employee.

As I had done when I was a man, I took the train into Grand Central and walked the ten blocks south to Stern. The revolving glass door spun symbolically as I passed through it; for a moment, the long, hard road from the man I wasn't to the woman I was seemed to be a circle, sweeping me back to the life I thought I'd lost. The escalator elevated me past laughing, smiling, chattering students, none of whom gave me a second glance. They weren't being polite; even those who'd seen me for years as a man didn't recognize me as a woman. Usually, it's students who worry about passing; today, it was me. Their indifference proved that they saw me as a woman, rather than as a man trying to look like one.

I checked my mailbox, ducked into the single-stall handicapped restroom, adjusted my clothes, necklace, and makeup, and charged up seven flights of stairs to the floor where I worked and taught. My office was heaped with the same stacks of papers, the same teaching anthologies, but the name beside the door said "Dr. Joy Ladin." It was a miracle. I—the real me—was here, in plain sight. I walked through the halls, waiting for my transition to matter to someone. It didn't. Teachers rushed to and fro, students talked on cell phones or swayed back and forth in prayer. Everyone had more important things to do than think about my gender. I couldn't believe it. Here, in the heart of the Orthodox Jewish world, a transwoman was neither a curiosity nor a monstrosity; I was just another middle-aged woman going about her business.

But to the *New York Post*, I was news. I had known the *Post* was going to write about my return to Stern. The author of the article was a former student of mine, and, though I had refused to speak to her on the record, she had shown me a draft, a thoughtful look at the process that had led to Yeshiva's decision to allow me to return to work that wouldn't have been out of place in the *New York Times*. The article said appropriately little about me. After all, I wasn't news; what was news was Yeshiva University's acceptance of my transition. So, when a *Post* photographer met me outside Stern, I smiled and turned away to the comforting work of academia.

The published article, splashed across page three, complete with before and after pictures, no longer bore any resemblance to anything in the *Times*:

A Yeshiva University professor left two years ago as a man—and returned last week as a woman.

> Literature Professor Joy Ladin, formerly known as Jay Ladin, 47, showed up for her first day of school sporting pink lipstick, a tight purple shirt and a flirty black skirt. . . .
>
> Many at the Jewish university are horrified by the presence of the transgender professor. Some fear the news could cut alumni donations.

My shirt *was* purple, my lipstick pink, and my skirt black, but the claim that the shirt was "tight" and the skirt "flirty" turned out to be quite controversial, with lively Internet debates among Orthodox Jews over whether, as the Post had implied, I was immodestly dressed. But even an immodestly dressed female teacher at Stern wouldn't make page three of the *Post* unless she, like me, had previously taught there as a man. "YE-SHE-VA," the headline gleefully shouted, spawning the first of many wit-challenged headlines ("Putting the 'Oy' Back in Joy," "Joy Returns, but All Are Not Joyful"). The *Post*'s quasi-literate sniggers weren't surprising. Cross-dressed men have been staples of Western humor since time immemorial (Thor even appears in Norse mythology in drag). The *Post*'s before and after photos and the article's assertion that I had "retained the most prominent part of [my] manhood" ensured that readers would get the joke—or, rather, would get the idea that I, as a transsexual, was something to laugh at. Thanks to the miracle of the Internet, Jews and non-Jews around the world were able to chortle over and weigh in on the spectacle of my return to teaching. Rabbis gave sermons about me in yeshivas in Israel; AM DJs around the United States ruminated on whether I looked like a "real woman"; newspapers as far away as Vietnam and China kept their readers apprised; bloggers and online commentators held forth on everything from the quality of my character (many, including a neo-Nazi group, agreed that I was a coward for waiting to come out until I had tenure) to the quality of my sandals (the consensus was that they were ugly but looked comfortable).

But, even for the *Post*, the joke of transsexuality is stale. Few New York–area transsexuals make tabloid headlines. What made my story tabloid-worthy was the incongruity of a transsexual, the quintessence of a secular individualism that says we are all free to define our identities, teaching at an institution for which identity, including gender, is defined in terms of divine law. Transsexuals (in tight shirts and flirty skirts, no less) and Orthodox Jews—what could be funnier?

Orthodox Jews, of course, weren't laughing. (Neither were members of the trans community, who were appalled by the *Post*'s dehumanizing portrayal.) Though Yeshiva University maintained official silence about me, the *Post* found a faculty member who was willing to voice Orthodox "horror" at my presence. Rabbi Moshe Tendler, who, as the *Post* noted, is "a senior dean at Yeshiva's rabbinical school and a professor of biology and medical ethics," didn't mince words about me: "'He's not a woman. He's a male with enlarged breasts. . . . He's a person who represents a kind of amorality which runs counter to everything Yeshiva University stands for. There is just no leeway in Jewish law for a transsexual.'"

Rabbi Tendler's comments suggest a startling (for a professor of biology and medical ethics) ignorance of the complexities of gender, and, as a number of Orthodox commentators noted, they violate Jewish laws that require that individuals be spoken of with respect and compassion. A number of Orthodox Jews publicly distanced themselves from his remarks; others applauded his willingness to publicly state that there is no place for a transsexual in traditional Judaism.

Much as I'd like to dismiss Rabbi Tendler's remarks as ignorant and narrow-minded, the fact is that they represent feelings that are alive and well among Jews and non-Jews alike. However inappropriate in tone, his comments crystallize issues raised by transsexual transition and attitudes faced by transsexuals, inside and outside the Jewish world.

The first issue, of course, is what, exactly, someone like me is: a woman, a "male with enlarged breasts," or something that explodes traditional definitions of gender? That question can be hard enough to answer in secular contexts—to this day my children argue about what to call me, and, no matter how transwomen look or live, the Social Security Administration won't acknowledge us as female until we present written proof of gender reassignment surgery. But no matter how confusing my gender identity might be, my children still consider me their parent, and the government accepts me as a citizen. Gender identity is so central to tradition-based communities such as Orthodox Judaism that it is more or less impossible for those communities to accommodate people who can't be easily identified as male or female. For example, unmarried Orthodox men and women are not supposed to touch one another; when observant Jewish men and women meet me, are they allowed to shake my hand?

Though people on the left tend to be less hostile than Rabbi Tendler when talking about gender, gender norms are embraced and enforced across the political spectrum. For example, Germaine Greer, the feminist writer, might be horrified to be told she had anything in common with Rabbi Tendler, but she has referred to transwomen as "ghastly parodies" of women. The Orthodox Jewish question of who, if anyone, should shake my hand is mirrored in feminist debates over whether transwomen should be allowed to attend women-only events and to appear in women-only groups and spaces. (One prominent event, the Michigan Womyn's Music Festival, states in its ads that only those born female are welcome.)

But Rabbi Tendler isn't only worried about what I am; he is worried about what I mean. Gender is a language, a way we tell one another who we are and how we fit into society. For Rabbi Tendler, my presentation of myself as female didn't say that I was a woman; it said that I embrace "a kind of amorality," because I reject the distinctions—male and female, light and dark, good and evil—that are the basis of traditional morality. If, as my transition proclaims, a man can "be" a woman, then there *are* no absolute distinctions and thus no basis for moral judgment.

Never underestimate the power of a tight purple shirt and a flirty black skirt.

But I don't mean to be dismissive. I've agonized over the moral implications of transsexuality longer than Rabbi Tendler ever will. I started as a six-year-old, tormenting myself for not being the boy my parents thought I was and for not having the courage to tell them the truth about me. For decades, not a day passed when I didn't feel the secret shame of presenting myself as someone I knew I wasn't. I tried to be a good boy and man—I did my homework, took out the garbage, was faithful to my wife, and supported her so that she could devote herself to her writing. I rose at 4 a.m. to work on my MFA thesis so that I would be ready to hold our first child when he woke before dawn; I typed my dissertation with one hand while standing up and rocking our second, who had colic. In short, I was a good man, the very embodiment of what Rabbi Tendler would call "a kind of morality."

But, for me, being a good man meant being a bad person. Every time I presented myself as a man—to my wife, to my children, to my students, to my colleagues—I was lying, being a coward, betraying the deepest truths about myself, choosing to live in misery rather than in the state of gratitude and joy that Judaism celebrates as the birthright and obligation of humanity.

My transition didn't resolve the moral paradoxes of transsexuality; it simply reversed the terms. Once I began living as a woman, I felt I was being honest and brave and living the only life I could embrace in gratitude and joy—but, by ceasing to live as a man, I was destroying my marriage and my family, bringing grief and confusion to those I loved. My transition exposed my employer, which had given me tenure on the basis of the reasonable assumption that I would remain male, to ridicule, controversy, and the risk of litigation, and plunged my colleagues and students into uncomfortable and uncharted social waters.

According to Rabbi Tendler, Judaism cannot help me navigate this dense web of conflicting moral obligations, because to be a transsexual is to automatically be excommunicated: "There is just no leeway in Jewish law for a transsexual. . . . There is no niche where he can hide out as a female without being in massive violation of Torah law, Torah ethics and Torah morality." Of course, Rabbi Tendler misunderstands transsexuality; I felt I was female before I transitioned, and, since Jewish law governs actions rather than feelings, no "leeway in Jewish law" is required to be a transsexual. He also misunderstands the nature of my transition. While some transsexuals erase their former identities when they transition, I would never have returned to Yeshiva—much less smiled for a

Post photographer—if I was trying to "hide out as a female." But Rabbi Tendler voices a fear that haunts devout trans Jews and other transpeople who long for connection to traditional religions and communities: the fear that, to become whole in ourselves, we have to amputate themselves from our religions, from our communities, from the deep wells of traditional wisdom that are the birthright of human beings who, unlike us, are comfortable with the gender into which they're born.

But Rabbi Tendler is wrong. Those who feel that "Torah law, Torah ethics and Torah morality" and other wisdom traditions offer transsexuals nothing more than condemnation might usefully remember Rabbi Hillel's famous questions in the first chapter of *Pirkei Avot* (*The Ethics of the Fathers*): "If I am not for myself, who will be? If I am for myself alone, what am I? And if not now, when?"

Hillel's questions confront us with the uncomfortable fact that, trans or nontrans, we all have to become ourselves—not just once, by growing from childhood into adulthood, but throughout our lives. Becoming can be terrifying. I avoided it as long as I could, and, when my gender crisis made avoidance impossible, I felt utterly lost. It was easy to find information about the medical treatments and social retraining necessary for people born and raised as men to act like and be seen as women, but I didn't want to simply act like and be seen as. I'd done that all my life. I wanted something more from transition. After decades of being a persona, I wanted to become a person.

And so, like generations of Jews before me, I looked to Hillel. His questions transformed what seemed to me metaphysical impossibilities into concrete choices. "If I am not for myself, who will be?" Hillel didn't have to know anything about transsexuality to know that the answer to that is "no one." No one expected me, needed me, or even wanted me to become myself. In fact, my family clearly needed me not to become myself. My journey toward becoming a person could begin only with the radical act of being-for-myself suggested by Hillel's question. Being-for-myself seemed selfish, solipsistic, even psychotic, for I would have to be for a self that didn't yet exist. But Hillel showed me, in the plainest possible terms, that if I wasn't for myself, my self would never be.

Hillel's first question leads inexorably to his second: being for myself was only the first step toward becoming a person, because "If I am for myself alone, what am I?" Over the years, I allowed myself moments of being for myself, of letting myself surreptitiously, guiltily, relax the rigid discipline that ensured that I would always sit and walk and talk like a male, and instead feel, for a second, like the girl or woman I knew myself to be. But those episodes were few and far between, and they always left me feeling empty. They didn't transform me into myself; they seemed to prove I had no self to become. Hillel wouldn't be surprised. We become ourselves with and through other people. My sense of myself as female was a private matter of being for myself. But being a woman is much more than a sense of being female. It is more than wearing certain clothes or sitting in certain postures, more even than having certain chromosomes and reproductive organs. Women remain women even after double mastectomies and hysterectomies. "Woman" designates a social status, the achievement of a mature female identity in the world. When I was for myself alone, what was I? A wish, a longing, a perversion, a disappointment, a half-remembered, shameful dream. No matter how fiercely I insisted that I was female, if I wanted to become a woman, I had to remake myself in the eyes of others, to be for and with them as the self I felt driven to become.

But Hillel's question is more than a call to come out of the closet. It is also a demand that we take responsibility for the consequences to others of our becoming. If I am not, cannot be, for myself alone, if I need others to become myself, then I cannot ignore the pain that results from my becoming. However much I've suffered, my self and my life are no more important than the suffering selves and shattered lives of those whose destinies are tangled with mine. People I love are in anguish as a consequence of my transition, and, unless I acknowledge that that anguish is as real as the anguish that drove me to transition, I will be for myself alone—and if I am for myself alone, what am I? The fact is that the best moments of the life I am making will always be intertwined with the worst moments of the lives of those I love. It isn't fair; it isn't what I want or intend; but it is true. For most of my life, I tried to be for others without being for myself—to be the man they needed me to be, to suppress and deny the woman I felt I was. Once I began to transition, I wanted desperately to do the opposite, to insist that, after all the years of self-denial I had given them, their feelings didn't matter, to demand that they embrace and support the miraculous, cataclysmic process of my transition from death to life. Hillel's question forced me to recognize that to become a person, a real person and not someone acting like a woman, I had to be both for myself and for others, to be as true, as compassionate, as present to my family and friends as I was to myself.

Being for myself, being for others—it all sounds very static. "Being," after all, is the most minimal possible verb; it doesn't specify any action beyond mere existence. Hebrew doesn't even bother to assign a word for it: there's no "is," no "am." And that is why Hillel's final question, "If not now, when?," is so important. It reminds us that being demands becoming, that without constant, urgent, complete commitment, we cease to be.

For most of my life, it seemed that the answer to "If not now, when?" was "never." My certainty that I would never be for myself or anyone else was so complete that I couldn't even think of becoming as a process. I imagined simply waking up in a magical now in which I suddenly was a girl or woman—and, since I knew that could never happen, I tried to accept that I would never, in Hillel's sense, be. Once I made the difficult commitment to transition—once I answered the question "If not now, when?" by saying "*now*"—I expected instantly to become myself. But transition didn't magically transport me from life as an imitation man to life as a real woman. I had to create that now—the now of becoming myself—not through one magic "Yes!" but through innumerable, sometimes agonizing decisions, choices, commitments. And, as I made those decisions, choices, and commitments and lived through their consequences, I found that I was slowly becoming the self I had waited my whole life to be—not a self alone but a self responsive and responsible to those around me, a self who was for them as well as for myself. That process continues, for every day I have to answer the questions that are the essence of becoming.

Transsexuals' lives may seem strange, even bizarre, but the questions we face in becoming ourselves are the questions life poses to us all: how can we become ourselves? How can we put the selves we are becoming into meaningful, moral relationship to others? And, when we finally become ourselves, who will we be?

*Part
One*

Who Will Be

1
Things Fall Apart

Summer 2005

A man is standing in the shower. It's the weekend, it's Saturday, it's sunny, he's in his thirties, his early forties, taking a long, hot weekend shower, listening to his family—first one child, then another, then three together—screaming happily with their mother, the woman he has loved and been loved by since he was seventeen. It's the weekend, it's Saturday, he is taking a long, hot shower listening to the intimate noise of his happy family. It's a moment of private, steaming leisure that happens over and over.

Some part of the man is glowing far away, or far below, or somewhere within. This glow is happiness, he tells himself. There is another feeling, too, a burning sensation, like magnesium blazing in water, a white-hot flame defying the cold, numb element— him—that threatens to smother it. That's love, he tells himself. He is burning with love for his family, glowing with happiness at the sound of their happiness, and yet he is far away, or far below, or somewhere within, watching the blaze of his most intimate connections shimmer as though through fathoms of water. These are among the strongest feelings he has ever had, and yet he cannot feel them.

Because he is the kind of person who always talks to God, he says to God, "You see how much I love them. You see that I'm happy. Thank you, it's enough for me, it's more than I ever imagined." And then he adds, "I'm so tired, God." And then, as the pain of the distance between himself and the life he is living overwhelms him, he prays a prayer he knows can never be forgiven: "If it's okay with you, and it would be okay for them, please let me die."

Eventually, the man gets out of the shower. The happiness, the love, the pain—so intertwined he can't imagine one without the others—sink to bearable levels. He settles back into his sleeve of numbness: skin, shirt, trousers. When he opens the bathroom door, he smiles. He knows this will happen over and over. It is a sign— the stigmata, he might have thought, if he had grown up on the right-hand side of the Judeo-Christian hyphen—of a good life, the very best life he can permit himself to imagine. And someday, he promises himself, this good life will finally be over, and he won't have to endure his distance from it any longer.

There are reasons for his distance, his despair. The sex of the body he was given is at odds with the gender of what therapists might call his psyche and religious people might call his soul. He calls it his "self," and, although it is faint, wispy, formless, without a life or a body to live it, although no one, not even he, has ever glimpsed it, it is the only part of him that has ever felt real. His insistence on—or is it knowledge of?—the reality of the least lived aspect of his life has terrible consequences for the other aspects. They hardly feel real—they hardly feel—at all. He knows that this absence of feeling, this unreality—and the ache and vertigo and desire for death that accompany it—is called "gender dysphoria." He knows that gender dysphoria has always been with him; he knows it will never go away.

What he doesn't know is that every day that he fails to live that unrealized self, his gender dysphoria will grow worse. More painful. More disorienting. Harder to live with. More costly to ignore.

I spent the summer of 2005 trying to learn how to make frozen coffee for my wife. During the semester I spent teaching at Tel Aviv University in 2002, my wife discovered that, when the temperature reaches the eighties, frozen—not iced—coffee becomes the height of pleasure. Frozen coffee is expensive, and, in a family of five subsisting on the income of a bottom-rung academic, it was a taste she couldn't often indulge. So she dug out the unused blender I had bought her as a birthday present in a display of husbandly obtuseness—"Why did you think I would want a *blender?*" she'd asked; oddly enough, the question had never occurred to me— and started throwing in ingredients. The results, she told me, were disastrous. I recognized a mission, a way to demonstrate my love by exposing myself to her criticism for the sake of giving her pleasure.

By that point, nothing I did gave her pleasure. Life as we had known it had ended in the spring, when my gender dysphoria became acute. I lost thirty pounds in a matter of weeks and found it difficult to eat, sleep, or imagine life beyond the horizon of anguish.

As luck would have it, my illness reached crisis about the time I learned that I had won a research fellowship from the American Council of Learned Societies that would enable me to spend the 2005–6 academic year writing at home in Massachusetts instead of commuting to and from New York City to teach. Our three children would soon be home from school, the weather was gorgeous, we had recently moved into the first house we had ever owned, and I was looking forward to a year of writing, parenting, and renewing a marriage frayed by years of commuting to a job two states away.

Few male-to-female transsexuals' romantic partnerships survive transition; the number of heterosexual women who want their life partners to become female is vanishingly small. Though I wanted my marriage to be one of the blessed exceptions, I knew it was unlikely. I doubted I would want to stay married if my wife started living as a man.

For my wife, as for many partners of transsexuals, my transition represented the ultimate rejection, a statement that I would rather deform a perfectly good male body and face social ostracism than spend my life with her. Her feelings were compounded by isolation. There isn't much support for transsexuals; there is almost none for transsexuals' partners. The literature, treatment protocols, and support systems, such as they are, focus on transsexuals' needs, transsexuals' traumas, the psychosocial drama or medical technicalities of transsexual self-realization. When partners are addressed at all, it tends to be in terms of how they can and should support the transition process. Nonsupportive partners are portrayed as problems to be coped with, rather than as suffering individuals in their own right. (Arlene Istar Lev's *Transgender Emergence*, a groundbreaking book for therapists working with transgendered people and their families, is a happy and hopeful exception.)

It wasn't clear how learning to make my wife frozen coffee was going to make up for my transition. But the coffee I made wasn't coffee. It was a dark, icy, too-sweet, nonfat-milk-laced embodiment of the love my wife could no longer believe I felt for her. If I kept demonstrating that love, if I kept taking care of her, if I kept doing things to give her pleasure . . .

I never figured out how to complete that sentence. My wife saw me as choosing self-mutilation over her, over the life we had painstakingly built up since we were teenagers, over our future, over our past, over the well-being of our children. Day after day, I was forcing her to witness the slow erasure of the man she loved. The hair on my head got longer. My body hair disappeared. My voice and manner of speaking altered. I was destroying myself before her eyes for the sake of a game of dress-up. "It's murder," she told me, "even though you will never be convicted."

We still shared the same small house, our daily lives were completely intermeshed, but we were now living in parallel universes. To my wife, every change I made was an obscene blow aimed at the heart of our love. To me, the changes I was making were too little too late. My brain was rejecting my body, as though it were an incompatible transplanted organ. I was constantly nauseated, suffered diarrhea no matter what I ate, woke constantly during the night, loathed the very feel of my skin on my bones. Jane Bowles wrote: "Most people spend their lives fleeing from their first fear toward their first hope." My first hope—to become myself—was inseparable from my first fear: that becoming myself not only would make me unlovable but would be fatal to those I love.

I spent my childhood trying to be what people wanted me to be. I taught myself to be nice rather than good, to be accommodating rather than honest, to be male rather than female. I'm still angry at that miserable, self-betraying child, who never managed to find the courage to tell anyone he was other than he seemed to be.

Maybe I should be more forgiving. He was, after all, only a kid. In preschool, he had literally run after girls, desperate to find a way to join them. They giggled and screeched and ran away, claiming he was trying to kiss them. He pretended they were right—that got tolerant nods from adults in the area, and at least he was playing with them. By kindergarten, he had taught himself to turn away whenever he glimpsed anything—a doll or a dress or girls laughing with each other—that might crack the façade of maleness and betray what he was within. By age eight, his discipline was absolute. He learned, via a sort of self-imposed hysterical blindness, to notice nothing of the girl-world that was the object of his longings.

Instead, he devoted himself to passing as a boy. (Learning to *be* a boy was a separate problem, one he never solved.) Of course, he was a strange boy, but he found ways to get by. In fifth grade, he called himself a pacifist so that he wouldn't have to fight and got beaten up every day by a gang of kids who wanted to see if he would stay a pacifist when they were pummeling his head and back. He never told his parents. He was ashamed of hiding behind pacifism when he knew there were other reasons he wasn't fighting. He developed nonathletic roles during team games—announcer was his favorite—but, as he got older, he found that disconnection from the body is a plus in contact sports. He didn't care how much things hurt, a fact his parents almost discovered one night when they saw him carrying a dinner plate in the wrong hand. He had broken his wrist at the bottom of a pile during "kill the kid with the ball" and kept on playing. It never occurred to him to complain about the odd feelings in his wrist. Hurting himself felt good—it was a kind of revenge on the body that was always hurting him, and a kind of freedom, a way of showing how little he and his body meant to each other.

But there was one situation in which his—my—dissociation cracked. Her name was Wendy. We used to walk home together in fourth grade. To me, we were natural best friends—two pale, freckled, serious, unathletic girls with curly hair who loved reading and talking about books. But to Wendy, and to everyone else, I wasn't a girl, and, as a result, no one quite knew what to make of our friendship. We were teased for being boyfriend and girlfriend. We knew that was ridiculous—but even Wendy and I didn't know how to describe what we were to each other. She moved away the following September—and when she visited a couple of years later, a visit I anticipated eagerly for months, we were estranged by incipient adolescence. To me, she was the one girl I had ever been able to befriend, the closest I had ever come to the life I longed for. To her, I was a boy, and she found my talk, my smiles, my very presence unbearable. She avoided me for several days and vanished forever.

Perhaps I should have told her what I was. After all, she was the daughter of anthropologists, and she loved polysyllabic terms as much as I did. Perhaps the word "transsexual" would have enabled us to cement the friendship the difference between our bodies destroyed. When I met Wendy, I had already known that word for two years. I was eight, haunting my mother's side of the parental bedroom. There was a women's magazine—*Good Housekeeping*, I think—on my mother's night table. Normally I averted my eyes from such things. But transsexuals have a sixth sense that leads us toward anything that might disentomb our buried selves. Something told me to pick up the magazine, to thumb through endless ads for girdles and feminine napkins until I reached the story blurbed on the cover, a first-person account by a mother coming to terms with the transformation of her son into her daughter. It was, no doubt, a touching saga of pain and reconciliation, but for me the most moving part was the information. This was the first time I had language for what I was, the first inkling that there were others like me. This woman's child had felt what I felt—and had found a way to do what I thought was impossible: to become herself. I read surreptitiously, as fast as I could, heart pounding, terrified I would be discovered by my parents. By the time I reached the end and slammed the magazine down—had anyone heard?—in exactly the same position on my mother's night table, I knew who I was and what I had to do. I was a transsexual, and there were hormones I would take and an operation I would undergo that would someday turn me into the true self that no one, not even me, had ever seen.

I didn't know when this transformation would happen. Though I was quite sure *my* mother wouldn't embrace me the way the woman telling the story had embraced her child, after reading that story, I tried again and again to screw up the courage to explain what I was to my parents, to ask them to help me become myself. After days of silence turned into months and months of silence turned into years, I gave up. The child who was often criticized for never shutting up couldn't find words to explain what he was and how much it hurt to be that way.

Adolescence began to deform me. I dressed in the dark and avoided mirrors like a vampire, and for the same reason—I wasn't there in the reflection. I often arrived at school in shirts that were inside out and backward. I didn't brush my hair—even at fifteen, my mother had to—and it grew wild in all directions. I couldn't bear to cut it, like a boy, and I couldn't permit myself to arrange it, like a girl. I refused to show any concern for my body, even so much as wearing a coat during the upstate New York winter. I walked the two miles to high school in a denim shirt over a T-shirt. My body was a no-man's-land, like those places between buildings that fill up with garbage and snow.

Though I never became an addict, I consumed more than the average amount of drugs. Hallucinogens were my favorites, because they dispelled the pain and fear that were always with me. Once, tripping on acid, my body relaxed into the forbidden postures that for me meant female. For the first time I could remember, I felt at home in myself. Of course, I had occasionally cross-dressed as a child. When I was alone, I would go into the attic and try on clothes my sister, three years my junior, had outgrown, jamming my flesh into the too-small garments. But that wasn't coming home to myself. To wear clothes that could never fit was a ritual of despair. My acid-inspired moment was different—instead of acting out my failure to fit any definition of femaleness, I suddenly, briefly, experienced myself as the girl I was beneath the skin that distorted and denied me.

The moment passed, and I lost myself again. Everyone is lonely, many of us achingly so, but I think there is a special kind of loneliness for transsexuals. Strip away your skin and bone, the distinctive shiver of your vocal cords, the way you sit and smile

Things Fall Apart   27

and walk, every gesture, everything that expresses and makes you who you are. What you have left is what I meant when I said "I," a purely theoretical sliver of self-reference with no basis in flesh, no ability to act, no history to define it, something that never had a birthday, never could be kissed, that existed wholly in negative, as an inescapable sense that I wasn't anything anyone could know.

Sometimes it felt as if I wouldn't have existed at all, if it weren't for the pain, the fear, the loneliness. But how could nonexistence be so painful? How could the choking terror of discovery accompany the pain of nonexistence? How could absolute loneliness translate so directly into fear of being discovered? I still don't know—but I know they can, they do, and I know that people can get used to them, accept them as a condition of life, a kind of unvarying internal weather.

Sometimes the need to exist, to become a self like other selves, with a life and a body to live it, grew so overwhelming that I literally started clawing at my flesh, trying to rip it open, to get at the girl within. Some transkids follow such feelings all the way to knives. I took more drugs and told myself I was transcending my flesh.

Many years later, during my first weeks of living as a woman, I was shooting the breeze with two other transwomen, when talk turned to recreational self-mutilation—mutilation engaged in for entertainment purposes, because being disconnected from your body means being disconnected from pain. I shyly mentioned hurling myself face first into pricker bushes for the amusement of neighborhood kids. R laughingly reminisced about doing stunts that risked broken bones or death. J, a six-four martial arts teacher and blacksmith, held out her open palms. "I used to nail them to the ground," she said.

She did. We could see the scars.

All things considered, I was a surprisingly functional adolescent. I graduated from high school in two and a half years, turned seventeen on the kibbutz in Israel where I spent what would otherwise have been the spring of my junior year, and a few weeks later heard that I had been accepted to Sarah Lawrence College—a not-very-well-integrated former women's college (the choice was not coincidental) where, ironically, my maleness gave me an affirmative-action edge in terms of admissions and financial aid. During orientation, I met the woman who would become my life. We spent more and more time together, and, after a false start or two, in February 1979, the beginning of our second semester, we became—each other's. We arranged for adjoining rooms as sophomores and the next year began living together for what, after the first decade or two, we thought would be the rest of our lives.

One afternoon, after making love, I told her what I was. We were both eighteen. I didn't know how to explain what I felt, and she responded with curiosity that soon subsided into indifference. In our junior year, we moved into our first real apartment, an overpriced dump on the Lower East Side that I (the official male in our heterosexual dyad) was renovating—painting, sanding floors, engaging in all sorts of manly crafts that made me feel hysterically incompetent. (I'm sure the floor still dips where I left the sander running.) Not coincidentally, during this transition to life as a partnered man, I found myself in the midst of the worst bout of gender dysphoria I had ever experienced. I started shaving my legs, talked constantly about wanting to be a woman, and tried therapy with a transsexual psychiatrist who, unfortunately for both of us, was mentally ill. (In our second session, she offered to strip to show me how good a trans body could look.)

My brand-new life partner—we didn't get married until late 1982, after we had graduated from Sarah Lawrence and moved to San Francisco—made it clear that, although she could accept that I had transsexual feelings, she could not accept any expression of them. Within a few weeks, we had completed the first cycle of a fitful pattern that would recur throughout our twenties. I would be consumed by gender dysphoria and unsuccessfully seek professional help; my wife would offer me a choice between becoming myself and being loved. It was a horrible choice but not a hard one, and with practice it got easier—almost as automatic as averting my eyes from girl-things when I was a child. I didn't know what life as a woman would be like, but I knew what life was like without my wife's love. I chose her love every time, burying my fledgling sense of female identity in the soul *cum* graveyard that already held so many aborted girls.

The last of this series of gender crises took place near the end of the 1980s and our twenties, in the midst of another crisis—make-or-break arguments about whether we should have a baby. I was dead set against it. In addition to the usual male objections—we didn't have the money (we didn't), the space (we didn't), the security (we didn't), the careers (we didn't)—I had my own unspeakable reasons for not wanting children. I knew my wife's pregnancy would confront me with realities of gender that I was desperate to avoid. Playing the male role in the drama of reproduction would seal my nonexistence, make my capitulation to biology official. I was bitter that my wife wanted me to fulfill her life's desire when she had denied me mine; overwhelmed by jealousy that it would not be *my* body swelling, birthing, nursing; and afraid of passing on to our child the gender anguish that so often left me longing to die.

One night, we hosted a party for a friend who, like so many people we knew in San Francisco, was dying of AIDS. He wasn't strong enough to return to his home across the bay, so we put him up for the night. Sound carried in our three-floor postindustrial space, and we could hear his muffled groans and labored breathing as we lay in the dark, talking the evening over. It had gone well; the food had been praised and devoured; our friend, for a few hours, had seemed happy. The rhythm of our pillowed intimacy merged with the harsher rhythm of his failing respiration. Simultaneously, as though by prearranged agreement, we turned from postparty chitchat to the most serious talking we had ever done in a decade of hyperintellectual self-reflection. Life, we agreed, was what was important. Nothing else mattered. Not careers, not money, not the disappointments that always seemed to dog us. The truth my wife had been trying to tell me broke through my jealousy, rage, and confusion: our children needed to be born.

As we made love to the rasp of our dying friend's breath—slow love, sweet love, love we both knew was intended to summon back into the world the life that was leaking out of him—I decided that my gender problems would be mine alone; no matter what I was going through, no one would ever know.

Over the next fifteen years, I tried to make good on my promise. I ignored my gender dysphoria; I ridiculed it; I repeated transphobic jokes like mantras; I told myself how ugly and clumsy and incapable a woman I would be; and, when the Internet arrived, I cruised it late into the night, compulsively searching for stories of gender transformation through which I could live vicariously.

I became the kind of male who haunts the outskirts of women's lives. My officemates complained freely to me about periods, boyfriends, and husbands. I couldn't respond in kind, of course, but I listened with what they seemed to take as empathy, desperate for every scrap they revealed of the life I yearned for. I joked compulsively but rarely laughed. Laughter dissolves boundaries. I was afraid to laugh.

Our son was born in May 1994, our second child four and a half years later, in December 1999. When ultrasound revealed that she would be a girl, I told myself that her life would be enough to compensate for the life I was determined never to live. A girl half made of me was coming into the world. Yet, when my wife went into labor—it was almost midnight—there I was, cruising the web, nauseating myself with transformation fantasies.

By spring 2005, when our third child, another daughter, was a year and a half old, I had started planning my suicide. My regimen of self-abuse and self-indulgence wasn't working anymore. Gender dysphoria was no longer a periodic problem; it was a constant crisis. My life—our lives—depended on my ability not to exist. Wasn't that the truth, the profound truth, that had welled up through my friend's labored breathing? Life mattered; my life didn't. One life for four. In any case, that was the deal I'd made, a private wedding vow to have and to hold my family till death did me part.

My wife was happily planning our sabbatical year. The weather was getting warmer. It was almost time for frozen coffee.

But I wouldn't be doing my family any favors if killing myself left them destitute, so I took out an additional life insurance policy in April 2005. There was only one catch. The policy had a two-year no-suicide clause. If I killed myself too soon, my family wouldn't get a cent.

I started counting down the weeks.

But, almost at the same time as I took out the insurance policy that defined how long I had to live, I took my first step toward a new life by coming out to Annie, who, in the months that followed, became my best friend. I had met her in Israel, when she and I were both visiting at Tel Aviv University on Fulbright scholarships. We had met for coffee, and I felt an immediate sense of connection. That was puzzling: she was a graduate student in her twenties, I was a male professor in my early forties, and her side of the conversation made it clear that she was very conscious of the demographic gulf between us. As always when I met women with whom I wanted to be friends, I felt awkward and sad, squirming inside my male identity as though it were a gorilla costume. I tried to meet her again, but she was busy being wooed by a young Israeli human rights lawyer; she moved to Israel and married him soon after I returned to the United States. We kept in touch by e-mail, trading poems and discussing the vagaries of building academic careers. A few weeks before I told my wife about my gender crisis, I sent Annie some poems written in a female voice. She asked me about them, and I wrote back something about having a rather unusual relationship to gender. She was curious: did I mean a theoretical relationship to gender? No, I said, and told her that it was something that I couldn't explain via e-mail. We set up a time to talk on the phone. Our house was too small for me to talk privately, so I carried the cordless phone out to the forest behind our house. And then I told her.

Annie had never heard of transsexuality, but her quizzical, compassionate questions confirmed the sense of connection I had felt since I shook her hand at Tel Aviv University four years before. I—the real me—had made my first female friend, and I soon saw Annie as the thread of empathy and love that would lead me through my crisis to a new life. She e-mailed me multiple times a day, spoke to me daily on the phone, drove herself to the edge of nervous breakdown in an effort to keep me going. She knew what transition would do to my family. As an Orthodox Jewish woman soon to be the mother of twins, she considered the family a sacred trust, a visible manifestation of divine love; she and I shared the language of Judaism, of God. Though she had never heard of transsexuality, I knew she would understand when I explained, with inescapable logic, why I felt that God, to spare my family the shame and pain of my transition, wanted me to die. She listened quietly; she understood, she said, but she didn't agree. Then she said words I will never forget. "People," she said, "do this." "People"—as though I were a person; "do"—as though becoming myself were something that could be done; "this"—as though she felt no disgust, no repulsion, no need to distance herself from what I was.

Annie suggested—at the time it seemed like madness—that I find a therapist. There weren't many in my area who had experience with gender identity issues, but, after several referrals, I found Susan. I was terrified, but the voice on her message machine sounded down-to-earth and kind, and it had become clear that neither my wife, who had been plunged into despair by the revelation that I could no longer repress my conflict, nor Annie, who tried but couldn't be on call seven days a week, could talk me through my maelstrom of feelings. In my first session, I begged Susan to help me save my family. By the end of summer, I was begging her to tell me how to reduce the intensity of the dysphoria, to slow down the process that was unmaking me from the inside out. "I feel like I'm dying," I told her. "I feel life pouring out of me." It was true. I would lie immobilized, curled in fetal position around an invisible wound from which vitality seemed to be spilling like blood. "You *are* dying," she said. "Your male persona is dying, as your new self is being born."

That should have sounded hopeful.

My wife begged me to stop dying, to preserve the happy life we had enjoyed until a few months before, to take pity on the four lives—hers and the children's—I was destroying. "How can you choose this mental illness over us?" she asked again and again. "I'm not choosing," I repeated stupidly, as life poured out of me.

My frozen coffee was getting better—I kept monkeying with the number of ice cubes and scoops of cocoa—but my gender dysphoria wasn't.

My wife and I agreed on only one thing—the children mustn't know. I tried to behave normally no matter how sick I felt. She tried to behave normally no matter how sick I made her. I played with the kids, cooked and cleaned, laid stones for a patio area, mowed the lawn. I woke up early and stayed up late to work on the books that were supposed to be the focus of my sabbatical year. It doesn't matter how I feel, I kept telling myself, praying that it—that I—would soon be over, one way or another.

So there we were, my wife and I, clinging side by side to the crumbling edge of the transsexual precipice. If you loved us, you wouldn't destroy our lives. If you loved me, you wouldn't make me choose between being myself and being loved. Our lives will end if you do this. My life will end if I don't.

It isn't easy to unmake a quarter-century of intimacy, but betrayal by betrayal—for that is how we experienced each other's rage and anguish—my wife and I managed it. Things fell apart. The center couldn't hold.

By the end of the summer, I had perfected frozen coffee. But something had happened to the pitcher. As I poured in the liquid ingredients, they ran out the bottom.

It didn't matter. She didn't want my frozen coffee anymore.

One night, after the kids were asleep, I went down into the basement and committed my first visible act of becoming. It was fall 2005. The basement was dark, cold, and cluttered—the perfect birth canal for a life that felt like pure loss. This is it, I told myself. I turned on the electric razor. Moments later, the beard and mustache that had blurred my face since adolescence were gone. The cheeks and lip beneath were pallid, unhealthy, the face in the mirror unfamiliar—and disappointingly male. Some part of me had imagined that beneath the sparse beard I had plucked out, one hair at a time, for years, a woman's face was lurking—the face of the woman who would blaze forth, fairy-tale-like and ready to be loved, once she was released from the curse that had smothered her in fur.

The man in the mirror looked lost and naked. He kept touching the strange smooth curve of his cheeks. Then, abruptly, he turned off the light and went back upstairs. It was done; something was over, someone was gone, but no one, it seemed, had taken his place.

The next morning, I rose, as always, in the dark. My beard was still gone. I felt relief, a touch of sadness, then panic. No one had seen me yet. No one had caught a glimpse of that bare, pale face. Reluctantly, I opened my son's door to wake him for school. As usual, he was stretched out on his back, knees up, sleeping the heaviest sleep in the family. He made a sound; he was dreaming. I lay down beside him, propping my head on one hand, staring at the indistinct, dream-stirred moon of his face. It shone faintly even in the dark. He has always shone—people have commented on it since he was an infant—and suddenly I was afraid that I, or what he would go through because of me, would put out that light.

What would he see when he opened his eyes? The parent who had loved him his whole life or some unknown, unloving, unlovable stranger? I remembered holding him as an infant on my chest, rocking him for hours in moonlight, trying to get him to sleep. He was so small, so present, so intensely alive, so strange and yet so much a part of me, as though his life had budded, paramecium-style, from mine. It was love, but love at the cellular level, the level at which one body recognizes another not as other but as part of itself. And, even as I drifted back, I felt myself drifting forward, into the future in which I would stand before my son as the woman he had never seen and couldn't imagine. Time had collapsed around the axes of love and terror. Both moments, past and future, fused in the predawn darkness, as I gazed at the long, vague form of the twelve-year-old boy sleeping beside me. He, too, was changing. The self I had known, the child-self whose body had melted into mine, was falling away, and the outlines of the man he would become were slowly coming into focus. Adolescence was pulling us forward at the same time, though in opposite directions, and neither of us knew who we would be or how we would see each other when we finally became ourselves.

I kissed him. "Good morning, darling," I murmured. "Time to open your eyes."

2
Being a Man

Fall 2006

"W hat's so bad about being a man?" my wife asks me. I've been living in the house for months since shaving off my beard and mustache and starting to wear androgynous but female-marketed clothing. At first, we talked compulsively, night after night, for hours at a stretch. Now, though we hardly ever discuss anything but household business, there are moments—the habits of a lifetime are hard to break—when we still find ourselves trying to talk our way across the chasm of gender.

"What's so bad about being a man?" My wife has repeated this question for months. Sometimes her tone is joking, almost light-hearted. Those are the times that hurt the most, when it seems for a moment as though our marriage is still intact, as though we can laugh together through my transsexuality the way we have laughed through every other crisis. She waits for me to go along with the joke, to clap my forehead theatrically, as though the light has just gone on, and say, "Hey, you're right—being a man isn't that bad" so that we can fall into each others' arms and reunite in the joy of renouncing the terrible mistake I'm making.

I hesitate, hoping she will realize that she is inviting me to laugh at my need to become what she has always been: a whole person. Then, trying to match her tone, I say, "There's nothing so bad about being a man." I try to sound like I'm joking when I add, "as long as you're a man."

In the silence that follows, I hear her heart breaking again.

It's easier when she's angry, when she hurls the question at me like a knife, when it isn't a question but an attempt to gouge me into realizing that I have thrown our lives away to become a patchwork parody of a woman. "I hope you'll be happy," she says. "I hope you'll be happy, knowing that you've destroyed four lives to walk around in a dress."

"I hope you will be happy." That's what thrown-over wives are supposed to say—what better mirror to hold up to a husband's faithlessness? To her, I am sacrificing our family for a panty-hosed version of a typical male midlife crisis, abdicating relationships and responsibilities to roar off on the Harley-Davidson of transsexuality (the metaphor is hers) toward a fluffy pink Shangri-la of self-centered gratification.

But I don't see myself in her bitter mirror, because I'm not transitioning for the sake of happiness. I have no illusions that becoming a jobless, homeless approximation of a middle-aged woman is a recipe for bliss. This isn't a typical male midlife crisis—it's a typical transsexual midlife crisis.

That's what's so hard to explain. I don't think there's anything wrong with being a man—at least, I have nothing to add to the complaints women traditionally make about the opposite sex. What's bad about being a man is that I'm not one.

"I don't walk around smiling because I'm a woman," my wife points out, meaning, if being a woman isn't a big deal to someone who really is a woman, why should it be a big deal to me? In our culture, men and women have almost the same options in terms of behavior and life choices. What difference does it make whether I'm living as one or the other?

The answer is there when she looks in the mirror.

In our small New England college town, it's common to see middle-aged women of the housewife-and-mother variety in Levis, work shirts, sneakers or boots, and no-fuss shoulder-length hair. My wife isn't one of them. Though she hates blow drying, she blows her long, dark hair dry no matter how hot it is. Though she doesn't wear much makeup, she spends longer putting on hers than I ever have. When she dresses up, she almost always wears dresses or skirts. Even when she wears pants and a T-shirt, the fabric and cut of her clothes—not to mention her earrings—proclaim her gender. And, like many heterosexual women, my wife is strictly homosocial—her friends and acquaintances, no matter how casual, are women. My wife's share of our household labor is similarly gendered. She plans the meals, maintains the social calendar, takes primary responsibility for the children's schooling, activities, and clothes, decides all matters that require taste—and leaves yard work, car maintenance, household repairs, computer problems, vermin removal, and business arrangements to me.

In short, though my wife is an independent-minded, college-educated feminist, there are few aspects of her daily life that don't reflect her gender—not because she has been forced into a narrow set of social conventions but because she freely locates herself, represents herself, expresses herself, and thinks of herself in terms of the feminine side of the gender spectrum.

Masculine behavior patterns, like masculine hairstyles, are simpler, cheaper, and lower maintenance than feminine behavior patterns, which is why so many heterosexual women in our area opt for them. Yet my wife never does.

My wife's gender doesn't define her; it enables her to define herself. Gender permeates her most intimate gestures, shaping the way she cries, laughs, suffers, rejoices, falls in love, rages, gets her heart broken. Even now, when my wife and I discuss the destruction of our life together, she's the one who cries. If tears start in my eyes—and they often do—I automatically stifle them. When my wife and I are together, she's the woman and I'm the man.

When we decided to start having children, I stopped complaining to her about being a man. I had decided, once and for all, to be one, whether I was or not. This seemed to me a supremely moral decision, a form of transcendence, a triumph of mind over matter. In the deepest sense, I was living my life for others, and isn't that the way it's supposed to be? Years of parenting turned this lie—I was as selfish and self-centered as anyone, despite the hollowness of the self I was centered on—into a semblance of truth. Like most parents, I *had* to ignore my own needs to care for my children's. After decades of practice, I had a well-prepared repertoire of male gestures, tones, even conversational topics that I could trot out as the occasion demanded; I had become expert at translating my smallest impulses into an acceptably male idiom. As a man, I was a father, a husband, a teacher, a writer. As a woman, I was nothing.

But, though I tried for decades, I never managed to die inside or to put my nascent self, the self that actually felt like me, into a permanent state of suspended animation. Against my will, beneath my awareness, life grew inside me, shower by despair-soaked shower. My life, the life that would include me. The life that would cost me all I knew of life.

The more I outwardly surrendered my life to those around me, the more I thought about gender. When I walked to the bathroom, I thought about gender; when I sang my daughters to sleep, I thought about gender; when I sat in my office, I thought about gender; when I stood in the classroom, I thought about gender. Finally, I realized I was thinking about gender every waking minute. There was no relief anymore, no moment when I was unaware of my estrangement from my skin.

Every now and then, over the fifteen years since we had made love to the sound of our dying friend's breath, I would lose control and become consumed by the desire to be a woman. Sometimes it lasted hours; sometimes days; sometimes weeks. Nothing else mattered to me but fantasies of transformation. The realities of my life, my career, my family seemed like shadows on a distant wall.

After each gender breakdown—that's what I called them—I restored my sense of self-control by imposing acts of penance on myself. After one breakdown, I ended a fifteen-cup-a-day coffee habit overnight; after another, I resolved to eat only when someone else offered me food. Being a man became a gulag of neurotic compulsions. I was the only guard, the only prisoner, the frozen ground and the barbed wire fence. Give up, I told myself. There is no escape. And besides, what's so bad about being a man?

In the name of being a husband and father, I had turned gender dysphoria from a chronic discomfort and occasional crisis into a system of torture. For years, being a man had been a habit. Now, being a man was a matter of constant self-denial, a desperate failing effort to control the rage for transformation that seemed to be all that was left of me.

When the walls of my private concentration camp finally collapsed, in spring 2005, it was almost too late. I couldn't eat—couldn't feed "it," as my body now seemed to me, couldn't keep "it" alive when "it" was smothering me. Electricity seemed to be shooting through me, a current of transformative energy that ricocheted around my nervous system in frustrated circuits that had no outlet, no outcome. My absence of connection to life—that numbness where a feeling of physical presence and aliveness should have been—shattered into two overwhelming, contradictory imperatives: the need to become the true self I had never been and the need to die before that self's emergence fatally injured my family.

Being a man, for me, was a performance, and most people were not only willing but eager to take that performance for me. The person I had loved the deepest and the longest refused to take me any other way.

How can I blame her? To her mind, my insistence that I wasn't really a man meant that I was erasing not only the future she had believed we would share and the present whose blessings we should have been enjoying but the entire life—thirty years—we had built with and around each other. It didn't matter that I had told her I was trans when we were sophomores in college or that I had erased myself for decades for her sake. For me, that erasure was the ultimate testimony to my love, the greatest sacrifice I could make. I had done everything I could to turn myself into a facsimile of the man she needed me to be, to savagely suppress the budding of any other, more "real" self, to ensure that I was giving my wife the only self I had.

As our twenties turned into our thirties and forties, I burnished my male self, adjusted it to meet her needs. But I couldn't infuse it with vitality, with joy. When my wife would enthuse about some plan or fantasy, taking a trip or buying a house, I would smile and nod and try to say the right things—but she always knew my heart wasn't in it. Every couple divides the physical and emotional labor of their lives. In our couple, joy and excitement, desire and frustration and fulfillment, were a privilege and burden she bore alone.

My wife knew something was wrong with me, but she believed—she wanted to believe, and I worked hard to enable her to believe—that the problem wasn't a threat to our life together, that it was a character flaw or a neurosis, a willful refusal to allow myself to be happy. Happiness was right there, all around me, like a fragrance, if only I would let myself breathe.

But, for me, being a man meant holding my breath. If I couldn't breathe as myself, I wouldn't breathe at all.

When my gender dysphoria became a crisis I could no longer keep to myself, my wife was faced with a terrible choice. Most literature on transsexuality implies that there is a moral obligation for others to recognize the supremacy of the transsexual's needs, as though, like fetuses, the imperatives of our becoming take precedence over everyone else's needs. All my wife had to do was heed the voices urging her to become a willing, supportive party to the destruction of the life and the man she loved, and she could hold on, probably, to whatever was left of them when I was done becoming.

But she had grown up with voices telling her to sacrifice her life for others'. For women, these voices never seem to fall silent. There is always someone becoming, someone needing, someone hurting, someone grieving, someone whispering and sometimes screaming the tenets of female self-sacrifice.

My wife had survived by shouting down those voices and insisting on her right to her own life. From the first, I had admired in her the courage I had never displayed.

So, rather than swallowing her pain and focusing on mine, she decided to fight for her life. If I had been faithless, she would be faithful. If I denied the reality of the man she loved, she would mourn and defend him.

What's so bad about being a man?" my wife asks me again. I'm in the kitchen, washing dishes she dries and puts away. The old teamwork is still there, the seamless dance of those whose lives have been entwined so long they can't remember living any other way. For some reason, this is always where we are when she asks this question. She's serious this time, neither joking nor raging, and, though I know it's too late to salvage our marriage, I have a sudden, desperate intuition that if I could only answer, really answer, she would finally understand that I am not rejecting her, and we could begin to heal, to forgive.

But it's hard to find words for feelings that she has never experienced. Before this last, now permanent crisis, even I hadn't understood that gender dysphoria could make life unlivable. I'd read stories of middle-aged men, stockbrokers and auto mechanics, telephone repairmen and Marine corps sergeants, who would appear without appointments or prior transition at gender reassignment clinics demanding to be operated on immediately. I couldn't imagine transsexuals behaving so badly. Where was their detachment, their dissociation, their discipline? What could be so bad about being a man?

She's waiting for me to answer. There's a blue plastic plate in one hand, a dish towel in another. Her makeup is off, her glasses are on; we are both in blue jeans and sneakers. There's so little difference between us. Surely she can see through my dilapidated male façade to the soul whose suffering is causing hers. Any minute now—I'm suddenly sure of it—she will realize, without having to be told, what is so bad about being a man.

A body is there, but it's not yours. A voice is coming out of your throat, but you don't recognize it. The mirror contains another person's face. When your children wrap their arms around you, they seem to be hugging someone else. Every morning you wake up shocked to find that parts of you have disappeared, that you are smothered in flesh you cannot recognize as yours. That you have lost the body you never had. This isn't me, you say to yourself. This isn't me, you say to anyone you trust. Of course it isn't. There is no "me," no body that fits the map, no identity that fits your sense of self, no way to orient yourself in a world in which you exist only as an hysterical rejection of what, to everyone around you, is the simple, obvious fact of your gender.

You are a man. And what's so bad about that?

3

Girl in a Bag

Winter 2007

W hat's *in* those?" my friend asks, her eyes swiveling toward me and then back to the road.

"Birdseed," I answer. "Birdseed in panty hose." She laughs. We are talking about my breasts. For a transgirl on my budget—$0— birdseed in panty hose is probably the best option for low-maintenance, relatively authentic-looking breasts. Hormone therapy won't start in earnest till next month, and no one knows how long it will take before my body starts changing—or, for that matter, if it will ever change much at all. The two small bags—the snipped, filled feet of cheap hose that turned out not to fit—are sitting in the palm of my hand. Unlike most women, I can have breasts as large or small as I like, but I want to be realistic: the effects of estrogen on a middle-aged male body are not usually very dramatic.

We're in my friend Janie's car, starting our weekly commute from our homes in western Massachusetts to our jobs in New York City. She's blunt and kind, a working-class girl who worked her way up into a high-level executive position in a major metropolitan health organization. It's a dark autumn evening. My hours in this car are among the few that I can dress as myself each week, and my need to materialize my female self has become so great that I willingly endure the humiliation of constructing it in front of Janie. She keeps her eyes on the road. Neither of us knows the etiquette for switching from male to female in someone else's presence. This mutual discomfort, a strange and strangely companionable combination of intimacy and distance, is the best we've come up with. My transformation is brief, awkward, and unsatisfying. At this point, there isn't much about me that looks female. I'm hairy, muscular, with short messy hair. Though clean shaven, my face is always shadowy with stubble, and my body has not been visibly changed by five months of progesterone treatments.

My entire female identity can be, and is, stuffed in my computer bag.

I take off the sweater that concealed my blouse from my family and clip on my earrings. I got lucky. One of my friends didn't get her ears pierced until midlife, and her ex-husband bought her gorgeous clip-ons that she passed on to me. The left one goes on easily, but my fingers are clumsy, and I struggle with the right, crying a little as I twist and retwist the tiny gold screw into the lobe. Eventually, I will get used to it, but now I'm still new to the fulfillment end of my lifelong wishes, and the pain and disorientation that accompany what I always imagined as bliss take me by surprise.

I put on a cheap watch with a stretchy, black-and-gold braided band that I bought a few weeks ago in San Francisco, in Chinatown, the first time I went out as a woman. Unlike most people, I remember when I first saw the light of day. It was October 13, 2006. I was at a literature conference and had a hotel room to myself. It took me all morning to prepare to go out. I blushed my cheeks uncertainly—I had never put on makeup alone before—trying to remember the proper relation between color and bone, squinting through the dim yellow light to see whether both sides were symmetrical. I tried to remember the theory of eye shadow—does the medium tone or the light tone go on the lid?—and kept smearing and resmearing the darkest powder into the crease. In that light, it didn't make any difference, but I was sure that imperfect eye makeup would instantly mark me as an imposter. I straightened my skirt, brushed and rebrushed my hair. I stared into the mirror. My reflection kept shifting, slipping from male to female. Every now and then, I just looked tired. Sometimes I was smiling.

It took a long time to find the courage to open the door. There was a woman outside, with a cart of cleaning supplies. I smiled nervously at her and fluttered to the elevator in shoes that had already begun to torment my feet. The lobby was crowded and dark, which was exactly the way I wanted it. I shouldered shyly through the tourists clotting the hotel entrance and stepped onto the pavement of a new world. It was a clear, bright San Francisco day, the sky a depthless, noncommittal blue. I had done it. I was out. I was free. I felt as though mummifying bandages had been cut away, leaving my skin, vulnerable but grateful, exposed to the unfamiliar air. It wasn't a dream, but something had finally come true.

Me. The sun shone full on my face as I climbed the picture-postcard hills, and, as men and women returned my smiles—I couldn't stop smiling—for the first time in my life I knew that no flaw in makeup or bone structure would keep me from being seen and accepted as a woman.

That was only a few weeks before this ride, but it seems like years have gone by. Not that being myself has lost its luster—far from it. Every time I put on skirt and blouse and makeup, I feel myself spreading out into my arms and legs, filling my body, shuddering from death into life.

In my fantasies, I had imagined transformation into a woman as a one-time, permanent affair. But, since the moment the bandages of masculinity fell away in San Francisco, I've learned that I have to keep wrapping them back around me. The embalmed carcass of male identity is still my home, even now that I've tasted sun on my skin.

I swipe foundation over my five o'clock shadow—I'm already an old hand at this—add powder to set it, and slowly—the car keeps bouncing—outline my lips in red. No eye makeup this time. I'll be wiping my face off in a couple of hours, when we arrive.

It's time to put on my breasts. I slip one birdseed bag into each cup of my sports bra, then adjust them according to my rather hazy notions of how breasts should hang. Not that it matters to anyone else. It's dark, and my friend's eyes are glued to the road.

But it means everything to me to see a shadowy face that looks like mine in the makeup mirror, to look down and see the shape of breasts where I usually see amputation. To stop cringing within my body. To feel, for an hour or two, the excitement—the greatest excitement I've ever felt—of being.

If my friend were looking, what would she see? An imitation of a woman? Or me?

She's the only person who will ever witness this transformation. Over the remaining months of my public life as a man—a life due to end with the spring 2007 semester, when I tell my dean that I can no longer teach as a man—other friends will see me enter a bathroom as one gender and emerge as another, but no one else will sit beside me as I remake and unmake myself—if a self is something that can be remade and unmade with items that fit in a shoulder bag.

There is a lot of talk in the academic world about gender as a performance, something we do with and for and sometimes to each other, rather than as something we *are*. In some respects, this is exactly right. The moment I finish putting on my makeup, I feel better. When my friend glances at me, despite my intense self-consciousness about my appearance, I feel she is seeing something, someone, who looks like me. Not very much like me, perhaps. A sketch, a rough draft, a work in progress. But, instead of the male façade that has always been taken for me, the blurred attempt at womanhood my friend glimpses in the car-dark reflects the person I feel myself to be. Like the bandages Claude Rains's invisible man wrapped around his face, my makeup, blouse, and jewelry make visible the outline of the self that otherwise cannot be seen.

But, for those committed to seeing gender as a performance, there is no "self that otherwise cannot be seen." What is seen, what is performed, is what you are. Though my female self is nothing if not a performance, for me, gender is more than performance. If it weren't, then someone like me, raised as male, perceived as male, and consciously performing as male, would simply *be* male; my lifelong sense that there was a true female self behind my male mask would be a delusion.

That sense of who I really am isn't enough anymore. My true self needs a face, a voice, a body, needs to *be*. And being my true self means acting like someone—a woman—I've never been.

So here I am, sitting in the car, trying to decide whether being my true self means crossing my legs even in this cramped space. My genetically female friend would never give leg-crossing a thought; she would do whatever felt comfortable to her. But nothing feels comfortable to me now. Every gesture is new, unfamiliar, a test of whether, now that I am free to stop pretending to be a man, I do what "real" women do. But how can I do what real women do, when being a real woman means not having to think about acting like a woman?

A week or two ago, one of my students told me her favorite women's-magazine headline: "Five Hundred Unique Ways to Express the Real You." To her, the idea of looking to a mass-market magazine for "unique ways to express the real you" was comic, but, staring at her through the mask of maleness I wore as her professor, I couldn't share her laughter. She could laugh, because she *has* a "real you" to express, a core sense of herself as a woman that doesn't depend on whether or not she crosses her legs in a given situation; her breasts aren't filled with birdseed. For better or worse, when she looks in the mirror or in the eyes of those around her, she sees her gender identity reflected back at her, confirmed and reaffirmed. A few years ago, when she was just beginning to negotiate the physical and social dislocations of adolescence, she and I probably had more in common. My leg crossing and uncrossing—I must have done it five times in the past five minutes—is a symptom of adolescent self-consciousness, the squirming self-doubt and reluctantly public practice that most girls go through when they, like me now, are learning to "be" women. For her and her friends, the throes and misfires of fledgling femininity, however painful, were normal; I feel achingly alone in practicing gendered riffs the average genetic girl has down pat by her late teens. In terms of becoming a woman, adolescence was a test she couldn't fail, because, unlike me, she had the chromosomes, the body, the social history, to make her real. I'm sorting through five hundred—or five thousand—ways to express the unreal me, the me I am trying to make real in the glow of the instrument panel of a speeding car, and these ways are anything but unique. I'm cobbling my real self together out of clichés and conventions of femininity, magazine ads, family traditions, ancient archetypes and TV reruns, supplementing these staples of female adolescence with advice from trans manuals and tips from first-person accounts of transition that assure me, for example, that the more I swing my arms when I walk, the more feminine I will seem—as long as my elbows stay close to my body. I constantly examine the women I see, including my students, looking for bits of femininity to try on when I'm alone. I've discovered, somewhat to my surprise, that, while some women's gender expression leaves me drooling with envy, others'—equally "real"—leave me cold. In the fantasies of transformation that sustained me over the decades, I was happy to turn into any woman, but, now that I've begun being for myself, I find that I want to be me. Even though there are no "unique" ways to express my inchoate female identity, I've realized there is a unique combination I'm searching for—and that combination may be the closest I come to having a real me.

No matter how much I want to—and it would be hard to overestimate how much I want to—I can't ask my friend how I look. That's the problem with going through adolescence in my forties; none of my friends are going through it with me. My female friends have little interest in talking makeup, body image, breast development (or lack thereof); they either got over or learned to live with such insecurities decades ago.

"Is my voice okay?" I ask.

"Your voice is fine. You sound the way you always sound when you're you."

It isn't much in the way of self-image-nourishing feedback, but I know it's all I'm going to get, and so I milk it for all it's worth. Was that boredom in Janie's voice, or the slight edge that signals someone trying to politely conceal a negative opinion? Is her boredom actually a testament to my established mastery of the difficult (for those with male voice boxes and vocal habits) art of speaking like a woman? Or, since I work daily on my voice, isn't "You sound the way you always sound" a criticism, a contradiction of my fantasy of progress? What good are those voice exercises if they don't produce noticeable improvement?

Transition is like playing chess against yourself. You constantly second-guess your own moves. You have no choice: your life depends on recognizing the weaknesses in your own presentation, and few people are interested in conducting verbal assessments of how convincing they find someone else's gender presentation. But we constantly, unconsciously assess one another's gender, instantaneously measuring the people we see against cultural checklists of male or female appearance. Do they have a beard? Breasts? Long or short hair? Skirt or pants? If we don't notice any gender-discordant characteristics, we read a person as "male" or "female"; if we do, they seem androgynous, or indeterminate, or just plain strange. Even when I started to feel confident that I could pass as a woman—if I didn't, my somersaults back and forth between male and female could literally cost me my life—I didn't know if I was actually becoming a woman, whatever that meant. The only people to whom I could say "Do you really see me, respond to me, as a woman?" were people like Janie, who primarily knew me as a man. The closest I could come to the confirmation I longed for was the occasional, indifferent "ma'am" of strangers.

At this point in transition, when my womanhood fits in a bag, I am excruciatingly aware that my success or failure at becoming myself is in the hands of strangers. When they accept me as a woman, I become, for a moment, a woman.

But most of the confirmation of my identity is negative: people who don't beat me up, stare, smirk, jeer, or scream when I enter a ladies' room have probably—probably—accepted me as female. In the months ahead, I will feel like a woman when I have failed to evoke these responses in an ever-larger number of places— in Westchester strip malls, at rest stops in Connecticut, on Peter Pan buses, at scholarly conferences, and in Waikiki tourist traps (albeit *not* in swimwear), ordering in restaurants, attending Friday night services, paying parking-garage attendants, asking for directions, making small talk with cab drivers, and attracting the amorous attentions of mentally deficient gentlemen. I will glow for hours after being ma'am-ed by credit-card telephone representatives, hotel clerks, auto repairmen, and homeless men and women—to name only a few of my inadvertent authenticators. I will lay my gender identity on the line by initiating woman-to-woman chats with strangers in lines and in restrooms. I will change from male to female on streets, in café bathrooms, in parking lots, and in the restroom of a moving bus, and one day I will set a personal record by shifting between male and female five—count them, five—times at a literary studies conference, without raising a single eyebrow on either side of the gender binary.

Though I can't yet know it, sitting in this car, at the very beginning of my wobbly walk from male to female, only once in my journeys to the forbidden end of the gender spectrum will I know that I have been read as anything other than female. Oddly enough, it will happen in the dark, at a distance, in gender-bending Greenwich Village, after a successful evening of passing in a long skirt and sweater at the Village Temple. There, under the blazing lights of Reform Judaism, among people who saw me walk and heard me sing and had every opportunity to inspect my makeup, no one would pay me the slightest attention. But, on a darkened street, a man who seems to be drunk will call out from twenty feet behind me, "Miss? Excuse me—are you a man or a woman? Come back, honey, it doesn't matter to me. . . ."

It matters to *me*, I'll think, swallowing a sob.

But there is one gaze under which I regularly fail to pass, and that is my own. Transition requires sacrifice, and one of the first things to go was my self-image; as soon as I shaved off the beard I'd worn since my facial hair began to grow, I lost my sense of what or who I look like. Every time I glance in a mirror, I see someone else: old, young, male, female, familiar as a long-lost relative, shocking as a stranger. During one identity meltdown, I had to beg a friend to come to my office to tell me whether I look male or female. She found me sobbing behind a locked door, lost on the gender spectrum, unable to tell anymore which side of the line I was on. "I know you will have complicated feelings about this," she said gently, "but you do look like a man."

Though I'm still nervous about my voice, once I'm dressed, I start to relax in the cramped darkness of Janie's car. We talk for the next three hours without a pause, laughing, sometimes crying, exchanging intimacies—since I've come out to her, there are few topics beyond the pale—in the dim glow of the instrument panel. This is another, deeper form of becoming. Though I tried to be the best man I could, the fact that I never felt I was me gave me a moral escape clause, a way of deferring judgment on my actions on the grounds that I didn't really exist. To the extent that I exist now, that loophole has closed: it is time to be the best woman, the best person, I can be. These conversations are the proving ground for this unproven self. How open, how honest, how compassionate, how generous, and, above all, how present will I be? Now that the veil has been ripped away, who is the person that I want everyone to see? Someone who jokes less and laughs more; who talks with hair-raising directness about whatever topic is at hand; someone constantly surprised by the generosity and grace of those around her. Someone grateful, vulnerable, much too old and barely born, present and accounted for.

At this rate of intimacies per hour, it doesn't take long to get from Massachusetts to New York. That's where the hard part starts: unmaking, unbecoming the self I have just cobbled together. While my friend idles at the curb and keeps talking, deliberately, about other things, I take off my earrings, then my watch, then wipe ruthlessly at my makeup until my face comes off.

My breasts are the last to go. I hesitate, not because I'm enamored of the feel of birdseed in nylon against my chest but because I want to take in another moment of seeing the swell of chest that mysteriously but undeniably makes me feel that I have a body that fits my brain—that expresses the real me. Neither my brain nor my body is fooled by this artifice, but removing the little bags of birdseed feels like an act of self-mutilation. My deflated blouse looks like aftermath—the aftermath of being.

When I pull my baggy fleece over my head and look in the mirror, the face I see is that of the man I never really recognize. He looks hard, and sad, and angry.

"I'm finished," I tell my friend. My voice has flattened into male monotone again. I'm "doing drab," as it is known in the M-to-F world: the masculine, joie de vivre–destroying yang to the liberating yin of drag. I call it "erasing myself" or, in lighter moments, turning back into a pumpkin. The ball is over, midnight has struck, and, as the magic fades, it turns out I wasn't Cinderella at all. I was the coach she rode in on.

I hoist my enormous duffle over one shoulder, the oversized computer bag in which I carry the accessories I call my self over the other, and thank Janie as best I can, tears throttling my already overburdened voice. We both know there's nothing she can do for me. We won't speak again for three days, till our return trip reopens the vibrating steel bubble in which our friendship has blossomed. I will teach as a man, then hurry downtown to unisex bathrooms from which I will emerge as my current approximation of womanhood and wander the cold, crowded streets trying to gauge whether the lack of interest I arouse is indeed a sign of the consolidation of my identity. I'll feel lonely and homeless for a while and then return to the hostel I am now checking into and unmake myself again.

I'm not sure I'll make it to our rendezvous.

Janie isn't sure, either.

I hand the hostel clerk the bearded photo ID that identifies me as the holder of the reservation, sign in, and haul my bags up steep steps that look like they were confiscated from the set of a movie about high school delinquents. I dump the bags in my sleeping chamber, pull out my toiletries, and head for the shower. This is the hardest part. Not because the water temperature often swings from frigid to scalding; not because the lights, controlled by motion sensors, stay on for only five seconds at a time. Because the image I see in the mirror in those five-second intervals and the body I feel under my hands are unambiguously those of a man. I have wiped off, removed, and packed away every trace of my true self into my bag.

If this is one of the bad nights, I will double over in the shower, freezing and scalding and pounding the numb flesh that is mine but isn't me. If it's one of the worst nights—they are ever more frequent—I will be unable to stop sobbing and fantasizing about what those silly pink razors women use for depilation could do in terms of slicing skin. If it is the worst night of all, the one I have approached but never yet experienced, I will finally find out.

No razors tonight, but it takes a long time to lift myself off the floor and towel dry. It takes even longer for me to make it back down the short dark hallway and longer still to get my hands to stop shaking long enough to unlock the door of my sleeping chamber. I take off my clothes and stretch out stiffly in the dark, arms pressed to my sides so they don't fall off the edge of the bed, listening to the breathing of men on either side of me, fists clenched, nails, which have gotten quite long, digging into my palms in a way that I wish would cause this unfeeling body pain, realizing—can it be called realization, when it happens so often?—that I am impossible, that there is no I, that "I" is a pronoun pointing toward an empty space in which no self of mine will ever exist.

Sometimes I miss the numbness of those comparatively peaceful decades of nonexistence, the sad but serene state of dissociation from which I could wistfully, benevolently gaze at the lives of the people—the real people—around me. Sometimes my friends ask me whether I am making a mistake. I'm not going back, I tell them, anger—toward what? toward whom?—blazing homicidally within me. I'll die first, I tell them. Meaning: I'll kill this flesh I'm stuck in before I'll go back to pretending it's me.

4

In the Image

Spring 2007

The usual Starbucks where I change for work—the one with two bathrooms—is under renovation, so I head across Union Square to its cozier northwestern counterpart. The line there is ten deep, and it's already midmorning. E-mails from undergraduates anxious for responses to their latest poetry revisions are piling up in my inbox, so I decide, for the first time, to change in the street. I've gone the other way before, unzipping my androgynous coat to reveal a blouse, putting on earrings and makeup as I walk, but that was in the semidarkness of the New York evening. I've never gone from female to male on the street in broad daylight.

No woman will be surprised to hear that it's easier to become male than to become female. I'm already wearing pants and shoes. In approximately ninety seconds, I've taken off my jewelry, wiped off my lipstick, and pulled a baggy black top over my white shell.

No one gives me a second glance. After all, this is New York, and Union Square has seen stranger transformations than mine. The same cannot be said for my workplace. Modern though the orthodoxy of Stern College may be, I have no doubt that its modernity does not extend to acceptance of transsexual faculty members. When my more pious students and colleagues find out what I am, they will consider me—well, the term "abomination" is a bit archaic, but so is the response I expect. Transsexuality has

55

bestowed on me the unusual distinction of knowing that soon after being granted early tenure, and in the same year that I was nominated for professor of the year, I will probably be prohibited from setting foot on campus.

That seems to be the way life works these days. Up is down; success, failure. My success as a teacher will make it impossible for my employers to tolerate my transition. Even if they can overcome their discomfort and the discomfort of the student body, their donors will be outraged. The same inverted dynamic is operating in my family. The intimacy achieved over a lifetime of monogamous devotion makes it unbearable for my wife to witness the emergence of my female self. When, in a few months, I achieve the sine qua non of transsexual transition—living full time in my new gender role—I will complete the midlife crisis trifecta of simultaneously losing my career, my marriage, and my home.

One minute I am there; ninety seconds later, I have disappeared inside the image of the washed-out male face, framed by badly overgrown hair, staring back out of a darkened shop window.

Some people glory in gender mutability, gleefully remaking themselves according to mood and occasion. I, however, am old-fashioned—a garden-variety transsexual, rather than a postmodernist shape shifter. The ease of my transformation—a real luxury among male-to-female transsexuals—gives me the willies. It's hard not to wonder if an identity that can so easily be erased qualifies as an identity at all. But, for me, as for other garden-variety transsexuals, gender is always a paradox. On the one hand, gender is at the core of my identity—my sense of being female is the most jealously guarded secret of my life. On the other hand, gender is utterly superficial, a matter of clothing and gesture and the other artifices that prompt others to see the image, male or female, I want them to see. When, in a few months, I find myself alone, homeless, spouseless, jobless, who, exactly, will I be alone with? A trick of cloth and makeup or the person I truly am? And will anyone, including me, be able to tell the difference?

But I have more immediate problems. It isn't enough to simply look like a male—I have to function as one, in front of students. I love teaching; it's the only form of intimacy I've found that requires no embarrassing self-disclosures. In fact, my lack of a real self has always seemed like an advantage in the classroom. It enables me to listen more closely, to recognize the often profound implications of my students' comments, to focus on their insights rather than my own.

For years, this communion compensated for my inability to feel fully present in relationships. For the hour or two I spent in class, I was as present as anyone needed me to be. But, in keeping with the Alice-in-Wonderland logic of transition, the closer I have come to being my true self, the harder it has become to really be with my students. The pervasive sense of nonexistence that enabled and inspired me to be a teacher is now making it hard to listen to my students at all. I, who have always found class time too short, keep stealing glances at the clock like the most restless undergraduate. Sometimes I find myself blinking back tears, nodding in what I hope is a convincing semblance of response while I struggle to get my pain and disorientation under control. Only thirty minutes left, I tell myself. Only twenty. Only ten. Unfortunately, the countdown to my release from my impersonation of the male professor my students know is also a countdown to coming out as a transsexual and, I'm sure, ending my teaching career. Only eight weeks as a professor left. Only three. Only two.

But today the clock is still at six, and I can't honestly say if that's a good thing or a bad one. Every day, functioning as a male is harder. By that clock, six weeks is a long, long time. But having struggled through two graduate degrees, innumerable teaching positions, and the accumulation of a mountain of debt to achieve tenure at an institution I love, the six weeks left of my career seem like an eye blink.

My wife, understandably anxious at the prospect of the imminent loss of the livelihood that supports our family, can't understand why I need to come out at work. "Teaching," she argues, "has nothing to do with being male or female." Well, yes—in the sense that one doesn't have to be one or the other in order to teach. But when I teach as a man, I become sick. Very sick. Which is what I am getting as I walk the remaining twenty blocks to work. The feeling of being alive is ebbing out of me, the numbness is seeping back. I'm having trouble crossing the street—partly because the waves of disorientation (what am I? who am I? am I?) make it hard to work out the physics of rushing bodies and vehicles, partly because being flattened by an oncoming delivery truck seems preferable to walking, talking, and otherwise functioning as a man. Gender is everywhere I look, smeared across every face, wrapped like a flag around every body. Gender shouts at me from shop windows, shrieks from racks of magazines, holds hands shyly in doorways. Every gesture, every tone of voice, every one of the hundreds of bodies in my vicinity is marked as male or female. I am the only creature that is both and neither.

It's a lovely spring day, warm without being hot, though homeless people still huddle in masses of donated blankets, tossing and turning in the winter night that, for them, never completely ends. I give money to a man I've passed in both my guises. "I know you," he always says, and then "Thank you, honey" or "Thanks, guy," depending on whether he sees a man or a woman on the other side of the dollar bill. My female identity is so fragile that sometimes a stranger's "honey" or "ma'am" is the only confirmation I have that I exist, that others can see me too. A single "sir" can ruin my whole day—even when I'm presenting a male image. Today the man, deep in conversation, ignores me as I put money in his jar. I'm grateful to be spared his gendered gratitude.

The shattered feeling that always follows the change from female to male recedes into a blur of grief. Once again I have—what is the old gangster phrase?—rubbed myself out. I don't know if other transsexuals feel this way. Transsexuals don't seem to talk much about the tumult of mid-transition, when we swing back and forth between male and female, like clappers in the ever-tolling bell of gender.

I pass the last bagel vendor—I was hungry, but now the thought of food disgusts me, as does everything connected with my body—and turn the corner. My building is up ahead. The guard at the desk is the first person who sees me. His gaze, his recognition, snaps the lid shut on the sarcophagus of maleness.

I don't have far to go, but, after making my way through the crowd of effortlessly female students, by the time I reach my office,

I am very, very sick. The walls are spinning, I've started to cry, and I thank God (in my way, I'm as religious as my students) that I have a door to close behind me. Until this year, my door was always open. This year, it is always closed, and that has enabled me, on more than one occasion, to curl up in a fetal position and give myself over to pain. It also enables me to share my crisis with the small, exhausted group of friends who have decided to keep me alive. Bravely they ask, when they e-mail me or pick up the phone to my strangled imitation of a female voice, how I am. Bravely they listen to the latest update on my agonies. Often they don't know what to say. I'd be happy to advise them, but I have no idea. None of us has ever gone through this before. They tell me I exist; they tell me not to hurt myself; they tell me my voice sounds fine; they tell me I don't look deformed no matter how deformed I feel. Sometimes they make me laugh; sometimes they make me promise; sometimes they tell me to wait, they will be right there. Keepers of a future I still can't imagine, they tell me things will not always be this way. They hope for me; they wait with me. They tell me I *will* make it through the next class. They remind me that I always have.

It's time. I pack up my books and other teaching materials, trying to remember what's going on in each class, what we were discussing, what I have assigned. When I designed the syllabi, the readings fit into a coherent intellectual journey; now, the readings seem like a series of ordeals, rather than stages of learning. What are my students' names? I have taught them for months, teased them, critiqued them, e-mailed them at midnight and dawn, but now my mind is a blank. I look at the roster, trying to remember the faces that go with the names. Bits and pieces sift back, through the dysphoric haze. Tears fill my eyes. I'm losing them, losing all of them, losing everyone.

I take a deep breath and open the door. Start smiling, nodding. I thank the student who dragged the heavy desks into the circle that is de rigueur for creative writing classes, trying not to hear the voice that comes out of my throat. The voice is deep, rough, affectless, a man's voice, the voice of a man wrapped in an irritable haze of self-absorption. I know that's not right. I love teaching, I don't want to sound this way, but my voice is no longer mine. If I think about how I sound, I will pass out. They'll try to revive me, and they'll see the truth that is under my clothes, and when I wake up everything will be over. The abomination—the unemployed abomination—will be revealed to everyone.

But I'm not passing out. I'm talking—or, rather, the voice emerging from my throat is talking. The teacher role is taking over. I can't quite understand what my students are saying—the din of gender dysphoria crashes like surf, intermittently drowning their voices—but, by following their faces and gestures, I can fake my way through these brief conversations. I clench my travel mug as hard as I can. I want to feel something, pain if nothing else, but I can't. No one is there to feel.

I open my mouth. Jokes come out, minutiae of assignment and attendance. I uncross my legs, I straighten my head, I clasp my hands in front of me, doing my best to project an image of maleness. Don't worry, I tell myself, just do what you've always done. To them, you're the man you've always been.

Someday, I tell myself, students will see *me*, the real me, and not an image I am hiding within. When I say "I," I won't be lying to them.

But when that day comes—when they see me not as a man but as someone born male and living as a woman—will they be able to recognize me as human? To see my paradoxical relation to gender as an expression rather than a perversion of the image in which they and I believe God made humanity? Genesis 1:27 seems to decree transsexuality a theological impossibility: "God created humanity in God's own image: male and female God created them." Kabbalistic mystics have read this verse as implying that the first human, Adam Kadmon, the primordial Adam, was a hermaphrodite, embodying, like God, both sides of the gender binary. But no voice in Jewish tradition has ever suggested that God is a transsexual. If maleness and femaleness reflect the image of God, what image of God, what form of humanity, does transsexuality reflect? None, I'm sure, that my students would accept.

My wife is probably right: gender shouldn't matter in academia. But gender *does* matter to my students. Gender shapes the lives of women who follow traditional Jewish law as pervasively and as profoundly as gender has shaped mine. For everyone in this class-room, gender and learning are intimately, inexorably entwined. Today's topic is personae—fictional identities that simulta-neously conceal and reflect their creators. When I designed the syllabus, I didn't realize how painful the irony I had built into it would be. Without my male persona, I couldn't stand here teaching these students. But, for Jews, teaching is a sacred act, a way of revealing the image of God. Is the male image I'm hiding behind revealing or concealing my Creator?

I wish I knew. I wish I could stop talking about personae in poetry and tell my students the truth—not just the truth about me but what that truth has taught me about the image of God. I wish I could tell them how hard it can be and how necessary it is to embody that image, to find it in oneself and to find the self that can make God visible in the world. When you look in the mirror, I want to say, you see your own faces; when I look in the mirror, I see the mystery of God's creation. Look at what makes me so hard to look at. If you can see the image of God in me, you'll see God everywhere.

5
Suicide

So there I was, a week or two later, howling on hands and knees on the terra-cotta tiles of my globe-trotting friend's West Village apartment, finally ready to die. Jumping would be the easiest way to go; I wondered how hard it would be to unlock the floor-to-ceiling windows of the ninth-story penthouse. I lifted my head from the tile on which I had been banging it and brushed enough tears from my eyes to see the little iron railing outside the windows. A balcony. That meant the windows were designed to be opened, that if I could crawl from the kitchen area through the dining area to the living room area and make my way behind the couch, I could open them and throw myself out.

Nine stories should be enough. And the sky was warm and blue and empty. I could almost feel myself falling through it. I had waited so long to let go.

I never much wanted to live. Wait, that isn't true—but, since English offers only one gender-neutral first-person pronoun, it's hard for me to make sweeping statements about my life. I never wanted to live as the male I was, and I never wanted the male I was to live, and, as long as I was living as a man, the I who could say "I want to live" didn't exist.

When I was a child, the only "I" I had was always hoping aches and illnesses would blossom into something terminal.

Alongside the usual childhood longings for bicycles and Barbies, I longed, in a childish way, for death. Death, I thought, would solve all my problems—not just the problems I struggled with but the problems I could feel radiating out of me, turning my nuclear, lower-middle-class family into a shadow-puppet theater of smiling fear and good-humored misery.

My parents didn't seem to notice, but something was terribly wrong with us, and I knew it was me.

Sometimes death seemed close. An atypical reaction to a new measles vaccine landed me in the hospital for a few feverish weeks. Laying the ground for what I hoped would be a heroic demise, I joked through every pill and poke—and, to my disappointment, got better. No doubt there were other children on my ward, children who *wanted* to live, who were actually dying, but it wasn't going to be me. Once I passed out at a county fair—but it turned out to be dehydration. When I was nine or ten, though, things looked up. I began to suffer from headaches so severe I had to leave school early most afternoons. I would get dizzy, my head would throb, the blackboard would pulse closer and suddenly slide away. Space and time rang in my ears; my schoolmates raised their hands in slow motion, behind air that had thickened into glass.

Nowadays I would ascribe such symptoms to gender dysphoria. Then, my heart quickened at the thought that life was becoming unlivable. My hopes for a tragically early exit received a boost when my pediatrician, an elderly German man who typed so fast with two index fingers that the prescriptions he banged out on his manual typewriter sounded like mass executions, referred me for an electroencephalogram—which meant, I decided, that I must have a brain tumor. Of all the childhood deaths I'd heard of, that seemed the most fitting, because death would grow in the same space, out of the same tissue, in which my strangely twisted sense of self had formed.

As they hooked the contacts to my skull, I was sure that any minute I would hear the wonderfully ghastly news. The technician, I imagined, looked worried; no doubt he could tell I had a tumor just from the shape of my skull. The pens tracing the electrical activity in my brain scratched and whispered like the fingertips of death.

Though my brain obviously wasn't, the electroencephalogram was completely normal.

Twice I tried to take matters into my own hands. The first time, I was six. I was trailing a gang of older kids who lived on my block. We ran through yards and houses, starting and stopping according to rules I could never fathom. The frantic parade paused in someone's mother's laundry room. A bottle of Clorox sat on a washing machine, dirty white plastic on dirty white ceramic. But it wasn't the matching décor that caught my attention. "Would you die if you drank that?" I asked the oldest kid. "Sure," he said, and, following a signal I hadn't noticed, raced off with the others. I was alone. The cool, quiet air smelled damp and clean. I stretched up on tiptoes toward the Clorox bottle, pulled it down to my chest—it was almost empty—and unscrewed the cap. The smell was awful. That startled me. How could death smell so bad? I hesitated for a moment, then put the bottle to my lips. Soon some grownup would find me stretched out on the basement floor, bravely clutching the now-empty bottle of Clorox. A sour, stinging taste flooded my mouth.

To my shame, I put the bottle down.

My other attempt was equally revealing of my lack—so it seemed to me—of the courage that enabled children I heard about on the news to hang or shoot or stab themselves. It was a dark and snowy afternoon. I came home from school at the usual time, put on my coat and gloves, and headed out among the dim, starry drifts. I didn't know where I was going at first, and then I did. I lay down in a hollow between snowbanks. I could see the shine of the streetlight in front of my house, the suddenly distant yellow of its windows, but no one could see me. I decided to lie there until I fell asleep and froze to death. It seemed easy enough. I was tired. "Come, sweet death," our third-grade music teacher had taught us to sing in German. A strange choice for eight-year-olds, but I found it reassuring that some long-gone grown-up named Ludwig had felt the same way I did.

It takes a while to freeze to death in a coat and boots and gloves. I hadn't realized how boring and uncomfortable it would be. How lonely when no one came to look for me.

When I got back to the house, no one had noticed I was gone. I don't want to give the wrong impression. I was no pint-sized Lady Lazarus. For most of my childhood, I was mildly, not violently and certainly not effectively, inclined to die. The idea of dying excited me; the idea of living didn't.

A therapist once reduced me to tears, in the pre-estrogen days when I never cried, by asking if there had been any good times when I was a child. I wasn't crying because the answer was no; I was crying because the answer was yes.

As twentieth-century childhoods go, mine was among the blessed. Unlike millions of children, I lived in a house, with a room of my own, in a place that was physically safe, under the care of two parents who kept me fed and clothed and saw to my education. There were pancakes and waffles and ecstatic glides through summer dusk on my bicycle beside my father. There was a snowstorm when the lights went out and we had to make a fire in the rarely used fireplace to keep warm. We roasted marshmallows and sang songs because there was nothing else to do in the dark. The next day, the world was too white to look at, and the snow was so high my father had to shoulder open the screen porch door. There were comic books and science fiction and little plastic soldiers (dolls, of course, were off limits) and armadas of walnut shells floating over the body I fantasized about transforming during long, hot baths. My father built me a headboard that I plastered with glow-in-the-dark stickers from cereal boxes. When I turned out the light, the stickers would bathe me in a dazzling green glow. On weekends and vacations I always slept in, with the enthusiastic encouragement of my mother, who never seemed prouder than when I "slept myself around the clock." Apart from a series of small, unfortunate green turtles and my own fantasies, death didn't touch my life until I was twelve, when my mother's mother, a woman I barely knew, succumbed to the dementia that had years ago consumed her mind.

Anyone who knew me would have been astonished to hear that I wanted to die. But, then, no one really knew me.

Dying would have been relatively easy when I was an adolescent—trans teens do it all the time—but, apart from typical, spur-of-the-moment, here-I-am-crossing-a-bridge-should-I-jump sorts of impulses, I rarely thought about suicide. My own, that is. But I was riveted by Karen, a girl I knew in ninth grade who briefly achieved popularity by announcing, every few minutes, that she was going to go kill herself. For weeks, a select group of initiates replayed, with heroic sincerity, the drama of saving her life. We hung out in an abandoned railway tunnel alongside the Genesee River, a conveniently apocalyptic setting that offered several credible options for Karen to make good on her threats. We talked endlessly about her problems, attempting to browbeat her into self-esteem. But eventually her suicide announcements became boring. What she longed for, we realized, was not death but attention—and all of us were dying for that. And, if she wasn't really about to kill herself, then we weren't really saving her. The fellowship in which we had been basking, the camaraderie that grows among first responders and others on whom lives depend, were as empty and self-indulgent as her threats. Once we realized she was going to live, Karen ceased to be a Noble Cause, and, as one, we turned away from her.

Karen taught me the short social shelf life of suicide threats. I taunted myself in my suicidal moments by imagining myself as her, running down the dark, concrete-strewn tunnel, looking over my shoulder to make sure someone was there to pull me back. If I didn't want to be Karen, I shouldn't start down that tunnel unless I was going all the way.

By the time I got to college, my suicidal impulses had subsided into a nagging feeling of failure—I had neglected to do something important, something I really had to get to sooner or later. The urge to kill myself surfaced most frequently in the temper tantrums with which I responded to anyone who pointed out I was less than perfect. It never occurred to me that there was anything wrong with responding to criticism—almost always well founded—by saying to myself and, occasionally, to my criticizer, "If *that's* true about me, I really just need to die." For me, feeling suicidal came more naturally than taking responsibility for my behavior. Taking responsibility made me feel small, embarrassed, woefully unprepared for adulthood. Feeling suicidal, on the other hand, made me feel important, courageous, as though my life were always on the line and a single misstep could push me over the edge.

Fortunately for both of us, my future wife had no patience for any of this—that, I realized, years later, was one of the qualities that drew me to her. She wasn't taken in by me—which meant that I couldn't continue be taken in by myself. As long as I was with her, I wouldn't kill myself simply because dying was easier than acting like a grown-up. If I was going to kill myself, I wanted to kill myself heroically, to relieve the pain of others, not just to escape my own.

There is no direct connection between transsexuality and suicidality. You don't have to be suicidal to be a transsexual, and you certainly don't have to be trans to want to kill yourself. But feeling like a stranger in one's own body makes it hard to feel alive: not just to feel the physical thrill of life, the delight of filling and flexing a body, of tasting and touching, smelling and seeing, of sound waves shaking the tiny hammers of the ears, but to feel the visceral determination to exist that makes human beings, no matter how miserable, fight so hard to live. I'd never felt that determination, and so it had come as no surprise when I read that suicide is common among transsexuals—as many as one in five of us, according to one of the many unreliable statistics on transsexuality, dies by our own hands.

Even as a child, I knew that suicide was considered a sin, and, even as a child, I decided that the God who had made life feel so wrong to me would accept, if not welcome, my determination to end it. In fact, for years, on Rosh Hashanah and Yom Kippur, the holiest days of the Jewish year, days set aside for remembering and repenting for sins, I would weep and beat my breast both for the sin of not delighting in life and for the sin, as it seemed to me, of failing to end the life in which I couldn't delight.

All those years, I believed that if I ever began to be for myself—to live as a woman—my desire to die would vanish. How could I keep wanting to die if I'd finally started to live?

But, as my trans friend R says, transition is like filleting yourself: you turn your former self inside out, eliminating all the structures and routines that gave you shape, and revealing every contradiction, vulnerability, and unresolved problem. So, perhaps it isn't surprising that over the year and a half since I had told my wife that I could no longer bear the pain of dysphoria, as my lifelong fantasies of transformation gave way to my first wobbly steps as a woman, I found it almost impossible to separate my craving for life from my craving for death. Like some hideous dog-eared teddy bear, the wish to die comforted me, kept me company, whispered to me in the dark when no one else was there.

My therapist urged me to take antidepressants. Unfortunately, most antidepressants made my suicidal impulses worse. One conjured a voice in my head that suggested, with inarguable logic, that I should kill myself as soon as possible to spare myself and others the tedium of my existence. Another made every step, every breath, every sight and sound feel leaden, as though life had become gravity dragging me down toward death. A third kept me awake all night with an almost irresistible urge to cut myself open. I began to find the search for an antidepressant more depressing than being suicidal.

Everything looks different when you are getting ready to kill yourself—more beautiful, more painful, impossibly distant and too close to endure. Life becomes black and white, everything and nothing, a yin/yang of absolute gratitude and absolute despair. There were times when every gleam of light, every squeal of tire, seemed perfect, too perfect, aspects of a magnificent whole that hung before me like a sphere of crystal, impossible to look away from, impossible to enter. There were times when I saw nothing but pain: the mother's indifference to her baby's babbling; the impersonal slam of a taxi cab door; the needs and yearnings embodied in supermarkets and restaurants and clothing stores that dogged and dragged down everything human.

There is a surprising generosity to death; it offers itself everywhere. One morning, on my way to work, I had my choice of two easy, no-fault denouements: a truck that accelerated through a changing light as I stepped off the curb and a pain in my nose that I knew from experience meant the recurrence of an infection that, if left untreated, had excellent chances of spreading through my sinuses into my brain. Both deaths would seem accidental to my children rather than self-inflicted—my therapist had explained again and again what happens to children who lose a parent to suicide—and, though friends might guess the truth, the insurance company wouldn't.

Both deaths, though, were inconvenient. The truck would smear me all over the pavement; it would be hard for my children to mourn bloody asphalt. The nose infection would leave my body intact, but the dementia preceding death would force my children to witness a particularly ugly unmaking.

Once I started seriously planning my demise in the first frigid weeks of 2007, I found that inconvenience is an inescapable aspect of suicide. The more violent forms, like the truck, make messes that spatter many lives. Poisons would make it clear I had killed myself. I had heard that injecting an air bubble into my bloodstream would induce a natural-seeming heart attack, but how would I hit the vein, and how would I know how much air to inject? Google was no help—all that came up under "methods of suicide" were websites devoted to discouraging people from killing themselves—and I could never figure out how to circumspectly ask my friends in health care for a tutorial in self-destruction.

As weeks of longing for death stretched into months, I realized I had reached a sort of détente, a kind of equilibrium. No matter how much I wanted to die, I knew that, for the time being, I would not make a conscious decision to end my life. That was depressing. Suicide was the closest thing I had to hope, my guarantee that, no matter how much my existence hurt me or my family, I could always pull the plug. But, though I had renounced what you might call rationality-assisted suicide, I still clung to the prospect that I might, on the spur of some particularly excruciating moment, irrationally take my life.

The particularly excruciating moment had arrived. There I was on my friend's terra-cotta tile floor, with the clear blue sky of death a few yards of wood floor and a few inches of glass away. The sounds coming out of me were neither male nor female; long, trailing animal howls ended in guttering gurgles, mewling whimpers, a thin keening whine, like a newborn kitten starving. I had snot all over my face, and I sputtered as I dug my long, ragged, recently and badly polished nails into my stomach, trying to drive them deep enough to rupture the bubble that was me.

Oddly enough, even after months of planning suicide, I never expected to find myself in this condition. I had come to New York for refuge. Though at the end of the semester I would begin living full-time as a woman, I was still living as a man with my wife and children. When I was in Massachusetts, I had little opportunity to "be myself"—to put on any of the small cache of hand-me-down skirts, blouses, and dresses I had pieced together and stuffed into a dark, unused corner of an unused room of our basement. Besides, I had come too far for surreptitious cross-dressing to feel anything other than demeaning, as though I were engaging in a shameful fetish, rather than a process of becoming. These few spring days in New York would give me a few days, whole days rather than stolen hours, to be myself.

The penthouse my friend had lent me was three floors of unfussy luxury. I had no responsibilities, no one to think about but myself, nothing to accomplish but rest and recuperation. For once, there was no anguished oscillation between female and male. I lay down as a woman and I rose as a woman, I dressed at leisure, choosing among clothes that had been hung on hangers rather than stuffed in a bag. I put on makeup in a private bathroom, with no one banging on the door, and did my voice exercises in private, where no one could hear me. It was a glimpse of the future I longed for, a few days of the uninterrupted selfhood nontranspeople seem to take for granted, seventy-two hours of being me.

I had never done this before—left my family for no purpose other than to take care of myself. But, then, I had never really taken care of myself. During my three-day teaching stints in New York, I sat at my desk from 7:30 a.m. till 10 p.m. or later, leaving only to teach classes and use the bathroom. I kept food at my desk—nutrition bars, dried cereal, apples, baby carrots—so that I wouldn't have to spend money or time on eating.

In theory, three days of leisure in New York would give me both a much-needed rest and my first chance to live without the painful pretense of masculinity—my first chance, I thought, to really feel well. The first day I drifted pleasantly around the city in what I didn't yet realize was an unfashionably long skirt. But, on the second day, I came down with the flu. For the past couple of decades, I had been amazingly resistant to illness; when I was sick or hurt, I coped as I coped with living as a male, by dissociating from my body, so that I felt little or nothing. It was easy to dissociate when I was living as a man—I didn't want to feel my body anyway—but I couldn't dissociate now that I was living as a woman. That, I suddenly realized, was one of the consequences of having a body—there's no easy escape from its discomforts. I was too sick to relax, too sick to stroll, too tired and nauseated to do anything but doze in a twisted heap of covers. Instead of solidifying my flickering sense of self, I was lying alone, surrounded by someone else's life. If I had been home, I would have coped by forcing myself to take care of the kids. But here there was no one to take care of but myself, and what kind of raison d'être was that?

I called my children. Are you coming home tonight, Daddy? my middle daughter asked. You always come home on Thursday nights. I'm sorry, honey, I told her. I'm too sick to get to the bus. Are you coming home to me? my three-year-old asked. Why do you want to miss me?

I don't want to miss you, I sobbed, too quietly for her to hear.

It was a long time before I was able to hang up, though I could barely speak.

I had run away from my children to be myself, and now the self I had run away to be had become a useless heap of organs.

I called Elizabeth, the friend who had become my designated sanity. "There's nothing you can do for anyone now but get better," she said. "If you can't sleep, read or watch a movie." Reading was out of the question. But I did have a portable DVD player with me, and a few selections I'd taken the day before from the penthouse's library. One had interested me for years: *Ma Vie en Rose* (*My Life in Pink*), a French film about a little transgirl who comes out to her suburban family. The alternative to *My Life* was *The Star Wars Trilogy*, and my desire to watch light-saber-mediated male identity crises had plummeted with my testosterone level.

My Life it was.

It was immediately clear that I had made the wrong choice. Sitting on my stomach, a few inches from my face, was a miniature French version of the transgirl I should have been—a girl too brave, too honest, too strong, too much of a person not to be herself. At the age when I was training myself to look away from dolls, this girl was donning party dresses for huge family barbecues, practicing makeup techniques, and offering charming affirmations of her identity whenever her parents stopped shouting at her. When I was a kid, I couldn't risk becoming someone my family would despise; she couldn't risk becoming someone *she* would despise. In a few minutes of digitized celluloid, she displayed more courage and integrity than I had displayed in a lifetime.

I am told that those who aren't in the midst of a gender-dysphoric nervous breakdown find *Ma Vie en Rose* a gracefully written, well-acted, and imaginatively photographed comedy. If you ever watch it, please let me know what the happy ending is. I never got anywhere near it. When the transgirl's mother and father, whose easy, affectionate intimacy reminded me of the relationship I had once enjoyed with my wife, started screaming at each other that their marriage had been a mistake, the overburdened borders between *My Life* and my life collapsed. There they were, co-starring on the five-inch silver screen: the abject cowardice of my childhood self and the familial destruction my attempt to get beyond it was wreaking.

The truth was as clear as the subtitles that lingered beneath the looks of hatred the husband and wife were exchanging over the heads of the boy who had turned out to be their daughter: *You have failed your family.* No matter what they screamed, that seemed to be the translation. My children needed me to come home, and I couldn't even pull myself out of bed. My children needed an intact home, and I couldn't stand to be anything my wife could stand the sight of. My children needed me to stay male, and I couldn't. For decades I had told myself that my constant sense of failure was the result of living the wrong life, that there was, or at least could be, a real me for whom failure would be an occasional occurrence, rather than a mode of existence. But this *was* the other life; I *was* the real me.

Every failure of my failure-strewn life streamed back to me, settling over my limbs like migrating monarchs weighing down trees in Monterey. But these failures weren't migrating; they had reached their origin and their destination. They were here to stay.

I shut off the DVD player. Sun poured through my friend's many windows, gilding the miles of city embraced by her views. My stomach lurched and my head spun as I struggled into sitting position. I had to get up, to find a way out of the feverish tangle of sheets.

Soon my children would know what I was; soon they would know what I had done to our family; soon they would realize what I had done to their lives.

Soon they would be relieved when I didn't come home.

I lurched past the bathroom toward the narrow counter that demarcated the kitchen area. I was screaming now, battering my ribs and stomach with my fists. I fell to my knees and began banging my head against the terra-cotta floor. How could I have let myself live? If I had died decades ago, when I was supposed to, none of this suffering would ever have happened.

Suicide had been my duty as a child; now it was my obligation as a parent.

I wondered suddenly how thick my friend's walls were. The neighbors must be hearing my howls.

I dug my nails deep into my skin. The stabs of pain cleared my head a little. I didn't need to get to the windows. I was lying in a kitchen. All I needed to do was stand up, open a drawer, grab something sharp, and drive it into my stomach. That would relieve the failure that was digging—that had always been digging—from my insides out.

I realized that I had stopped howling. I imagined my cell phone ringing a few feet away from my dead body. My children would call, and I wouldn't answer. I would never answer. Even my heroic suicide would be a failure. My effort to spare them pain would hurt them more than ever.

I found myself crawling toward the bedroom, curling in a fetal ball around my cell phone, speed-dialing every friend I had.

No one answered.

Suicide　　　73

I curled tighter. I was crying again, but very softly.

The phone rang. Someone had gotten my message. All I had to do was unclench my fists and answer.

In the fall of 2005, when I was still longing for transition, craving the transformation I feared would never happen, a female-to-male friend of mine assured me that, someday, people would tell me how brave I was. "When they say that to me," he said, "I tell them it doesn't take much courage to run *out* of a burning house."

After a lifetime of fear and hiding, I can't, in good conscience, make much claim to courage. I avoided transition until I was no longer capable of pretending to be what others wanted me to be. If living as a man hadn't become physically intolerable, I would still be living my old half-life, a ghost, yes, but a friendly ghost, blessed with the ability to care for those I loved even though they couldn't really see me.

My friend was right. It doesn't take courage to run out of a burning house—it takes courage to stay there for the sake of those you love. Which brings me back to the half-born creature howling on my friend's terra-cotta tiles, wavering between windows and knives. I had "chosen"—if that's the word for following the deepest, most painful promptings of existence—transition because that was the only way I could relieve the pain of being. I had run out of the burning house, and now my family was going up in flames.

I would like to think that crawling to the phone was the moral equivalent of running back into the burning house, that I survived because I realized I had more to give my children than my own destruction. But all I know is that I left my friend's windows closed and never touched her cutlery.

"Transition" is what doctors and midwives call the fiercest part of labor. Caught in the birth canal, I couldn't go back and couldn't stay put. What held me for years, what nurtured me and kept me safe, was collapsing all around me, pushing me forward toward— and that's where the metaphor left me, in the violently contracting darkness of becoming.

6

Truth

So, did *you* go to an all-girl school?" the elegantly dressed woman asks. Since I started my transition, I've been asked a lot of questions by friends and fellow travelers, but this is a new one. Not only did I not go to an all-girl school; I only recently started to use all-girl bathrooms. Life as a woman is still weeks away.

We're sitting at a small table crowded with cross-cultural vegetarian food, in the second hour of a Greenwich Village dinner. This is the third time I've met Alana. We are at the stage of acquaintance when people exchange stories of youth—where we grew up, and how, and how those beginnings led us to become the people we are today. It's time to exchange mild intimacies that demonstrate how open and honest we are willing to be with each other.

Alana is gay, the best friend of one of the members of my little life-support network, and a widely traveled executive at a major international firm. Between her connections and her sophistication—not to mention my own awkwardness in straddling the gender barrier—I had suspected that by now she saw me as trans.

Apparently, I was wrong.

A young heterosexual couple is wedged approximately fourteen inches from our elbows; the young woman is openly listening to our conversation. I steal a glance at her boyfriend. She's right. We are much more interesting than he is.

This is it, I tell myself. This is the moment I've been waiting for. In intimate visual and aural proximity to a perceptive woman who, as a New York lesbian, is certainly aware of the range of variation in the gender spectrum, I pass. This is the woman-to-authentic-woman conversation I've fantasized about for years. My true self is being accepted as—my true self.

"No," I say. "I never went to an all-girls school." I had just been singing the praises of sororal bonding at the women's college at which I teach; that's what prompted her question. "I went to public school. I guess I romanticize the idea of female community."

There, I've told her the truth—the whole truth, and nothing but the truth, at least with respect to the topic at hand. She now knows my unmonied origins, my educational background, and my tendency to project utopian fantasies onto the female world I have longed for from afar for years.

So why do I feel so utterly phony?

I take a careful bite of food—I still haven't figured out how eating as a woman is different from eating as a man—then drink some water. I'm drinking a lot of water. It's a warm night, and the restaurant is even warmer, but the real reason is my voice. Something about the act of swallowing confuses the muscles in my throat, making it hard for me to regain feminine pitch and timbre when I speak. The whole meal has been the vocal equivalent of walking a tightrope in tights and tutu—and, believe me, I know how bad I would look walking a tightrope in tights and tutu. With every bite, I lose my footing and start to plunge toward the failure I fear every moment I present as a woman: the failure to convincingly approximate my true self.

But if I'm finally presenting my true self, why am I so worried?

I spent days preparing for tonight's appearance. I planned to leave work by five and walk downtown at a leisurely, non-sweat-inducing speed, check into the barebones youth hostel I stay at when I'm in New York, and get dressed and made up in relative luxury. Usually, my outfits reflect combinations of colors, fabrics, and styles that have never been vetted in a mirror. This time, I not only planned my outfit in advance; I also tested it on my therapist and received her unqualified approval. Tonight I would arrive looking and, I hoped, feeling like the woman I truly was.

Fantasy has always been my favorite genre.

Impromptu after-class student meetings left me running forty-five minutes late. I hurtled south along the crowded rush-hour sidewalks, shedding my *kippah* and the few masculinizing accoutrements that could be publicly removed without either breaking stride or rupturing the male persona I needed to maintain in order to check into the hostel as someone who at least putatively matched the bearded face on my driver's license. Not that the hostel staff hadn't figured out the truth. They'd seen me enter as one gender and leave as another so often that the clerk who worked the night shift regularly broke my heart by calling me "sir" no matter what I was wearing. But tonight I didn't want to risk a tête-à-tête about my gender identity. I could take off my *kippah* and brush out my hair, but I had to stay on the boy side of the gender line.

By the time I got downtown, sweat was pouring off me. My damp shirt clung to the sports bra I wore to minimize my minimal breasts. The hostel, of course, didn't have air-conditioning—it barely had air circulation—and I had only forty minutes to get myself into plausible female guise and all the way across town. My "room" was dark—the only light source was a bare, dim fluorescent bulb—and stiflingly hot. I stripped off my boy clothes with one hand, while the other alternately swabbed my body with a towel and frantically pulled crumpled bits of my true self out of my bag. Makeup and clothing flew; sweat kept sliding down my odd, boy/girl curves. My skirt and blouse, carefully but clumsily folded before being hauled across three states, emerged as masses of wrinkles.

Vainly hoping to cool—and dry—off, I put on jewelry first, clip-on earrings and cheap necklaces spilling across the narrow, nun-worthy bed. When I finally pulled on my blouse and skirt, I found my only pair of panty hose was ripped and laddered. Fortunately I was wearing a long skirt, but the tears near the toes would be a problem with sandals. That's when I discovered that I had forgotten to pack my sandals. The only shoes in my bag were high heels I had worn once before. Perfect choice for a mile-long cross-town sprint.

The process of assembling my true self had gone so fabulously badly that it was almost anticlimactic when, after struggling to put on makeup in the flickering fluorescent light using a tiny compact mirror, I got the shakes the moment I started on mascara. Small but disfiguring black blobs settled gently just beneath and to the sides of my lashes. Any fashion flaws I had avoided—there weren't many—were more than made up for by the enormous, worn leather computer bag on my shoulder. I had also forgotten to pack my purse.

I hoped the restaurant would be dark.

It wasn't as hard to run in high heels as I'd feared, though the flouncing gait I developed—a cross between *That Girl* and Quasimodo—frightened pigeons and small children from one side of the Village to the other. Panting, sweat-drenched, and late, my true self tottered into the crowded restaurant and gave the waitress Alana's first name coupled with a last name randomly selected from my hyperventilated memory. The waitress corrected me with a professionally tolerant smile and led me through the bustling dimness.

Tall, slender, sweatless in silver and black, Alana sat waiting at the narrow table, exuding a Zen calm that was dauntingly distant from the maelstrom of crisis that over the past two years had become my natural element. Self-assured, successful, in a stable, long-term relationship, she was about to enjoy a relaxed dinner with an interesting acquaintance.

It didn't seem like we had much in common.

For a moment, I wondered why I had so looked forward to this meeting.

But, when it became clear that Alana didn't know I was trans, I knew why I was there. This was my moment of truth. Alana was the first friend I had made as a woman—not as a man or as a transsexual but as a woman—and, as such, she had the power to confirm that my lifelong wish to become myself had finally come true.

For her to authenticate me, of course, I had to be authentic with her. I had to tell her the truth.

But—not *that* truth. Surely I could find other things to talk about.

"So how are things going at home?" my companion asks tactfully. She knows things are going badly, but she doesn't know why. I met her when her need for a cat sitter matched my need for a free place to stay in New York. The cat and I got along so well that she asked me if I would be interested in adopting him. *I* would, I told her, but things were very difficult with my, er, partner just now. I had already mentioned my children, so she had a general idea of a troubled homescape. Now she'd given me the very opportunity I was looking for, a chance to offer actual and even painful intimacies in return for her tales of a complicated youth in the hinterlands of a troubled African nation.

Nibbling my grilled seitan skewers, I start with the undergraduate romance and work my way to the present, with its fading hopes of a consensual divorce settlement and growing danger of being legally barred from seeing my children.

"I'm sorry," I sniff, apologizing for the weight of emotion under which my voice is threatening to crack.

"Of course," she says. "You're their *mo*ther."

Suddenly I realize that by hewing strictly to the gender-free truth, I have told the biggest string of lies in my highly falsified life. My companion not only thinks I'm a biological woman; she also thinks I'm a married (she knows I live in Massachusetts) gay mom struggling to assert my adoptive rights despite the opposition of my children's birth mother. In telling the story of my marriage, I have inadvertently laid claim to being in the vanguard of lesbian life. After all, I committed to my partner when I was seventeen, an age when many gay people are still sorting out their sexual identities; I had three children with her, when even the most reproductively oriented lesbians tend to stop at two; and I not only got hitched in the relatively short time since the Massachusetts Supreme Court had made marriage possible for gay couples but almost immediately rushed to become one of the first gay spouses embroiled in a nasty divorce.

Dinner, thank God, is over, and neither of us wants dessert. We continue to talk over tea (mine) and coffee (hers). I'm exhausted. Telling the truth—the failure of my attempt to tell the truth, the truth of my failure to find a non-gender-related truth, my failure to establish a true nontrans female life—has erased any dream of receiving from Alana the blessing of authenticity. It doesn't matter what Alana or anyone else thinks. No matter how carefully I arrange my personal history, I will never be the born and raised woman I want so much to be.

I insist on paying, though I and the four people who depend on my income are at the brink of financial disaster and my companion is a well-paid executive with no dependents. I need to own up to the fact that this wasn't a dinner between friends. It was a staged test of the degree to which I had and could become a woman. By swallowing my lies so faithfully, my companion has pushed me to take a teetering, high-heeled step toward the truth that will define my new life: to become who I am, I must admit— no, affirm—what I have been.

7

Choosing Life

I call heaven and earth to witness against you this day:
I have set before you life and death, blessing and curse.
Therefore choose life, that you and your seed may live.

Deuteronomy 30:19

The answer to the problem of being human fits on one small stone. I'm looking at it now: a rounded triangle of Jerusalem stone, its bone whiteness streaked with browns and grays and veins that gleam pink when the sun strikes at the right angle. It's gone through a lot, this stone. One of the corners has shattered, revealing the depthless crystal within. The surface is scored with scratches, lines, and curves so densely clustered they suggest a message in an ancient language. That's the way it is with Jerusalem, a city and an idea inseparable from the damage it has endured and occasioned.

Dina gave me this stone on a sunny Saturday spring morning in Manhattan. She had just returned from Israel. I had just returned from hours of walking from her West Village penthouse to the very bottom of Manhattan, the oldest part, where packed ferries make the circular pilgrimage to Ellis Island.

Dina had slept a few hours—she never sleeps more than a few hours—and was dancing in pajamas through her apartment, which, as usual, was filled with light.

It was the morning after I had decided not to kill myself in her apartment. Fortunately, I didn't tell her about that until after she gave me the present. It's just a little thing, she told me, pulling a crumpled brown bag out of her duffle. It was heavier than I expected. I opened the paper slowly and found myself face to face with the gouged white face of the stone. There were letters painted on it, Hebrew letters, dusk blue outlined, scribal style, in black: *u-va-charta ba-chayim.* And therefore choose life. Underneath, in spidery black ink, was a Hebrew word I'd never seen. I sounded it out slowly to myself: *L-j-o-ee. L'joee.* To Joy.

There it was, the name Annie had given me because, she said, it reflected the way she understood my transition: not as a radical transformation but as an internal adjustment, a shift at my heart as subtle and as crucial as the shift from the "a" in "Jay" to the "o" in "Joy."

It's the hardest thing I've ever done, choosing life.

That sounds strange. Our bodies are so predisposed toward living that they make it hard to experience life as a choice. We can't stop breathing (believe me, I've tried); we can't stop waking; no matter how convincingly our hearts break, they refuse to stop beating. Most of us second our bodies' predilection for existence. The traditional Jewish birthday wish is "May you live to one hundred and twenty." Christians believe that eternal life is the ultimate telos of human existence. The health of nations is measured by life expectancy, and medical science takes the extension of life as an axiomatic mission statement.

But I've never wanted to live a long time. When I was a child, the idea that my tortured little consciousness might go on forever was a prospect of hell, not heaven. Though I often entertained grandiose fantasies of fame or accomplishment, I had no actual ambitions; I couldn't imagine any future and didn't especially want to.

I thought that in this, as in so much else, I was alone, something other (I was wildly ambivalent about whether otherness meant superiority or inferiority) than human. So it startled me when I arrived at the passage in the Torah in which the aged Moses, knowing he is about to die without entering the Promised Land, exhorts the children of Israel to choose life—which meant that he felt, as I did, that life was a difficult choice.

It was a Saturday morning service. I was ten or eleven, sitting among the old, heavily accented, reflexively Orthodox men who made up the *minyan* of our synagogue. My parents weren't religious—my father was an atheist, while my mother carried on Jewish traditions but was noncommittal about why she did so. In my Jewishness, too, I was a mutation. Judaism had always seemed to me alien, exotic, and ineluctably mine, and week after week I felt drawn to sit with the old men and listen to the incomprehensible drone of their prayers. While I did so, I read the Torah—the Hertz edition, a historic apologia published after World War II, whose every commentary seemed to me to whitewash the terrible and terribly compelling problems posed by the text. The prayers droned on, I turned the page, and there it was, in a narrow column of tiny black and white letters beside a thicker block of Hebrew:

I call heaven and earth to witness against you this day:
I have set before you life and death, blessing and curse.
Therefore choose life, that you and your seed may live.

To me, it was clear that the old man's bullying—here's the blessing, here's the curse, choose correctly or die—was a form of desperation. Moses expected everyone to exhibit the hesitation, the confusion, the cowardice that I had thought were mine alone. Staring into the future he wouldn't live to see, Moses was begging us to do what he feared we wouldn't or couldn't do—to distinguish between life and death, and to choose the former.

His honesty still takes my breath away.

For many transsexuals, it's hard to choose life—at least, life as ourselves. Authentic life is neither natural nor automatic for us— it is a choice we make only when we have no other, a fate that has seemed worse than death to some of us. I believe that this will change. I think it is already changing as the public visibility of transsexual people makes the phenomenon familiar rather than frightening and parents become more accepting of their children's fractured genders. Slowly but, I hope, surely, the terrible cost of choosing to live by the gender of our souls is diminishing.

But there is always a cost to choosing life, even when the lives we choose fit socially recognized parameters. To become ourselves, everyone has to go through processes analogous to transition: to remake our lives to reflect truths we have come to embrace as ours; to come out to those who know us differently than we know ourselves; to give up well-worn paths and wander toward the new, sometimes unimaginable places where our inner promptings tell us we belong. Some of us are applauded for choosing life; some of us are punished; but, as a transwoman I thought had had it easy once assured me, we all suffer losses.

Which brings us back to Moses, who, though he lived to be one hundred and twenty, didn't seem to enjoy the life that God had thrust upon him. In fact, Moses wanted nothing more than to live out his days as a Midianite shepherd, which is what he was when he happened to notice, out of the corner of his eye, the flickering tongue of flame from which God first spoke to him. Moses listened politely as God set before him visions of life as a leader, as a savior, as the world-transforming instrument of power beyond comprehension—and just as politely refused. Send whomever you want, Moses said. No wonder God almost killed him on the road to Egypt. Not only because of the gall of a shepherd cold-shouldering an offer from God—but because Moses wouldn't willingly choose life unless the only alternative was death.

But perhaps Moses's reluctance, like the humility that led him to prefer leading sheep to leading a nation, was a necessary qualification for his job. For a nation of slaves to become free— not merely free from bondage but actually free to become themselves—they needed to learn to choose life over death, blessing over curse. The automatic animal reflex of being that had carried them through centuries of servitude wasn't enough to make them partners who could enter into the moral covenant that, from

God's point of view, was the purpose of their redemption. God may have brought the people out of Egypt, but, to actually free them, God needed a human agent who knew what it meant to choose life over death. To set life and death, blessing and curse, before the children of Israel, Moses had to know firsthand the temptation of the unchosen, unlived life, the life that is nothing more than happenstance and duration; had to have recognized that as a form of death; and had to have chosen instead the unknown, unimaginable life in which eighty-year-old shepherds chat with God, slaves walk through water to freedom, and individuals become what everything around them proves they cannot be.

I was grateful to Moses for admitting that it was hard to choose life, and, somehow, despite the clear meaning of his words, I convinced myself that he would understand and even approve of my refusal to choose it. After all, life wasn't available to me in any form in which I could bear to choose it. And, besides, I thought that there was a sort of morality in my refusal to choose life. Years of self-repression had taught me that less of me meant more of everyone else. When I was small, I was a talker. I always had something to say, something that simply *had* to be said, and I was always saying it. But the self-consciousness that enabled me to act like a boy gradually taught me something that had nothing to do with gender. My chatter was drowning out others' voices. When I spoke, others were silenced. I started to count the words I said in a day, in a week. I clenched my jaws, I bit my tongue, I did everything I could think of to school myself to silence. The closer I came to silence, the more I heard the people around me—and the more I realized that my voice was an intrusion, an interruption of the seamless singsong of life. When I held my tongue, life seemed— whole. When I spoke, it shattered.

The lesson was clear: the less of me, the better. Therefore refuse life.

Moses might have wanted to smite me. By blurring the boundaries between life and its opposite, I was assaulting the core of his teaching. I couldn't choose between life and death, because I had chosen not to distinguish between them. By turning death into a way of life, I had turned life into the shadow of death.

Though I still didn't know much about real life, over the two years since spring 2005, when my gender dysphoria became a crisis, I had become quite familiar with the varieties of death. There was the physical death I tiptoed toward during my months of suicidal longing; the death of my male identity; and the growing sense of having been dead for decades that drove me toward life. Sometimes I longed to stop the transition process and embrace that death—perpetuate my body while annihilating myself as a person. Exist without needing to *be*. That would solve everything. I imagined the shell of male flesh smiling, teaching, changing diapers, washing dishes, gliding through its day without a twinge of suffering self. The entire family would be happy. They would have the man they wanted, and I would no longer have to be him.

The Emily Dickinson Diet, I called it: first chill, then stupor, then the letting go. I had spent a lifetime dissociated from my body, so chill was easy. I was used to unplugging whenever I felt too much. My commuting friend, watching me dissociate from overwhelming pain—one moment I was sobbing in her car, the next moment I was joking—said, "That would be useful. Can you teach me how to do it?" "No," I told her. My voice had the ironic, emptied-out quality that goes, for me, with dissociation. "The only way I know involves years of trauma." Even if I could have taught her, I wouldn't have. It's better to suffer than to choose, as I always chose, to split into anaesthetized fragments.

Stupor was harder. To compensate for my dissociation from the feelings that orient most people in daily life, I had to think all the time, and, since I began my transition, my thoughts had speeded up. Even during the simplest conversation, I often found myself cycling through innumerable reflections on the peculiar triangulation that linked the man I seemed to be, the woman I wanted to be, and the dissociated consciousness I actually was. Stupor meant not thinking, and that scared me. I wouldn't know, anymore; wouldn't care; the gerbil wheel of being would squeak into silence.

But, during the sabbatical months that began with my telling my wife that my gender problems had become a protracted crisis, months during which I had no time and no place to be myself, nothing to look forward to at the end of the day but heartbreaking conversations about how my transition was destroying our family, stupor began to seem attractive. It was becoming too hard to think myself through existence, to believe that I was the woman I told myself I was becoming when I had to devote every minute to acting like the man I told myself I'd never been. "You sound like you're fading away," my friends would say when I stole a few moments alone. I was, but I wasn't fading fast enough. Whenever I thought I had finally lost myself in the whirl of domestic chores, whenever thinking seemed to have devolved into the brute routines of being, something would reawaken my awareness of the difference between what I was and what I needed to be.

My frustrated desire for stupor brought me to the brink of letting go. When the younger children were asleep and my son was settling in beside my wife to watch yet another dramatization of the FBI's prowess at locating missing persons, I would walk along our unlit country road, praying to let go, once and for all, of the need to be. Frogs sang from water-filled hollows; owls and bats swooped and screeched; squirrels and chipmunks snapped twigs and rustled leaves; trees whose branches eclipsed the sky gave way to sudden gasps of meadow. One night, I stood a long time beside a clearing. It had been night along the road through the forest, but, here, the evening brightness was still subsiding into shades of blue. There were no stars yet, but Venus shone white and steady above the fireflies' brief flares. The planet's light was calm and quiet, beyond the humid frenzy of the earth. The fireflies, though, had only a few hours of darkness in which to find, among the damp black grasses, the mates that instinct told them would fulfill their lives.

The air was thick with the sounds of creatures. None of us, no matter how desperate or scared we were, could give up being alive.

For me, too, it was the shadow of death that taught me the necessity of life. A few weeks before the end of my male teaching career, I was lying in my New York hostel, trying to sleep. Sleep wouldn't come. I lay in the dark thinking about knives. "Yes," I whispered, "*yes*," gouging myself with my ragged nails, enraged by my humiliating failure to be—anything. Anyone. Me. The time had come. I sat up in the dark, mentally rummaging in my mind through my luggage for something sharp enough—would a little razor do it? a belt tongue?—to cut me open. That's when I heard it, for the first time in my life: the voice of self-preservation. "You can kill Jay," it said distinctly, "but you can't hurt Joy."

Okay, I thought, but killing Jay without hurting Joy was easier said than done. The male self I had constructed had been dying for a long time, and yet he was still there. I zipped myself into him when I went to teach; I sank into him whenever I reentered my family sphere; I signed e-mails and checks as him, I collected rejections and the occasional acceptance on his poems, I saw his face in windows and mirrors floating above the body that was beginning to become mine. I wanted so much to be rid of him, but the truth is that I still needed him, and his death throes were surprisingly hard and sad. In ways that none of my trans fantasies had prepared me for, it *hurt* for my male self to die. As my wife had to witness the dissolution of the man she had loved, I was being forced to witness the dissolution of the man I had been, to watch him fray, fade, fall away: the walk, the manner of speaking, the stance—ironic, distant, but, I hoped, compassionate—from which he had regarded the world.

Now that I wasn't commuting to New York anymore, I was living with my family, enduring what I knew were my final full-time days as that frayed, fading, falling-away man.

You have to get out, my friends told me as I whispered hoarsely into my cell phone about how little I wanted to live. I can't leave my children, I whimpered, trying not to imagine the amputated life I knew was coming closer. I had never lived alone as an adult. Commuting had made nights away from the family a feature of every workweek, but my real life, such as it had been, was with my family.

Now, that family would be better off without me. Though my wife, like me, dreaded our separation, she had needed me to move away since my crisis had started. How could she start to heal, when I—what was left of me—was always there? Though I doubt she saw me as a woman, it had been a long time since I looked like the man she loved, or any man, for that matter. Even when I flattened them with a sports bra, there were noticeable bumps on my chest. My face had thinned, my Slavic cheekbones grown more prominent. There was as little hair on my face and body as laser treatments and daily shaving could leave and enough hair on my head that a lock hung down, fetchingly or ludicrously, over my right eye. My wife could hardly bear to look at me.

My children, too, needed me to go. My son was frank when I asked him. It would reduce the stress, he said. He wasn't violating the unwritten teenage-boy code of cool that required him to disown his own feelings; he was only referring to the obvious stress that radiates from any couple living together in the midst of divorce. That was the safe stress, the impersonal stress, the stress that reflected our family situation, rather than his private pain. But having your father try very hard to turn himself into a woman when you are trying very hard to turn yourself into a man is one of the worst things that can happen to a thirteen-year-old boy, and "stress," I knew, was barely a snowflake on the submerged iceberg of anguish he was trying to deny. Like mine, my son's feelings were too big for him; he was scared that, once he began to acknowledge them, they would swallow him whole. His rage was all he would let me see. It came out in play, when he would hit me or fantasize aloud about putting bullets through my head. It came out at times that would previously have been intimate, when he would sit stiffly at a distance or make a point of reading when we shared a meal by ourselves. My wife was the only one who fully shared his loss—the loss of the maleness of the man he loved—and they had grown very close over the past months. He needs you to leave, I told myself. Don't worry—he won't be left alone.

My youngest child was the least disturbed by my transformation. Every morning, around dawn, she would cry out to be taken from her crib. My wife would nurse her in what used to be our bed, and I would lie on the couch under a blanket, in the watery, thickening light, and wait for the happy thump of her feet as she ran down the dark hall to find me. "Photos," she would say, or "Books," or "Yogurt on the counter," and I would say, "You haven't hugged me yet," and she would clamber up onto my stomach and squirm her way under the blanket, and I would hold her, knowing that if I wanted to, I could count the days remaining when she and I could hold each other like this, rocking together at the edge of dawn, when I could feed her her first bites of the day, read her the first book, be one of the fixtures that, to her, meant home.

Soon I would be gone, and it was hard to tell what hurt more, her loss or mine.

But, for her, it was too soon to mourn. Her concept of gender was still fluid, and the fluidity of my gender was something she had grown up with. Soon she wouldn't remember me as a man, except from the reams of bearded pictures my wife had taken. Those, of course, were increasingly confusing to her. She would wake me up in the morning and order me to look with her at family photos, and she would keep demanding "pictures" all day. I don't know what she saw in them, but I know what she was looking for: the stable, smiling constellation of what used to be her family. It was still there, inside the crisp white borders; outside them, she knew, it had already vanished. But loss for her meant physical absence, and I—some fading version of me—was still physically present. To make sense of this ambiguity, she had become obsessed with who was in the house, who was alone, who would miss us, whom we were missing. "Don't go alone," she begged me, when I told her she couldn't accompany me to my endocrinology appointment. "Then you'll be the missing one."

But, with a knowledge that my son had grown too old to trust, she also knew that I—some version of me—would always return to her.

She needs you to leave, I told myself, so she can see you coming back.

My middle daughter suffered the most visibly. For a while, she tried to stop eating. She had studied nutrition in second grade and told me calmly, "I don't want to live, and if I don't eat, in a week, I'll die." It was better when her anger was turned against me. "Now you'll tell me you *love* me," she would say, her seven-year-old voice dripping the sarcasm of a bitter fifty-year-old. "Now you'll say whatever I feel is *okay*." She would stop, smile horribly, and laugh. "But then, everything you say is a *lie*."

My daughter survived these outbursts, but they didn't reduce her pain. She was determined to hold my wife and me together, in her own psyche if nowhere else, and so she tried to embrace our utterly incompatible views of transition. When she was with me, she would invite me to speak in my "girl voice," brush my hair, coo over feminine frills her mother considered anathema for me. Preternaturally observant, she would register the awkwardness of situations in which I was forced to act male with empathic winks and whispers. When she was with my wife, she threw herself, with equal sincerity and love, into the opposite perspective. She would talk about how uncomfortable my changing appearance made her, the pain I was causing, the way I was destroying our family and her life. How, she would ask, could I do this to them? All of these feelings were true, but, as long as I was there, she could never experience them as hers, only as my wife's and mine, opposite poles of a world that was splitting beneath her feet.

She, too, needed me to leave.

If my wife's and children's anguish were the only reasons for me to leave the house, it would have been much easier to go. But I not only needed to leave for them; I also needed to leave for myself.

Without the weekly respite of walking around as myself in New York, life at home had become intolerable. When I sat up in the morning, I had to make sure the bumps of my breasts weren't too obvious, that no one would see my shaven legs. When I walked, I had to stop myself from swinging my hips. When I spoke, it was in a voice that seemed to come from some affectless abyss. It scared my friends, that voice; I had to use it when I answered the phone to them in front of my kids. I rationed my words as I had when I was a child, not so that others could speak but so that I wouldn't have to hear the sounds coming from my throat. I would go days without using my real voice, the voice that I was working so hard to make real, and increasingly I would forget what my real voice sounded like. Soon, I feared, I would lose it forever. It nauseated me to exist. I went to sleep sick and woke up sick and played with the baby sick and did grocery shopping sick and vacuumed sick and cooked sick and ate sick. Life had become a form of illness. You are fading away, the distant cell phone voices told me. You have to get out of there, or you'll die.

I couldn't bear to surrender a moment of my children's growing, their fussing, their quarrels, the daffy singing into which they would break spontaneously, my son's deepening bellows, my older daughter's sudden and violent artistic inspirations, the thud-thud-thud of our youngest running down the hallway at dawn to smile me into meeting her first imperious demands of the day. Surely it was better to die among them than to leave them behind. Isn't that what parents are supposed to do? To stay with their kids no matter how much it hurts?

Three thousand years late, I had finally reached the steppes of Moab. There, before me, were life and death, blessing and curse. The choice was finally clear, but now I couldn't tell which was blessing and which was curse, and for whom. How could the death of our lives together be life to me? How could a life that was a curse to them be a blessing to me? Easier, infinitely easier, not to make any choice, to deny, as I had so long denied, the possibility of choice, to choose, if I had to choose, to simply fade away. . . .

But that wasn't the choice I made. I posted an ad on the Internet, and someone offered me a room. Moving day—June 26, 2007—was approaching, the day when life, whether blessing or curse—and somehow I knew, contrary to Moses's peroration, that it would inevitably be both—would no longer be a circumstance I suffered for others but a choice I had made for myself.

I didn't need much to live alone, but the little I needed seemed impossible to determine. I had already separated out the summer portion of the hand-me-downs, thrift-store acquisitions, and clearance items that composed my female wardrobe. They were in the basement, except for my underwear, which was upstairs in a dresser drawer in the bedroom I used to share with—No. If I was actually going to move out, I couldn't afford that kind of thinking. But how could I figure out what I needed when what I needed most was to stay with my family? And, since that was no longer possible, what did it matter what clothes I took or didn't?

It mattered. Clothes were my passport between male and female, my means of concealment and revelation, and also my way of traveling between the new life as a woman I hoped I would be starting and the old life, with my children, to which I intended to return every day. No one in my family was ready to see me as myself. Though living as a woman would now be my norm and dressing as a man the temporary aberration, I needed enough clothes to pass on both sides of the spectrum.

And toiletries—after years of commuting I must have a pretty good idea of what to bring, but somehow I didn't.

Then there were books. I didn't read anymore—at least, I hadn't been able to read more than a few pages at a time since my gender crisis had started, and I often wondered if I would ever again experience someone else's voice or world coming to life inside me. It was a humiliating disability for an English professor. Of course, since I had just sent my coming-out letter to the dean, I didn't know how much longer I would be an English professor. ("Dear Dean Bacon," I had started. "This is the most difficult letter I have ever written. . . ." I still hadn't received a response.) But I couldn't live without books . . . could I? Had I really changed that much? What about the shelves and shelves of poetry I had acquired over the years, most of them—the best ones—gifts from my wife? What about the books I needed to complete my critical study of modern American poetry or for the essay I had started months before for *Parnassus*?

Yes. No. Maybe. Teachers need books. Poets need books. Scholars need books. But, for the past year, I had taught and written with fewer books than I had ever imagined possible. You will read again, my friends assured me. You will teach again. But, even if they were right, what did I need to pack right now, for the three-week housesit that was my version of Columbus sailing over the flat line of horizon into a new, round world?

My answer to these questions was the heap of items that grew on the floor of the unfinished basement room in which I had stored the furtive fragments of my female life. Over the past months, more and more of my life had been dumped there—teaching materials, conference papers, books I would never read, books I needed to read, household finances, everything that had previously lived above ground, in the space I had shared with my wife and children. A small fraction of this miscellany made it into the heap that would travel with me from place to temporary place; the rest stayed, doing whatever abandoned objects in damp basements do when no one is looking. Other than clothes and toiletries, I didn't pack much. My notebook computer; manuscripts of the two poetry books I was revising; a science fiction novel I had read twenty pages of a few weeks before; prayer books and bibles; a portable DVD player.

What I needed to live didn't fill the back seat of my car. I found that out on the late June day on which my existence as a man ended. It was heartbreakingly hot. The temperature hovered around one hundred degrees, and sweat poured down me as I shuttled things from the cool basement to the convection oven in which I would soon drive away.

The omens for my new life weren't auspicious. That morning, I had found out that my ancient Altima wouldn't pass inspection without repairs we couldn't afford; I would have to drive with a bright red "R," for "Rejected," pasted on my windshield.

As I finished loading this vehicle of shame, a motion on the ground caught my eye. It was a large toad. I have to run and tell the children, I thought, but, even as the thought formed, I saw that the toad was struggling to escape from the mouth of a snake that had swallowed one leg and sunk its teeth into the toad's belly. This wasn't the sort of natural wonder I was accustomed to sharing with my children. In fact, though we live in the country, surrounded by the life-and-death struggles of creatures on the lower end of the food chain, I had never seen such a thing. The fact that it had materialized at the very moment I was embarking on life as myself seemed to demand allegorical interpretation. None of the obvious ones were very encouraging, though. If I was the toad, it suggested that I wasn't really going to get away—at best, I would tear myself in half, leaving part of me in the mouth of the living death I was trying to escape. If I was the snake, it seemed that my wife was right about me—my life was devouring the lives of those I loved.

I had a vague sense that there were other possible meanings, more abstruse and yet closer to the facts on the ground, in which life itself—the life I was finally, after decades, preparing to encounter— was both the toad and the snake, feeding itself on its own destruction, fighting its own insatiable hunger, living and dying in the same convulsive motion.

But such exalted acts of interpretation were beyond the sweat-soaked transsexual whose life was ending and beginning at the foot of what was no longer her driveway. I knew my duty—my last act as a full-time, live-in parent. I hurried to the screen door that had slammed behind me. "Come quick," I shouted into the dimness that held the woman and three children who were waiting for me to say goodbye. It was utterly wrong and, in some way, right. It was what my role as a parent had become in the past few months: to show my children the ugliness, the anguish, the inescapability of life.

A toad hopping in the mouth of a snake, a snake struggling to swallow a toad, I drove away. My Jerusalem stone, with its ancient, unqualified injunction, drove with me. The stone offered the same answer to everything I said to myself as the streets that had meant home disappeared behind me. I'm leaving my children, I said. *And therefore choose life.* I'm abandoning my family. *And therefore choose life.* I don't really exist. *And therefore choose life.* I'm homeless. *And therefore choose life.* I've lost everything. *And therefore choose life.* I can't stand the pain. *And therefore choose life.* I need to die. *And therefore choose life.* I'm going to—

And therefore choose life.

My life insurance policy's waiting period on suicide was up in two weeks. At almost the same moment, I had become free to begin or end my life.

As I crossed the bridge that separated the region in which I could now walk publicly as myself from the region in which I had agreed, for my wife's and children's sake, to shroud myself in maleness, the tears turned into sobs, the sobs into howls, the howls into screaming, shrieking prayers not to survive this act. It didn't matter that I would see my children the next day, and the next, and the next. I was someone, I would always be someone, who had driven away from those I loved to become myself. My family shrank behind me, shining and distant and fragile as a raindrop on a leaf. Ahead of me lay nothing—nothing I knew, nothing I could imagine, no one I had ever really been.

I stopped screaming. I stopped crying. I stopped feeling. A friend who was flying in to help me learn to live alone was due to arrive in a few hours, and, after all, the damage had been done. The snake's teeth were deep in my stomach; the taste of toad was in my mouth.

It wasn't any life I would have chosen. But I had chosen life.

Part Two

Adolescence

8
Adolescence

Summer 2007

Like a Dior fashion spread gone terribly wrong, the tangle of
sheer lemon dress and not-quite-female skin writhed in the
mirror, struggling to separate flesh from fabric without disturbing
the brown curtain that concealed it from the high-end consignment
browsers on the other side. The writher, of course, was me. The
need to see what I could be had driven me to wrestle the demons
of fashion in the dim glamour of a battered forty-watt deco lamp.
Not only did I need clothes—living full time as a woman presented
a whole different dressing challenge from doing three-hour stints
a few days a week—but I also needed to stare at myself in the mirror,
to learn, as we say in the basement of the fashion world, what was
and wasn't me.

I was particularly drawn to dresses, the ultimate in forbidden
female outerwear. The man in a dress is a staple sight gag in our
culture, and my wife scared herself and the children by conjuring
the image of me walking in broad daylight in a dress. Dresses are
designed to follow the female form, to separate the girls from the
boys; if I could look good in a dress, I would surely have at least
one toe in the Promised Land. Of course, many women, including
most of my friends, consider liberation from dresses one of the
advantages of adulthood. But I had never been forced to wear
dresses as a child, and now, in the dawn-dusk of my middle-aged

99

adolescence, they were the stuff of fantasy, transforming me into housewife or sophisticate, businesswoman or bohemian, flirty college girl or asexual matron, upscale theatergoer or dress-down sunbather.

The lemon dress was the gem of my morning's discoveries, an honest-to-God evening gown whose sweeping, simple lines would emphasize my slight bust. It had one normal and one spaghetti strap, an asymmetry that added flair to its classic severity. I had never wanted any garment more. Unfortunately, as I pulled it over my head, I realized that it was a size, or maybe three, too small. I twisted and turned and yanked to get it down over my very small but suddenly too large breasts, ignoring the pain that shot through the tender nipples. It took a long time, but I managed it and was rewarded by a vision of myself as . . . well, someone else, a distinctly grown-up woman of poise and the sort of existential ease that is the birthright of 1930s movie stars and anyone else who manages to squeeze into gowns like that. For all her ease, though, the woman did have one little problem: an unzipped zipper, agape under the left arm. I pulled, I wrenched, but the zipper wouldn't budge. I lowered my arm; perhaps it wouldn't matter that the gown was open on one side. But, no, the opening was wide enough for my left breast to slip out. The problem, I realized, was the breadth of my chest. I briefly considered surgery. If a couple of ribs were removed, the dress would fit, wouldn't it? Then I noticed how hard it was to inhale, even with the zipper open. There was no getting around it: the dress didn't fit.

The too-beautiful, too-small dress, if not a judgment from God, was an externalization of my ill-fitting body image. As I contemplated my mismatched reflection—the sleek lemon lines on my right side, the flash of pale, hair-flecked flesh on my left— it was obvious that I wasn't becoming anything but sweaty, breathless, and late for a therapy session I clearly needed. With a martyred sigh, I grasped the hem of my ideal of feminine beauty and hoisted it over my head, only to find it even more reluctant to come off than it had been to go on. I squeezed one arm through a strap, but that didn't help—now it too was trapped inside the dress. There were people right on the other side of the curtain, a male customer and a woman whose voice I recognized as one of the salespeople. I thought of asking the saleswoman to help, but a glimpse of my exposed underwear—frayed, pink, and not looking at all the way panties should on a woman's body—convinced me otherwise. There are some battles a transsexual has to fight alone. I worked my trapped arm back up through the strap. The fabric was thin; I could rip it a little, just enough to free myself—but I couldn't bear to destroy something that so beautifully realized the femininity of smaller, more authentic women. I considering buying the dress— it was only a dollar—and wearing it out of the store, then thought better of walking through town with my left breast exposed. I was trapped in a femininity I could neither fit nor escape. In a way, the dress was me, after all.

Clothes shopping was an education I had missed. Clothes had always descended on me from above, from my mother, to be precise, who had to force me into them and who would ask, futilely, whether I liked them, when it should have been obvious that I was doing my best not to look at them at all. Whatever they were, however they fit or didn't, they were not me, the not-me that the world insisted I live in.

But my existential retardation went deeper than clothing. To maintain my male façade, I taught myself to resist my impulses. Impulses threatened to express me, the real me, in unguarded ways, to expose me as the zipper on the lemon dress did. I envied boys who would just do things, burst into laughter or tears, tear off down the street, grab toys from each other, throw themselves into their mothers' arms and throw temper tantrums when they got there, dance with inexplicable delight, engage, as if by telepathic consent, in swirling, chaotic games whose rules and rhythms I could never follow. By the time I had figured out what they were playing, the game had flowed into something else. I taught myself to imitate their spontaneity, their joy—and never to let myself experience them.

How did they do it, I would ask myself, playing over the day's interactions as I lay in bed, breaking them down the way coaches analyze films of opponents' games, critiquing every way in which my performance as a male child had been lacking. But, no matter how carefully I analyzed, the next day, I was just as awkward. Other boys were real children. I was—something else, something hollow, a façade not just of boyhood but of personhood. Terror of discovery had trained me to control my impulses so well that it seemed I didn't feel anything at all.

We become who we are by making choices that expose our unruly selves to the world. I never made those choices, so now, as I told one of my friends, I was literally making myself up as I went along, practicing the impulsiveness I had spent a lifetime suppressing by descending the narrow consignment-store stairs to hunt for one-dollar clothes in the basement. Since I'd moved out to live full-time as a woman in June, trawling bargain-basement clothing had become my main form of recreation. I would paw through every bin, seizing on dresses, skirts, and blouses like a bear scooping fish from a stream. With a heap of clothes overflowing my arms, I would push behind the dressing room curtain to face the dim hermaphroditic reflection in the mirror. Too recent to recognize, too transitional to embrace, this was me, the real me, the me stripped of the magic of feminine fabric.

A few months before, the sight of my body would reduce me to tears. Now a different body faced me, softened, slightly narrowed at shoulders and waist and slightly swollen at the breast. Dark curls tumbled toward my shoulders. Hints of woman were visible through—no, in—the skin I had always hated. Separated by the curtain from the world of real women and real money, I would pull clothes on and off in a fizzy, guilty frenzy. I was getting away with something, many things, actually—not only clothes that were, as they say, a steal but also the impulsive freedom I had never thought to taste, freedom to buy clothes I wanted, freedom to want, freedom to imagine myself wanted, freedom to imagine a life I could recognize as mine.

I made mistakes, of course—that's the nature of impulse: the sheer negligee I took for an evening gown, the marvelously textured blouse whose cut spotlighted the masculinity of my shoulders, the flower-sprinkled velour dress that made me look like a Victorian armchair. Ineluctably drawn to every black skirt I saw, I soon amassed a collection of nearly indistinguishable items. But the mistakes didn't bother me; in a way, I was proud of them. For the first time in my life, I could afford to make mistakes. At one dollar apiece, my failures mattered less than my finds. The sophisticated little black dress with a double row of big white buttons, the long leather skirt, the V-neck black sweater that came as close as anything could to making me look like a French girl—I recounted each purchase to my long-distance friends, ignoring the boredom in their voices in the name of showing them that slowly, decades late, the girl who had never seen herself in the mirror was growing toward them.

As my first days of living as myself gathered into weeks, my impulses became stronger, clearer, more frequent. One day, after hearing that a friend was having her hair cut, I found myself making an appointment at a hair salon, telling the hairdresser that I wanted to try a style that would push me beyond androgyny. My lifelong fears screamed dire warnings about my wife's, my children's, the world's revulsion at an unmistakably feminine me. My junior-high-school-girl ego cringed at the thought of trying to look cute and failing. I ignored them both. Impulse whispered that it was time, that some buried piece of me would emerge beneath the stylist's shears.

Impulse was right. The cut was exactly what I needed, a mass of curls that made a virtue of my natural inclination toward chaotic coiffure. But no sooner had my hairstyle come into focus than my gray hair, which I'd cringed over since spring, became intolerable. A woman asked me during intermission at a local play if I was the mother of one of the middle-aged actors. I had put off doing anything about it, brushing my hair this way and that, plucking white strands, worried that coloring it—the obvious solution—would estrange me from my children. But a few days after my haircut, as I passed a cosmetology school that a friend had recommended, I found myself walking in, making an appointment, and signing a release holding the student and the school harmless for any damage done to my hair, my self-esteem, or my offspring. Blonde, red, orange—what color would I walk out with? I wanted to crumple the release and walk away, but impulse laughed at me. A couple of hours later, my hair was all one color—a slightly richer version of what it had been before I went in.

My wife said nothing. My older daughter said it was too dark. My reflection gave me a self-satisfied smile through a tumble of brown curls.

There are many disadvantages to going through adolescence in middle age. The odds of being the only one you know with acne are greatly increased, as are the odds of making fashion choices everyone else immediately recognizes as disastrous. The rejection fantasies that accompany hormone surges and visible bodily changes are more likely to come true the second time around, when you aren't surrounded by swarms of surging, swelling, angst-ridden peers.

The first time around, I had rushed through adolescence. After a couple of years of drugs and sex and poetry punctuated by weeks of being punitively ignored by my father, I left home at sixteen, volunteered for a few months on a kibbutz, returned, putatively, for the summer but kept leaving to hitchhike back and forth across the country until the college semester started. By the time I was twenty-two, my father had disowned me completely—he never told anyone why—and I had landed abruptly in the midst of adulthood: I was married, working full-time in an office, and living three thousand miles away from the stupid things I'd said and done a few years before. But the trappings of adulthood couldn't still the whispers and occasional screams by which my buried female self reminded me that I had never actually completed childhood, much less adolescence. Part of me—the part that felt most urgently, uncomfortably alive—kept trying to drag me back to the point when I had dissociated myself from the girl I had always wanted to be. I had simply pretended to grow up, and, no matter how settled my life seemed, it was always shadowed by my unfinished development.

The detritus of adolescence returned in bulk when I was in my early thirties. On one of her occasional visits, my mother brought with her a huge green plastic trash bag filled with everything I had left in my room when I left home. I hadn't been back to that house since my father stopped talking to me, and the bag gave me a strange sense of excitement, as though it were a polyurethane version of Proust's madeleine. I expected youth to come rushing back to me as soon as I undid the twist tie.

There they were, all the notebooks and papers I had amassed during my brief, turbulent teens. The smell that rose from the notebooks, some of them carried for months in sweaty hip pockets, showed that those years had provided fertile ground for mold; the words in them, alas, showed that they had not proved nearly so fertile for poetry. The writing, which had seemed so dazzling to me at the time, was—adolescent. For a teen who had done as many drugs as I had, there was distressingly little vision. One notebook held a series of letters from a girl I hadn't thought of in years, a freshman when I was a sophomore. She had flattered and terrified me by her assumption that I would understand her opaque, highly compressed utterances and be able to respond in kind. I had done the best I could, falling back on condescension when her attempts to engage me in abstruse discussions of poetry and life threatened to expose the fact that I had no idea what she was saying. She had talent, I remember thinking, but was very young, unlike me, who, I believed, had talent and was very advanced. The letters showed that I was wrong on both counts. At thirteen or fourteen, she had been a brilliant young poet—and I, like a teenage Thomas Wentworth Higginson confronting an even younger Emily Dickinson, had utterly failed to recognize that she was by far the better poet. And the letters revealed something else I had been too obtuse to see: she had been in love with me, and had taken my inability to respond to her as deliberate rejection.

Despite my longing to be female, I had done a marvelous job of acting like a real teenage boy, buoying my narcissism with sexist dismissal when a girl's talent threatened my self-importance.

I wished I could speak to her now—not to the woman she had become but to the girl who had tried so hard to find in me a kindred spirit. I'm ready now, I wanted to tell her. I'm finally old enough to understand what you were saying. For a moment, I wondered if, unbeknownst to myself, I had been in love with her. Then I wondered if I still was. But I had as little romantic interest in her as ever. I was grieving for the loss of her friendship, a friendship that gender would have prevented us from having even had I been ready for it.

I peered through our loft's small dusty window, staring down at the people on the street, overcome by longing to be down there with them, strolling through the summer dusk in a different body, a different life.

I piled the notebooks back into the bag and twisted the tie around its neck. A few days later, I hauled my adolescence to a dumpster, heaved it in, and walked away, muttering, "Thank God I'm done with that."

Adolescence must have snickered. It wasn't behind me, moldering in a dumpster. It was sauntering toward me, a future that refused to be thrown away.

My second adolescence—the one that erupted during my forties—began with walking. Long before hormones or laser treatments, before I had a stitch of female clothing to wear, during the weeks that followed my confession of my gender crisis to my wife, I would walk alone down the rutted dirt road on which we lived, leaving my family behind for an anonymity that tasted equally of amputation and liberation. Walking made me feel normal. When I walked, my body seemed unimportant, ancillary to the brain that bobbed sixty or so inches above my feet. My isolation, my difference, seemed as natural as that of anyone who walked alone. The pines, the stones, the stars, the flashes of goldfinch and bluebird, cardinal and oriole, the swell and sink of land whose hills had been Everests in Cretaceous times, the crunch of snow and the suck of mud—the world didn't care who or what was walking through it. The gender on which so much of life seemed to depend meant nothing here.

Nothing, that is, to anyone but me. On that empty strip of road, I started talking to God again about the subject we long ago seemed to have settled. Soothed by the rhythm of my feet, I let myself be flooded by longing to become. That longing terrified me. Become what? I asked God. Become who? Become, God whispered, like an echo. Become, my footfalls muttered. The road rose and fell, my family house receded in the distance and loomed up ahead, but that was all God and my body would tell me. Become.

At first, those walks, after the kids were in bed or while they were in school, were the only times I gave myself over to that longing. I couldn't, I realized, know who or what I would become without becoming, so I practiced swinging my hips the way the trans-advice websites I surfed assured me that men who wanted to walk like women should. When normal thirteen- and fourteen-year-old girls start to walk like women, they translate the ease and sprawl of childhood into the self-assured sway of maturity. I was trying to translate decades of self-repression into a gait that had no relation to my hipless, waistless, breastless body. The birds, the squirrels, the trees didn't practice their motions; they simply moved according to their natures. But I had no nature. Neither genes nor instincts nor the laws of physics could teach me to walk as the woman I longed to become. I had to teach myself to walk again, braving the gauntlet of silent jeers I couldn't help but hear in the windy silence of road and sky and tree. Sometimes, their silence entered me, the jeers died down, and my hips fell into harmony with my sketchy inner template of femininity. For two steps, or three, sometimes for a whole stretch of road, I would feel—who knows if it was true?—that I was walking like a woman.

Early in my transition, in the fall of 2006, Janie, who witnessed my transformations in her passenger seat from male to female and back again, gave me a good talking to. I had just begun taking hormones. "Be careful," she said. "You walk as a woman now." Unlike those who are born and raised female, it didn't occur to me to walk in fear. Masked by masculinity, I had felt invisible, safe in a world that I knew couldn't really see me. But walking as a woman soon taught me what growing up male had not. It was a cold October night. I hadn't yet figured out where I could safely change from male to female—Starbucks still meant coffee to me—so I walked into a large movie theater. A bored concessions girl eyed me idly as I walked with what seemed to me transparently false nonchalance to the men's room. I started shaking the minute I'd locked myself into a stall. I knew I was making a terrible mistake, one that could cost me the untenured livelihood that was all that stood between my family and homelessness. Being trans is not against the law, but the law is often against being trans, and trans-people are routinely harassed, humiliated, even beaten by police who consider patrolling gender norms part of their beat.

It's hard to get dressed and put on makeup when you are imagining a SWAT team preparing to blow open the door of your bathroom stall. It's even harder when the stall next to you is suddenly occupied by a man who is not there to change genders. The more I hurried, the longer it took. Finally, though, I managed to button what needed to be buttoned, smear still-unfamiliar cosmetics across the stubble I could see in my tiny compact mirror, and brush out my hair. It was time to open the door. I waited until the bathroom sounded empty, slid open the latch, and dashed in skirt and sweater into the hallway shared by both the men's and women's rooms. The popcorn girl eyed me coldly as I walked past; I wondered if she noticed that I was only swinging my hips every fourth or fifth step. More likely she was watching to see if I would try to sneak into the movies. I made it out the door without being screamed at, arrested, or beaten. I was on the street—safe.

But, as I walked along, clutching my thin jacket tight against the wind, I suddenly didn't feel safe. The avenue was getting darker, the rows of shops giving way to housing projects. Some streetlights were out; some flickered. Shadows thickened, and the young men who moved in and out of them seemed predatory, hungry. When a homeless man asked me for money, I jumped. I fumbled some change out of my purse—"Thank you, honey," he said—and ducked into a doorway. One of my clip-on earrings had come loose, and my fingers were shaking too hard to screw it back on. There was no doubt about it. I was terrified. But was I terrified of being attacked because I looked like a woman or because I looked like a man trying to look like a woman? The familiar dilemma—was I a woman or just a wannabe?—calmed me. The world and I were on the same terms, after all. I tightened my earring and walked from the block of darkness toward a block of light.

After I finally left the family home, in June 2007, walking as a woman became both recreation and self-exploration. I had no local friends yet in my new female incarnation. But, in the first week, I didn't walk alone. My friend Nancy had flown in the day I moved out. We walked for hours, rambling and ruminating about teaching and transition and girls' school novels and good shoes and the ethics of flowers. Toward the end of her visit, I was seized with an impulse to walk down Main Street in a dress. That act was the specter my wife had conjured to represent the horror of my transition. "You *want* people who know you to see you in a dress?" she had asked me incredulously. It seemed like a reasonable question at the time. I had never seen myself in a mirror, never put on makeup; my face still felt naked from the absence of the beard. But, once I had begun walking the streets of New York in mascara, lipstick, and skirts, the horror didn't seem so horrible. The more eyes passed over me without a second glance, the more smiles I exchanged with women on the way into or out of a restroom, the less I felt like an object of derision and the more I felt like—myself.

The day before Nancy left, I put on heels and the fanciest dress I owned. It was a flawless late June afternoon. Time had thickened into sunlit honey, day was spilling into evening, summer stretching into a boundless blaze of possibility, transforming the tired, afterwork crowd into leisurely flâneurs. Everyone was strolling or shopping or licking enormous ice-cream cones. It didn't bother me at all that I was the only one on that mile-long street in high heels and a dress. I was straddling the forbidden cusp of womanhood, in broad daylight, no less. Grinning like a delinquent intoxicated by her first shoplifted cosmetics, I made Nancy walk with me all the way down the street and all the way back. When the scene my wife had dreaded was over, the world as we knew it remained intact.

I repeated that walk, in more casual clothes, later that summer, but the experience was utterly different. Reflected in Nancy's eyes, I felt my new self unfurling. Now I had no one to smile at, no one to reflect my identity back. The fact that I attracted no attention slipped from being a point of pride to a form of loneliness. People who had known me for years passed without a flicker of recognition, and I let them, telling myself that their obliviousness was an identity-affirming success. By becoming myself, I had traded one form of invisibility for another, but now the person who was invisible wasn't a male persona. It was me.

My solitude was like an emotional echo chamber. It reverberated with griefs and longings, anguish and excitement I couldn't share. I was stunned by the intensity of all this emotion. Did people, real people, feel *all* the time? Feelings had always come to me singly, over great distances, arriving like dusty messengers exhausted by the effort of reaching the remote country in which I lived. Now there was no part of me that didn't feel. I felt too much to read, too much to write, too much to do anything but feel. "How do people function with all these feelings?" I asked Nancy, in one of our daily phone calls. My new housemate was away for three weeks, and on days when I didn't see my children, speaking to Nancy by cell phone was often my only human contact. From a thousand miles away, with sympathy and amusement, she watched me stumble into the life she had always known.

I started to quiet my mind while walking, to let go of everything but perception and feeling, to trust the waves of my own emotion. My body moved; sights and sounds and colors and smells and textures entered and passed through me, mixing with the terror and loneliness and awe of the self that I finally, with some justification, could call "I." I began to be familiar with my new emotions. I got used to being overwhelmed with pain, I became accustomed to moments when every brick on every building was saturated with significance, I realized that feelings were not natural catastrophes— they were how people, real people, give life to the world that gives life to us.

The yellow moon waxed in the humid August night sky, ripening, as everything was ripening, in the final flush of summer. Insects chittered in the branches above my head. Their rhythmic rattle seemed to swell inside me as I headed toward the lighted windows of the aptly named Café Evolution. It was Saturday night, jazz night, and as usual—this was my third time—I was done up for the occasion, even though I knew I would look ridiculous among the few other patrons who had happened upon the music wailing in the heart of this otherwise sleepy, semirural town.

I was wearing a new—from the one-dollar designer clearance bin—early-afternoon-blue chiffon skirt rimmed at the bottom with iridescent beads and a plain black T-shirt that set off the West African turquoise necklace I had bought on the street in New York, en route to my first poetry reading as myself. A phone conversation with Nancy dissuaded me from topping the skirt with a new pink T-shirt—"Pink and *blue*?" she asked, exquisitely balancing horror and tact—and, reluctantly, because I love wearing my newest clothes, I had settled for the safer combination, though I kept thinking that if Nancy could only see the way this pink and blue looked together, she would bless my inner urgings.

No one could object to black and blue.

Café Evolution had become the closest thing I had to a favorite haunt. Resisting the urge to sit alone at an out-of-the-way table, I would settle into a rocking chair near the couch that was always occupied by one couple or another. I would sip my tea, cross my legs, close my eyes, and nod into crystalline musical spaces. For once, the slowing down of time I had experienced since my gender crisis was an advantage. No matter how complex the musical conversation became, I had the leisure to untangle it, to consider each line individually and in relation to the others.

Of course, my appreciations were always interrupted by thoughts of how I looked to the people sitting a few feet away from me. I told myself that I looked like a woman who knew how to listen to jazz or who loved jazz too much not to lose herself to it and not like a woman who had dozed off or was afflicted with a slight rhythmic tremor in her neck or was pretentiously pretending to lose herself in the music while in fact she calculated the impression her apparent absorption was making on those around her.

I told myself they weren't looking.

Sometimes I told myself I looked beautiful. With my eyes closed, I could almost believe it.

The first two nights, the jazz had centered on a slender young pianist whose eyes looked closed even when they were open. His lids would flutter as his fingers fell on the keys. It was as though he were dreaming or as though the music were dreaming him. One night he had teamed up with a saxophonist, a shy Russian woman in her fifties with a habit of looking off to the side, as though the café and the people in it were a backdrop for a not-too-interesting play and she were looking into the wings, toward the reality behind the stage. She played with deep emotion, in tones that summoned ghosts she obviously revered, Ben Webster and John Coltrane and others omitted from my fitful self-education in jazz, while the painfully thin pianist—barely visible when he stood sideways—answered her introspective intimacy with gleaming, soaring chords.

Tonight, she was there, but my pianist—that was the way I thought of him—wasn't. She was teamed instead with a smiling gargoyle of a man, broad-chested, pot-bellied, shirt collar open to reveal a tuft of curly black hair, who treated every song as an occasion for whimsical, sometimes brilliant, emotionally empty virtuosity. The saxophonist responded to his lead as she had responded to his predecessor's, abandoning emotion for splashes of abstract sound.

I was furious with him for emptying out the music and furious with her for following him, for not realizing that, while he had the greater technical facility, she was the greater musician. I wanted to tell the couple on the couch exactly how I felt, to lean toward the man sipping the wine he'd brought in a brown paper bag and explain at great length what I disliked about this musical relationship. When I was a teenage boy, nothing could stop me from detailing my opinions about music to anyone in the vicinity—a shame, since, at the time, I knew nothing about it. Now I was once more swelling with the helium of adolescent self-righteousness, but I remained silent, nodding with my eyes closed.

It was lonely, stewing there in solitary adolescence. Half the tables were occupied by people who looked my age but were functionally much older. It had been decades since they had fretted about how and whether to cross their legs or fought the impulse to rush to the bathroom every few minutes to check their hair. The rest were occupied by twentysomethings whispering or laughing together, the girls bathed in a glow of fertility that lent its glamor to whatever they wore, the boys hulking, awkward, wondering how to make their presence felt.

I was too old to be that young and too young to be this old.

Midway into the second set, I had had enough. I stood, smoothed my skirt, and made my way as gracefully as I could between the close-set tables. No one paid any attention, but I felt as though a spotlight were shining on me, picking out every flaw in my performance as a woman and haloing everything I did right.

I reached the door, dropped a five-dollar bill into the contribution box, and stepped outside. The music faded behind me into humid black air; even the cars seemed hushed as they rolled along the small main street.

I turned onto a block overhung with enormous leafy branches. No streetlights there, no cars, only the sound of my heels and cicadas and insects whose names I didn't know. Things were growing in the darkness, gourds swelling, flowers gathering strength for late-bursting buds, vines creeping upward, roots stretching through soil toward veins of underground water. I too was growing, swelling, stretching. Tricked by the hormones I took every morning, my forty-something body had embarked on an adolescence that would continue into my fifties. My cheeks glowed like a young girl's, my waist—or what would have been my waist if I had the proper hipbones—had thinned enough for me to be able to figure out where my skirts should sit, and, after weeks of aches and stabbing pains, my breasts had visibly sprouted. In clingy T-shirts, they even cast a shadow. They were growing, though I could never catch them at it. For days, for weeks, I would notice nothing, and then the fall of a blouse or a bobble as I walked confirmed that they had expanded, fulfilling the potential that had slept in them for decades.

"You sparkle," said an old friend, the first time she saw the new—the real—me. "You're sparkling," my therapist confirmed. "It's like a layer of pain has fallen away," said a rabbi who had known me for years. I couldn't see that sparkle—I felt too awkward, too raw, too grief stricken—but I knew what they meant. I had seen that glow in my friend R a couple of months after her surgery. I had just started taking progesterone and barely started shedding excess body hair with laser, while the hair on my head seemed like it would never grow out. R had always been charismatic, a natural leader in the trans community, but now there was something else about her, something that arrested and dazzled me, as though the lines of her face and form had leapt suddenly into focus. "I'm sorry," I said, wanting to apologize for the unbegun person I had dragged into her presence. "Don't," she said. "I'm already living my life. You're still trying to imagine that yours is possible."

Light poured from her face. It was more than the sunlight slanting through the café windows; it was more than her heavy blonde hair. After a night that had lasted decades, the sun was rising inside her. Now that sun was rising inside me, thawing my frozen heart and limbs, shining in the swing of my steps, warming the humid August night that clung to my tingling skin. I'd left the jazz, but the night still sang with creatures like me, who hadn't existed before this summer, who didn't know who or what we were, who were happy to be alive.

9

Mothering

If your mother has never seen your face—if you have never had a face to be seen—if, in a sense, you have never been born— do you have a mother? And if your mother has always called you "son," can you ever really become her daughter?

For most of my life, I couldn't begin to ask such questions. My sister, three years my junior, was the only daughter in our family. To the extent that I had a place in the family—a place that became vanishingly small once my father stopped talking to me—it was as my mother's son. And, though I hated being a boy, it came with the usual advantages. I could be messy, dirty, ruthlessly self-centered, indifferent to my appearance, careless of others to the point of rudeness—behaviors my sister could never have gotten away with. Since I had to pretend to be the boy of the family, I was glad that others were so ready to mistake the self-neglecting symptoms of transsexual despair as normal male solipsism.

I hated myself for deceiving my family, and it broke my heart that they were so easy to deceive. I felt utterly alone, and, as so often when I was child, my estrangement from the world around me drove me to the Torah. There, amid the Bronze Age familial misery that makes up so much of Genesis, I found someone I recognized as the direct ancestor of my own unbearable tangle of love and lies. In a passage I read over and over, Jacob serves his blind, aged father, Isaac, his favorite dinner as a prelude to receiving his blessing. There's only one problem with this scene of filial devotion. Jacob is impersonating his twin brother Esau, who, older by a moment, is his father's heir. Esau, a vigorous, hairy, hypermasculine hunter, is his father's favorite. Jacob is smooth skinned, domestic, almost feminine. Lest his blind father become suspicious, Jacob conceals his smooth forearms under hairy swatches of fresh-killed kidskin that make his arms feel as hairy as Esau's. If his father recognizes that the manly Esau is really the feminine Jacob, Jacob will be cursed instead of blessed.

I hated the familiarity of this scene: the perversion of gestures of love into lies and betrayal, the apparent intimacy that is really utter estrangement, Jacob's terror—shouldn't this be his hope?— that at any moment his father might see him for who he was. Like Jacob, I wasn't the boy my parents meant to bless with food, shelter, clothing, love. Under the skins of masculinity—the pants and shirts I hated, the roles and games I forced myself to play—was something too smooth, too soft, too feminine to be loved like the male "twin" I pretended to be. Like me, Jacob barely hesitated before committing himself to deception, and, as in my family, he found that deception heartbreakingly easy; the crudest sign of masculinity—hair that isn't even human—made it impossible for Isaac to recognize the truth about his son. I lived that heartbreak every day: as long as I kept my hair short and wore pants and shirts, no one could see the girl cowering beneath.

But Jacob had something going for him that I didn't have: a mother, Rebekah, who knew him for who he truly was. It was Rebekah's idea that Jacob masquerade as Esau, Rebekah who dressed him in goat skin, Rebekah who knew that Jacob was destined to transmit Abraham's spiritual legacy to future generations. Perhaps more even than the young Jacob, Rebekah recognized Jacob's true self: not the grasping, amoral younger sibling but the progenitor of the twelve tribes of Israel that, in a few hundred years, would receive the Torah. She saw that Jacob was a first-born trapped in a second-born's body and that only by flouting law, convention, and family ties could he become the person he was meant to be.

Not only didn't my mother know who I truly was—I was sure that the moment she suspected, I wouldn't have a mother at all.

My skins never slipped. Lonely as it was to feel that my mother had never seen me, when I was a teen, I started to appreciate the pass my male mask gave me from the mother-daughter dynamics (as euphemistic therapists call them) in which my female friends were embroiled. Their mothers seemed to take every aspect of their behavior and appearance personally and intruded into every corner of their lives. My mother did little other than despair about my appearance, the ragged jeans and the mushrooming hair, and she left the behavioral battles to my father, who, according to gender conventions, was my designated foil. My father played his part with a passion unusual for him. I did my chores, completed high school in two and a half years, babysat and mowed lawns and was at least tolerably polite, but I stayed out late doing things that he imagined, correctly, violated his rules, his principles, and the law, and he stayed up late eating sunflower seeds on the couch so that I would know that he knew my life had become illicit and alien. Unlike other fathers, he didn't waste much time trying to control my behavior. Instead of grounding or shouting at or hitting me—disciplinary actions he knew I would find easy to ignore—he would stop speaking to me for weeks at a time. The ties that bound him to me were so slender that it was easier for him to deny that I was his son than to cope with the rage I roused in him. Once he told me that, if I couldn't be honest with him, I couldn't be his son and that, since he didn't need any more friends, he had nothing more to say to me. But honesty had never been an option for me. The dodges and deceptions that went with my forays into sex and drugs and so on seemed to me like a natural extension of the deception I'd been engaged in all my life.

After my father stopped talking to me for good, in 1983, my mother became my sole connection to the family. She visited a couple of times a year, and we spoke on the phone every month, but, by mutual, unspoken agreement, we communicated little of our lives to each other. Since we couldn't talk about my father's silence—when I tried to bring it up, she would start crying—and since my father's refusal to see or even hear anything about me meant that I wasn't included in family events, it seemed like there wasn't much to say.

The first time my mother and I really talked, I was forty-six, sitting on a box in a dim, cool basement storage room, surrounded by unseasonable clothes, old tax returns, and broken computer equipment. It was June. I was still living in the house but would soon be moving out. For my mother's sake and the children's—my mother was the only relative in their lives—I needed to warn her before I left. For my sake, I needed to tell her why.

An underground room for unwanted things was the perfect setting for the moment I'd been avoiding my whole life—the moment when I would finally face the rage, or the hatred, or the love that would erupt when I told my mother that I wasn't her son but someone she had never seen. I had lived that moment in dreams and nightmares, fantasies and wishes. Now I was about to live it in the flesh.

I was still new to coming out, so I consulted a gay friend who had gone through all this years before. Don't tell your mother in person, she warned—you don't want to have to see her reaction. And writing a letter is too cold, too distant. Tell her on the phone.

I almost never called my mother—the silence when my father answered was too painful. So I made an appointment to be sure she would pick up the phone when it rang. Though the area code has changed, my mother's phone number is the same one I grew up with, the one I memorized when I was five in case I ever got lost, the one I recited like a captured prisoner reciting a serial number if any adult asked. I had called it when the exigencies of adolescence meant that I would be late coming home. I had called it after I'd gotten married. I had called it when I learned my father wasn't speaking to me anymore.

I pushed the buttons and listened to the tuneless sequence of sounds. Maybe the line would be busy. Maybe my mother wouldn't be home. Upstairs, aboveground, in the world of my family, it was a hot summer day, filled with the shouts and laughter of children. Down here, it was cool and quiet. A few feet away was a box of male clothing I would never wear again. By my legs, a box of Hanukah toys and decorations. At the edge of my peripheral vision, a rough sea of mismatched winter boots.

Hundreds of miles away, in a house I'd never seen, my mother's phone was ringing. Don't answer, I whispered, as though, if I couldn't complete this call, I would somehow arrest the cascade of losses triggered by my transition.

She answered. "Hello. Jay?"

"Yes," I told her, "it's Jay. I need to tell you something, Mom. Something hard. But first, you have to promise me that what I tell you won't affect your relationship with the children. You'll stay in touch with them, right?"

My mother was baffled. "Of course. I'm their grandmother—nothing is going to change that."

"Good," I said. "Because soon I'm—I'm moving out. This will be hard for the kids, and they need you to stay in their lives."

"Of course," she said. "I'm so sorry."

I wished she would ask me why I was moving out, but she didn't, so I took a deep breath and recited the words—even I found them hard to believe—that I'd practiced. "Mom, our family is breaking up because I'm a transsexual, and I can't live as a man anymore."

Since my gender crisis had begun, time had often slowed and stretched, sometimes becoming so elongated that I would curse impatiently, waiting for the chorus of a song to end. But that wasn't why the pause that followed my revelation—the most honest thing I had ever said to my mother—seemed so long. Years crowded into the silence between us, years long gone and years yet to be lived. I thought I had prepared myself to lose her. After all, I told myself, you've never really had her. But, in that pause, when truly motherless years were only a breath away, I realized that I had never stopped clinging to the hope of her.

"I've heard about this," she said at last. Her voice, rich and low, trained for a radio career she had never had, was thick with feeling. "I know that you have to be who you are, and, no matter what that is, you will always be my child."

The air above my head felt empty. The sword that had always dangled above me, the terror of what would happen if my mother discovered what I was, was gone.

My voice rose to the pitch I had made my own, and, for the first time in my life, we really talked.

A voice on the phone is one thing. The sight of a son dressed as a woman—a sight my wife feared would permanently unbalance our children—is another. Until she saw me, I wouldn't really know if I had a mother.

A few weeks after our phone call, my mother came to meet me.

I had known for days what I would wear: my meeting-grown-ups-for-the-first-time-as-myself dress, the dress I had worn in March to my first poetry reading as a woman, a dark, demurely flowered navy dress with a neckline that sank almost to the slight swell of my breasts and innumerable small white buttons up the front. It fell to my calves and had a complicated, suspension-bridge-like system of loops and cords that, when correctly threaded and tied, gave me the semblance of a waistline. Thanks to my training in Starbucks bathrooms, I put on makeup fast, but for this meeting I took my time, which, as usual, meant making a mess. None of that showed, though. By the time I was done, I looked as feminine as I could. At the worst, my mother would see her son trying very earnestly to look like a woman. At the best, she would see . . . what? Was she meeting someone new, a daughter she hadn't known she had, or finally seeing her son as he really was? Would she see an object of horror, an object of pity, or an object of love?

I parked, opened the car door, gathered up my purse, and carefully swung my legs onto the asphalt. Though I knew my mother couldn't see me, it felt as though a single lapse in femininity would invalidate my entire claim to existence. How silly I had been to look to friends for authentication. Clearly, it was my mother, the source of my life, who would decide if I was real.

I hesitated in the parking lot, trembling as my own real-life variation on a scene from innumerable movies and TV shows began: the moment when the daughter who has always dressed in jeans and sloppy shirts descends the stairs (there are always stairs) dressed in the finest heterosexual regalia for her big date, or senior prom, or wedding, and her awestruck parents stare in mute recognition of her womanhood.

But, no matter how much of a tomboy she's been, the heroine's emergence into womanhood is always preceded by a girlhood. My mother had known me only as a male. The day before, when she had seen the kids, I had met her in the boy clothes I wore to spare my children the shock of my femininity: a black, short-sleeved linen shirt big enough to conceal my breasts, and loose white pants. Dressed as a man, I had felt simultaneously invisible and hideously exposed, as though I were greeting my mother naked.

But now my mother wasn't seeing the dregs of my male persona. She was seeing the woman I had become.

I knocked on the door. "Come in," she called. I pushed it open and stepped inside. She was standing a few feet away, beside her unmade bed, her night table piled with the detritus of travel. I stood stock still, feeling her eyes circle from my face to my body and back.

"You look beautiful," she said, in a choked whisper. Then she hugged me and started crying.

She was crying, and I was smiling, sagging with relief into her arms.

She had lost a son. I had gained a mother.

The hotel dining room was small and crowded with an unusually average-looking collection of Americans. I felt stiff, self-conscious. This was the performance of my life, my first act as a daughter. My mother, by contrast, seemed relaxed after the shock. She kept her eyes on my face, she let me refill her coffee, she didn't seem to notice whether I was crossing my legs or not. After every swallow of food or tea, I had to readjust my voice. My mother had already commented a couple of times on how shrill and soft my voice was. It sounded stronger, I noticed, when I made a sympathetic remark to the young woman struggling to keep the breakfast bar stocked in the face of the locust-like onslaught of tourists.

My vocal problems notwithstanding, we talked and talked: about my situation with my children, about my wife, about my father, dying of kidney failure and still unwilling to see me, about my sister. I was happy to see that my mother was proud of my sister, though I also felt the twinges of a new rivalry, utterly different from the older brother/younger sister struggle that she had won decades ago when I left home. My sister, I felt sure, was feeling similar twinges, wondering how the family dynamic might shift in the aftershocks of my transformation.

Time was growing short. In less than two hours, I would have to change back into boy clothes to see my children. But my mother and I had never shopped together—unless you count her dragging me along when I was small—and I realized, suddenly, that it was a crucial rite of passage. I hinted; my mother agreed; and I soon found myself trailing her along a bustling shopping street, following her into stores I had, till then, only stared at from the sidewalk.

The street was too hot and too bright; each store seemed a cool, dark cave of gratifiable desire. "Do you have shoes?" my mother asked. These, she told me, would be comfortable and practical. "'Naturalizer' is a good name," she said, apparently unaware of the meaning that word would hold for me, "but here they are too expensive." In a store that carried Mediterranean handicrafts, my mother's eye was caught by a woven cotton pullover. "This isn't my size," she said. "I can tell just by looking. And the one that is my size is different—no zipper." I drifted away, toward a wall display of sheer silk skirts in saturated colors, reds and violets and greens, the same price as the pullover my mother was considering. She was bargaining with the shopkeeper now. The price was down five dollars, and it seemed for a moment that the pullover might fit after all. But, no, it still wasn't quite right. "Too bad," she said regretfully. I felt the same way about the skirts, but I was a stranger to the art of daughterly coercion, having missed out on years of hinting, wheedling, disappointment, and fulfillment. She was in her late seventies, I in my mid-forties. It was too late to start wheedling now.

I consoled her for the loss of the pullover and nursed my own regrets in silence. It was time to go back to her room, time for me to change from her daughter into a washed-out, feminized approximation of her son. I changed in her bathroom, unbuttoning innumerable tiny buttons and stepping out of my dress, pulling on my white pants, buttoning—on the opposite side—my black linen shirt. The sink was outside the door. I scrubbed off my face—lipstick, foundation, concealer, eye shadow, the stubborn mascara like a bruise beneath my eyes that marked the violence I was doing to myself.

My shoulders sagged. My scrubbed face was dead white, spattered with flaws the makeup had concealed. My hair, as though it knew what was happening, had degenerated from a throng of curls into a frizzy, misshapen mass. It looked grayer than it had before I stepped into the bathroom.

I flushed with shame—I always flush when someone sees how fragile my femaleness is, how little separates me from the man I was.

I was ready; my mother was ready; it was time to get the kids.

She called out to me as I was stuffing my plastic bag of womanhood into the car.

"Jay!"

"Yes, Mom?"

"Your sandals!"

I looked down. She was right. I hadn't changed my sandals. A trace of me still clung to my feet.

I gave her the best smile I could manage. "You're new at this," I said, "but you're pretty good at being the mother of a transsexual."

10
Like a Natural Woman

There was no doubt about it: the Australian flashing me the I-know-you-feel-so-lucky-I'm-smiling-at-you grin was cute.

This was strange, not because he was Australian—voted, I am told, as among the sexiest males on the planet—but because, as I had just explained to the friend who was introducing me to him, now, at the height of my first summer living as myself, I had less sexuality than the average fire hydrant. The combination of a quarter-century of marriage, two years of deep depression, and eight months of suppressing testosterone and elevating estrogen had left me neutered.

Once upon a time, I too had been a sexual creature, though arousal as a man was always a complicated, quixotic process. I remember walking down the street on early spring days in my teens and twenties when women had finally shed their jackets, and breasts and hips hidden all winter had re-emerged into the light of day. Every curve and indentation seemed to whisper invitingly to me. My gender identity was female, but my hormones weren't, and, as tsunamis of testosterone washed over me, I felt like a groin with legs, a sperm delivery system looking for somewhere, anywhere, to erupt.

If I hadn't thought about what I was feeling, I might have been carried away by the waves of pure, impersonal male desire to, as

Allen Ginsberg puts it, scatter semen freely to whomever come who may. But, of course, I always *did* think. So this is male desire, I would reflect, watching lust throb within me like a xenobiologist examining an alien mating ritual. Fascinating. If I feel like this, does that mean I'm actually a man? Do I really want to penetrate that girl whose sweater exposes not only her breasts but also a little too much belly fat? She doesn't look that intelligent, but, still, she's pretty, and wouldn't I give anything to look like that? And then I would start body shopping, imagining alternate lives and selves, magical transpositions, while my testes frantically elevated my testosterone levels, arousing spasms of ever more excruciating desire, unaware that their clarion call to penetrate a female body had dissolved into an even stronger imperative to inhabit one. That's what always happened to me: my desire for sex was inseparable from my craving to become.

I had known sexual pleasure. Genesis calls sex knowing and being known, and that's what gave me pleasure in my marriage, the translation of love into the rub of bodies, the postorgasmic collapse of boundaries that made me feel touched, held, almost whole. But that pleasure too was complicated by my abstraction from my body, the sense that what was touching and being touched was not exactly me, that my body was something that I needed to pilot through the shoals of sex. As the late-adolescent waves of testosterone receded, my distance from my body widened, and it became harder and harder to feel, much less surrender to, desire. My wife grew more attractive, our intimacy more nuanced, but I was trapped in a clumsy marionette of flesh. To make that puppet perform sexually, I had to keep my intellectual hands on the strings, make sure that my limbs were moving properly and that my phallus remained in an adequate state of arousal. Making love became exhausting and lonely, the opposite of knowing and being known.

The last time I made love, my gender crisis had already ripped my marriage to shreds, and I was so nauseated by my own flesh that sex felt like rape. My wife hadn't forced me to have sex: I had raped myself, forced myself to endure the male role, the male arousal, that disgusted me. I didn't know how to explain how I felt to her, how to tell her, without insult or accusation, that I could no longer relate to her sexually as a man. So, although I knew, the moment she had come, that I would never violate myself like this again, I didn't tell her. After weeks of my avoiding her touch, she asked me point-blank why I wasn't responding. I told her, but by then it was too late. My long silence had made it impossible for her to understand that it wasn't *her* I was rejecting but the body I was in—that I no longer had a body with which to express my love.

That felt like the end of my life in the land of adult desire. I had become a virgin again.

When I began the physical part of transition, in the winter of 2006, people began asking whether I was hetero- or homosexual. I didn't know if I would ever become either or if I would spend my life in this maiden-aunt version of prepubescence, silvering on the sidelines of the dance of love.

My genetic girlfriends, by and large, thought I was lucky. Most of the time, desire is a pain, they said. Trans friends, further along than I, assured me that desire would be back. One had had several heterosexual relationships as a woman, after half a lifetime as a married man. The other was charismatic, attractive, and terrified of the intimacy she craved. For a male-to-female transsexual, hetero-sexual dating is a potentially life-threatening endeavor. Announcing what you are from the outset eliminates most potential partners. But establishing a relationship as a woman and then revealing that you were once a man is not only a turnoff; the reaction you trigger can lead to verbal abuse, beatings, even murder.

If misogynist urban legend is true and the odds of a middle-aged woman getting married are lower than her odds of getting killed by a terrorist, then the odds of a middle-aged, publicly trans-sexual woman getting married are probably lower than the odds of getting killed by a terrorist who is left-handed, albino, and her cousin. So, though I felt nostalgic for my lost sexuality, I decided that my genetic girlfriends were right. If I was going to be alone, I was better off without desire.

I didn't find the Australian as attractive as he clearly found himself, but I found him more attractive than someone without sexuality should have. His hair was close-cropped, salt-and-pepper, the light strands blond or gray depending on whether one read the wrinkles around his sapphire blue eyes as signs of outdoorsmanship or age. I had never realized that wrinkles and gray hair could be attractive on a man, but, suddenly, they were. I know the evolutionary biologists' explanation—humans are hard wired to associate female attractiveness with features that suggest youthful fertility and male attractiveness with features that suggest a mature, competent provider—but somehow that didn't explain the little flip-flop inside me as I returned his sandy Australian grin.

The feeling was gone in a moment, but it left behind ripples of unfamiliar sensation. I would never see this guy again—a fact that was no doubt for the best, since it was unlikely that a self-assured Australian businessman and a self-doubting American transwoman could share much more than hello, goodbye, and the ritual flashings of teeth that accompany them. But this stranger's reflexive gesture—he would regret it a few minutes later, when my friend explained who or, rather, what he was smiling at—made me, through a sort of heterosexual alchemy, feel like a woman.

Men, I am told, can do that to you.

At least, that's what Carole King says, in a hit that sounded to my teenage ears like a transgirl anthem. The fact that "You Make Me Feel Like a Natural Woman" could be written by someone who *was* a natural woman meant there was hope for unnatural wannabes like me. To be a woman, King crooned, is to be someone who is always hoping to be "made" to feel like a natural woman. That verb meant a lot to me. King and the women she sang for seemed, like me, to have given up on actually *being* natural women; the most they hoped for was that some guy—King doesn't indicate if hers was Australian, too—would give them the feeling of natural womanhood.

I found myself wondering if her problem was that she didn't feel natural or didn't feel like a woman or both. What, I wondered, did naturalness feel like? I certainly didn't know, but, though King sounded like she enjoyed it, even as a teen I wondered if it wasn't painful for her to know that naturalness was transient, that, when the touch of her lover stopped, she would revert to unnatural womanhood or natural unwomanhood or whatever constituted her clothed, quotidian state of being. I felt sorry for her but personally delighted. If to be a woman was naturally to feel unnatural or unwomanly, hormones and operations were beside the point: I was already a member of the club.

Now, standing on the crowded Northampton main street three decades and one gender transition later, I felt like I was finally learning the club's secret handshake. "This is Joy," my friend told the Australian, and he reached toward me through the warm late-afternoon sunshine and squeezed my hand. "Joy," he said, and smiled, and smiled again, the exact same sandy, marrow-melting smile, as flattering as it was noncommittal, when I thickly murmured goodbye and dissolved into the anonymity of shoppers, idlers, and toddler-wielding parents. His smile didn't make me feel like a natural woman—even King suggests that it takes more than a grin or two to achieve that—but it did make me feel like someone who was being taken for a natural woman, played with like a natural woman, treated, like a natural woman, as an accessory to the male ego.

Gosh, it doesn't sound nearly as fun when I put it that way. But, to me, the knee-jerk flirtatiousness that my lesbian friends would find insulting and my hetero girlfriends would find tiresome felt invigorating, authenticating, and like a dramatic improvement over the neutered femininity I had cobbled together.

I was aware that looking to a man to find myself was throwing away decades of hard-fought feminist progress. And I'd been aware of the feminist critiques of male-to-female transsexuality—of the very idea that I could become a woman—since about the time I'd started singing along with Carole King. As a teen, I came upon a tract by Janice Raymond—one of very few items under "transsexual" in the public library's card catalog—called *The Transsexual Empire*, which argued that transition represented the ultimate male cooptation of the female and that learning to live as a woman was simply internalizing and externalizing sexist ideas of femininity. Not only wasn't I a natural woman; according to *The Transsexual Empire*, my attempts to approximate one were inherently demeaning to those who were.

Though few people seem to have read *The Transsexual Empire*, as my only example of how "natural" women—genetic women, born women, the XX community—saw transsexuality, the book had a profound influence on me. For decades I repeated key passages to myself, the passages most scathingly dismissive of the idea that someone born male could ever become other than a man. You can't become yourself, I would tell myself sternly. You can become only an "artifactual female," a commercialized parody, an insult to women.

Leaving Raymond's paranoia aside—she seems to have sincerely believed that transsexuals were infiltrating and destroying feminism from within—my response to the Australian's smile would seem to support her case. By working so hard to become—or at least pass as—a woman, I was enthusiastically participating in sexist conventions, from makeup and jewelry to sunlit flirtations in which I gratified the male ego exactly as my smiling Australian expected. No woman should ever be one smile away from selfhood—and any aspiring woman who acts as though she is tacitly undermines the entire feminist enterprise.

Contrary to *The Transsexual Empire*'s predictions, though, feminism has survived tens of thousands of male-to-female transitions, just as femininity has survived the fashion errors that transitioning transwomen and other adolescents commit on our way toward taste. In fact, thanks to feminism, trans versions of womanhood, like those of natural women, have evolved considerably. Even those of us who fuss over makeup and blush when self-besotted rakes toss us a rakish grin hold down jobs, write books, run for public office, teach, bend iron bars with bare hands (one of my trans-friends is a blacksmith), and raise as much or as little political hell as our genetically female counterparts.

The day may come when I find myself wearing pants and leaving off mascara, or I might keep watching infomercials for those incredible makeup systems that enable middle-aged women to look *ten* (it's always ten) *years younger*. Either way, transition has taught me that conventions of femininity that many women find tedious, draining, and oppressive can be empowering, self-affirming, even liberating, as well.

But, liberation aside, I reveled in femininity. I loved the shapes and shades of lipsticks, the delicacy of eye-shadow brushes, the darkness of mascara; I loved watching makeup transform my drab, still vaguely masculine face into that of a woman with glistening lips and shy but vivid eyes; I exulted in the dizzying array of options my closet now presented, the variety of color palettes and body shapes. Of course, all my choices of color and shape were determined by feminine conventions I was doing my best to fulfill. But, for me, those conventions weren't limiting; they were my medium of self-expression and invention. By manipulating them, I could make myself masculine or feminine, younger or older, available or inaccessible, a beacon of confidence or a glyph of despair. The Australian's smile may have made me feel like a natural woman, but the feeling, the womanhood, even the natural or unnaturalness weren't his; they were mine. Even my fragile, makeshift femininity gave me the power not only to trigger this Australian's flirtatious reflexes but also to render my genetically male body transparent and reveal the female identity within.

Australian smile or no, I'll never be a natural woman. My identity will always grow out of the tension between what I seem to be and what I am. But, though that tension is often painful, it also adds an element of fun, of masquerade, of practical joking, to my identity. I loved imagining my unwittingly gender-bent Australian's reaction when my friend told him about my anomalous relation to womanhood. I couldn't help smiling as I wondered whether my success in triggering his well-oiled responses to womanhood would make him question those responses. If he could respond that way to someone who was still more or less anatomically male, what did that mean about manhood, womanhood, and his all-too-cozy assumptions about them?

Of course, just as the Australian (my friend confirmed it) assumed that I was a natural woman, I was assuming that he was a heterosexual male. For all I knew, he could be bisexual, gay, a cross-dresser, a transman, or a male-to-female transsexual playing out, with tragic elegance, a masculinity that smothered rather than expressed him.

But, somehow, I didn't think so. It wasn't as much fun that way.

Buoyed by that smile, I strolled along with an unaccustomed sense of well-being. The shadows were long; the sunlight had thinned to beaten gold. The rectangular lawns baked mysteriously in their sweet green juices. I was sweating a little, walking uphill, smiling at the world for no reason at all but the pleasure of feeling like myself. For the first time in weeks, I suddenly realized that I wasn't in pain. No—my sense of well-being went beyond the absence of pain. This must be what people mean when they say they are in a good mood, I realized. This must be what they mean when they say they love being alive.

A rabbi I've known for a decade or so was strolling on the other side of the street. It was Shabbat, and he was out for a late afternoon walk with his wife. I'd studied with him, schmoozed with him after services; he had officiated at the naming ceremony of my second daughter; but I knew he wouldn't recognize me. I was directly across from the rabbi now, smiling beneficently in his direction, glowing with pleasure in the world he and I so improbably shared, enjoying the sense of invisible visibility—of being invisible to those who had known me by virtue of finally being visible as myself—that so often had plunged me into despair. I wasn't trying to catch his eye—he and his wife were tilted toward each other, talking—but, though he didn't recognize who I was, he noticed me and broke off his colloquy with his wife to nod a greeting across the street. As his smile passed through mine, it, too, made me feel like a natural woman.

11

Anger

My wife called while I was driving with the kids. It was another in a string of blazing, humid summer days, and the car—the new used car they had helped me pick out when the Altima I had moved out in abruptly died—was cool and comfortable. Drives were often our best time together. I spent most of them telling stories. The two older children were addicted to narrative—my wife still read to them every night before bed, and losing "book time" was their most feared punishment. The youngest liked the idea of stories but really wanted to be talking herself. During drives, she would say, "Now *I'm* going to tell a story" and launch into an incomprehensible jumble of events involving mice, cats, and other animals—and, all too often, using the potty. "No, no," her older sister would shout. "That's enough! It's Daddy's turn!" Sometimes she would just keep talking, but today she had fallen silent, listening, or perhaps just plotting her next narrative coup.

We had crossed the river and were swinging in a wide arc toward Jenny's house. That's what we called the place I was living—Jenny's house. It wasn't my house and certainly not their house, but at least it was the house of someone they could name and know. I was recounting an episode of *Smallville*, a TV show that chronicles the troubled adolescence of Clark Kent before he was

Superman. Clark, a teen with a secret that forced him to lie all the time, burdened with the excruciating awareness of being something other than human, reminded me a lot of myself when I was growing up. As a kid who constantly had to rescue the adults around him, he reminded my children a lot of themselves. They rarely voiced their feelings about what I was doing to their lives, but they insisted I retell episodes of *Smallville*, sometimes chanting their demands in unison, and I had belatedly realized that Clark's struggles with relationships—"I know more about feelings than he does!" my older daughter once exclaimed—gave us a safe way of talking about things that were otherwise too painful to put into words.

The cell phone rang at a crucial moment—Lana Lang, Clark's on-again, off-again childhood sweetheart, had become a vampire. My wife called to schedule a doctor's appointment for our youngest just as Lana was biting Clark in the neck.

"What's going on?" I asked.

"Something came up at her annual checkup."

"She had a checkup?" I asked, suddenly unsure whether I was struggling to control fear about my youngest or rage that once again I had been excluded from her life.

"Yes, and the doctor said she thought—"

She broke off in a way that suggested both tact and overwhelming emotion. I wasn't buying either. "Tell me *now*," I said, and for the first time in many months my gravelly affectless male voice seemed an ideal vehicle for self-expression.

My wife told me what the doctor was worried about.

"Why didn't you tell me before?" I demanded. It was the sort of question I had practiced not asking, a relationship question, a question not about practical details of our still-intertwined lives but about where my wife and I stood in the wasteland that once, not so long ago, was our marriage.

"I didn't want to spoil your visit with your mother. You seemed so happy to see her."

During our children's previous medical crises—there had been several—whichever of us first found out what was going on would struggle with the burden of knowing, needing to tell but wanting to wait, to protect the other's innocence. Why spoil this good moment or make that depression worse, we would think, and wait for some neutral moment to deliver the news as gently as possible. It had been crazy to feel that we could protect each other from the hard facts of our lives, but it was craziness born of love. But, by withholding the information about our youngest daughter, my wife was not protecting me. This was rage, not tact.

"And—" she broke off.

"And what?" I demanded.

"I was worried that you would say something horrible if I told you."

"Something horrible? Like what?"

"Like that you wish she had never been born."

My wife's vision of me as a husband and father so selfish that I had condemned my family to years of agony to devote myself to an elaborate game of dress-up was seamless. My wife was the only person who had ever come close to knowing me, and now she was voicing my worst fear about myself, my fear that I was incapable of love, even for my children.

There was nothing to say. If I expressed my rage, I would only confirm her accusations. Our daughter might have a terrifying illness. To a loving parent, that should be all that mattered.

That wasn't all that mattered, but all I said to my wife was goodbye.

I returned to the story of Lana sucking blood from the love of her life. Clark, desperately in love with her, had always kept her at a distance, terrified that she would reject him if she discovered that he wasn't human. Now that Lana wasn't human either, she triumphantly pierced that distance. It wasn't only blood that she took in—it was truth, for Clark's blood carried his super power with it. Beams of heat shot from her eyes, and she exulted that she finally knew his secret. "Go, Lana!" my son muttered beside me. From the back seat, my older daughter shouted her agreement. Rage and fangs had given Lana powers of her own, and she was finally taking what she needed from Clark, rather than waiting for him to provide it.

Like Lana, my children were learning the link between rage and love by being subjected to involuntary transformations—in their case, transformation into the broken-homed offspring of a transsexual. My childhood, hysterically devoted to maintaining the happy-household fiction, had never taught me that lesson. I had lived in terror of my own anger. It seemed unforgivable to me, my rage at those I loved.

My marriage, particularly the difficult early years, taught me that anger wasn't fatal, that rage was a normal part of life. But now the commitment that had contained my rage was broken. There was no marriage, no trust, no relationship to embody whatever love might linger between us. Where our lives touched, when our eyes or interests met, we hurt each other. My wife's inability to accept my transition had destroyed the foundations of my life, forcing me from my home, separating me from my children, and now, by withholding the information about my daughter's health because she feared I would wish our child unborn, she was voiding any claim I made to be a parent. Rage sang in my ears, intoxicating me with promises of aggression without consequence, righteousness without reflection, promising to turn the pain I felt into pain I inflicted. Love had imprisoned me in awareness of my family's suffering. Anger would set me free.

Poor Lana. The only way she could regain her humanity was for Clark to plunge a large hypodermic needle into her heart.

The intern sat on the opposite side of the room, ignoring me and my youngest daughter, who was squirming in my arms, straining toward the sink. The intern couldn't take her eyes off my wife—or, rather, they couldn't take their eyes off each other. No matter what I said, neither glanced at the façade of masculinity I was struggling to maintain.

I wasn't used to being ignored as a parent. My daughter had spent much of her infancy strapped across my stomach or in my arms, and, even now, when she was four, I often found myself holding her while washing dishes or preparing food. When I wasn't away teaching, I was the one who fed her most of her solid food, changed most of her diapers, stayed up with her when she couldn't sleep, cleaned her messiest spills and expulsions of bodily fluids. She had called me "Mama" until Father's Day when she was two years old. Until she was three, she would occasionally ask me to nurse her. When I would say no, she would smile and say, "Your nurses are too tiny?" "Yes," I would say, "my nurses are too tiny." "But when you grow up," she would say encouragingly, "then you can nurse me."

Despite the pants and shirt and slump to conceal my breasts, the wretched rumble that I had made of my voice, and the way my wife and the intern were ignoring me, I was still my daughter's parent.

She was wriggling out of my arms toward the faucet, intent on getting both of us as wet as possible.

"I'll make a deal with you," I started, trying to figure out what I could offer that might make her change her mind about playing in the sink.

"Here's *my* deal," she corrected. "You turn on the water."

"Only a trickle," I said, desperate to assert what ought, by all rights, to be my parental authority.

"I want more water," she said. "That's my deal."

I held her squirming, triumphant body—she was using my lap as a launching pad to reach the faucet—and tried to limit the volume of drops raining down on us. My daughter was beaming. This was exactly what she had envisioned—filling and spilling the cup she had convinced me to give her, creating a geyser-like spray when she put her hand close to the running tap.

The intern cleared her throat. "Could you tell your husband— I've forgotten his name—that I have a few questions for him?"

My wife didn't have to tell me. Her husband was sitting a couple of feet away.

The intern's questions weren't about my daughter; they were yes-and-nos about the health history of my natal family. The instant the last monosyllabic answer left my lips, the intern turned back to my wife. Of course, my anger at being ignored didn't— shouldn't—matter. What mattered was my daughter's health.

As the intern rose to leave, I followed her out the door. I couldn't do anything about being dressed as a man, I couldn't stop my wife from shunning me, but I could let this intern know what a bad job she had done. "My daughter has *two* parents," I said. "You completely ignored me, even when I was trying to talk to you."

"Did I?" she said vaguely. "Sorry."

"I can't believe you did that," my wife hissed when I returned. "But I guess I shouldn't be surprised. No matter what's going on, it's always about *you*."

As I left the room, I heard my daughter asking to be lifted onto my wife's lap. "Read me a book," she ordered.

I went to check on the older children. They had been marooned for an hour in the large, windowless waiting room of the pediatric genetics clinic. The DVD player wasn't working, and they weren't interested in battered preschool books and scribbled-in coloring books. If boredom were a life-threatening condition, medics would have been all over them.

Beneath the glaze of boredom, though, my middle daughter was scared. Her eyes were brimming. It had been only a few months since she had learned that there was another person hiding inside her father, and here she was, waiting to find out what might be hidden in her little sister. My revelation had shattered her family. How would her life change now?

"I know," I murmured as she pressed herself against me. "Hospitals are scary. But everything will be fine. We just need to be here so we can make sure of that." I was babbling. I didn't know if everything would be fine with her sister, and I certainly didn't know how to take care of the avalanche of crises I had triggered by changing genders. I wished my daughter had a better, wiser parent, the kind who would say the right thing, instead of a parent who was too angry and too scared to do more than hug her tight and pray that the love brimming inside me would somehow find its way to her.

"Stay with me," she pleaded. "Stay with *me*." My son was flipping through a book meant for children ten years younger than he was. He knew better than to ask me to stay. He had learned when my older daughter was born that some part of me would be leaning toward whoever was youngest, listening for the next cry for attention.

"I can't, I have to go back," I said, wondering if that was true. Was I leaving out of concern for my youngest or out of my rage to be acknowledged, to show that my youngest was *mine*? She let her arms drop sadly and turned away.

My wife and I pointedly ignored each other as I sat down beside her. Our youngest reached out her arms to me, then snuggled back into my wife's lap to finish their book.

When the intern returned to say that the doctor was on her way, she spoke only to my wife.

Shortly after the trip to the specialist, the kids stopped asking me to tell them episodes of *Smallville*. In a way, that was a relief. The episodes had gotten darker and more violent, and I hated the male voice in which I had to recount them. But the sudden disappearance of their wish for one of the few things that I, and only I, could give them, upset me. Since I had moved out, the kids and I didn't share very much. We would visit the cats at Jenny's house and cruise Jenny's cable stations for kid-appropriate programming. My son would struggle, unsuccessfully, to convince his sisters to watch sports. My youngest daughter would insist on *Barney*, *Teletubbies*, or anything else that market research had determined would be irresistible to preschoolers. Once she forced us to watch *Mr. Rogers' Neighborhood*. "Mr. Rogers must die," my son wrote on the yellow pad I had given him. I would make the kids food, drink Diet Coke, and force slices of mozzarella down my throat, cuddling with my older daughter on the couch when I could. Sooner or later, she would whisper that she wanted to try on a pair of my earrings. We would go into the bedroom I used as a dressing room—it was right off the TV area—and she would choose a pair for me to fasten to her ears.

Though dress-up had always been one of her favorite activities and though she was thrilled by the jewelry I let her wear, it was hard for her to enjoy it. "Mama wouldn't like this," she would say uneasily.

The grim struggle between desire and fear played across her precociously grown-up face, a luminous, heart-shaped emotional stage framed by curtains of curls that tumbled to her ribs. Sometimes she would change her mind and lead me back to the couch, but, most days, the lure of jewelry, of dress-up, of this new, forbidden relation to me, was stronger than her fears of angering her mother, and she would slip on a pair of earrings for a few moments, fingering them and exchanging glances with me while her brother and sister watched TV.

Eating and watching, laughing and fighting, edging closer and pulling away, my son and older daughter were remaking their relationships with me, with the me they had always known and the new me, the house-wrecking me, the me they dared not look in the face but knew I was becoming.

One day after our trip to the specialist, my son startled me by asking what I had worn when my mother had seen me as a woman for the first time. Till then, he had shrunk in revulsion whenever my insistence on talking about my life made it clear that others were seeing me in women's clothes. Not without embarrassment, I told him what I had chosen. He was horrified that I had worn a dress that buttoned down the front. "Too old-fashioned," he said disapprovingly. "Never wear dresses that button down the front." He then asked me for an inventory of my skirts, evaluating them according to a fashion sense that I had never imagined he or any heterosexual thirteen-year-old boy possessed.

I recounted the conversation to each of my small circle of friends. "He's really starting to accept you," they said. "Yes," I said proudly, as though I had just told them that he'd been short-listed for the Nobel Prize.

The next morning, when I went to the house to see the kids, I thanked my son for his fashion advice.

"What fashion advice?" my wife, appearing in the kitchen, demanded, the moment the words left my mouth.

Though my wife had been in another room, the house was too small to speak above a whisper without being overheard. I had told myself not to say anything, to wait until we were out of hearing range, in the car. A moment later, I blurted it out anyway. It wasn't an accident. I wanted my wife to know that our son was growing toward me, that my new self had started to be something he could bear to imagine. Without regard for his safety, without respect for the risk he had taken in speaking of what was so difficult for him, I threw up his words to my wife as evidence that she was wrong about the effect she claimed my transition was having on my children.

"What fashion advice?" my wife repeated.

"I'm sorry, Mama," my son protested, backpedaling away from me as fast as he could.

"*You* don't have anything to apologize for," my wife said. I don't know how my son heard them, but to me her words felt like a blow.

"So he just started spontaneously offering you clothing advice?" she demanded, turning her back on my son and closing in on me.

"Yes," I said, stiffening into the truth-at-any-cost mode I had adopted long ago in the face of her rage. I've been lying and hiding long enough, I told myself. I have nothing to be ashamed of. I refuse to act ashamed, even with someone who sees what I am as shameful. "He just started offering me advice. It's a sign that he's starting to accept me."

"And you see that as a good thing?"

"My transition isn't a good thing for him, but, since I'm his parent, he needs to be able to accept it."

"If you thought about the children's welfare for even thirty seconds, you'd realize how wrong that is. This is what *you* want. It has nothing to do with what's good for them."

The children were cowering in their bedrooms, unable not to hear. My wife and I kept talking, saying things we knew would hurt them in the name of protecting them.

I apologized to them afterward. My older daughter didn't take her eyes off her book. My son told me, very politely, that he didn't want to talk about it now. "Now," he repeated, as though, if only I would go away, there would be a time in the very near future when talking about my betrayal of him would be exactly what he wanted to do.

The next time I saw them, my older children, as I had known them, were no longer there. My son was cold, pointedly indifferent to my comings and goings; my older daughter was rude, sarcastic, unwilling to hug or be kissed, uninterested in the attentions— they suddenly felt like manipulation, rather than love—I offered. Both took pains to criticize any mistake I made and to question loudly, in tandem, every parental edict I issued. "*Mama* doesn't do it that way," they would say. "I don't think Mama would be happy about that." Occasionally, my older daughter's sarcastic sangfroid would shatter into screaming or hitting. Once she thrashed at me for an hour. Once—this was the most communication we had had in weeks—she warmed up enough to tell me in detail what a bad parent I was. "Mama's a *good* parent," she said. "You're a bad role model. You've abandoned us. You've ruined Mama's life."

"We need to get her a therapist," I told my wife, between bouts of verbal and physical violence.

"I'm trying," my wife said coolly. "But she's never like this when you're not here."

My son continued to play games with me, but the games had become violent. I stopped him from hurting me, but I was never sure where to draw the line: if this was the only way he had to express his rage, it was better that he hurt me than that he turn it against himself.

"The children don't want to see you," my wife told me. "They tell me all kinds of things about how they really feel about you."

My wife and I had always divided the chores and pleasures of parenthood. I had imagined that, when I was no longer living with my children, I would get up every day at 4 a.m. so that I could be there when they opened their eyes, but now I knew I was no longer going to be there when they woke up and when they got back from school. I would no longer get them breakfast and feed them dinner and wipe out their lunch boxes; I wouldn't kiss them good morning or good night. The wound I had inflicted on the family had closed behind me. If I wanted a place in their lives, I had to create one.

I spent the rest of the summer in Smallville.

Everyone's orphaned there. Lana's parents had been killed by the meteor shower that brought Clark to Earth; Clark's parents had died in the destruction of their planet; Clark's adoptive mother was estranged from her father; Clark's adoptive dad died of a heart attack during Clark's first semester in college, and on it goes; even the villains are orphans.

By Smallville standards, my alienation from my children was small potatoes.

Clark and I had a lot in common. Neither of us could be ourselves without endangering the lives of those we loved. And becoming a parent had, in a way, made me a superhero. Like Clark—and like every parent—I felt that my triumphs were largely invisible and that my failures would haunt me for the rest of my life.

Clark's weakness—besides a level of emotional intelligence that would have embarrassed your average six-year-old—was kryptonite, pieces of his shattered planet that glowed balefully in his presence, sapping his strength and leaving him writhing in agony. My need to present myself as a male in order to see my children had a similar effect on me, though nothing glowed and I didn't have the luxury of writhing.

The closer we got to where we had come from, the sicker Clark and I became. Away from Krypton, Clark was faster than a speeding bullet. Pull out a chip of kryptonite, and he could be mugged by a goldfish. Away from what was left of my home, I was a success. I passed as a woman; I was publishing poetry and essays, I had been granted early tenure, and, though I couldn't set foot on campus, I had just been offered a graduate poetry class at Sarah Lawrence, which I had attended as an undergraduate male. Strangers welcomed the fledging woman my family couldn't bear to see.

In episode after episode, Clark and I were forced into devastating proximity to the homes we had lost, homes we couldn't save, homes that had expelled us into space, homes that tried to kill us.

We both longed to be human. Saving the town, the nation, the world only deepened the furrows on Clark's forehead, confirming that he was and always would be other than those he loved. The happiest day in his life was the day he discovered he had lost his powers. When he slammed his hand with a hammer, for the first time in his life, it hurt—and that only brightened his smile. When I was cruising the transsexual talk boards at the beginning of my gender crisis, a twentysomething on the verge of transition asked *the* question, the one that keeps transsexuals up at night: is the pain and upheaval of becoming ourselves worth it? "No one can tell you what to do," a series of older transwomen responded. "Be careful, be sure, talk with your therapist, take your time." Each voice of moderation made my heart sink a little deeper.

Then a young transwoman—I think she'd been on hormones for a year—weighed in. "Transition is going to hurt more than you can imagine," she wrote, "but you will have *real* feelings. You'll walk outside and feel the sun and the rain on your face. You may go through hell, but it will be worth it." Though I had never thought about transition this concretely—to me it still seemed like one of the magical transformation fantasies I had lived on for years—her words had a shockingly familiar quality. This was the voice that had called to me all my life. No more numbness, the voice had whispered. You, too, can be human.

The transwoman and the voice were right. I did have real feelings. I felt pain, loneliness, terror, hope, exhilaration, triumph. I might not be a woman, but I had become human.

And being human, as Clark discovered when he was shot through the heart, means being vulnerable.

No matter how dramatic the rescues Clark effected at the end of each episode, no matter how widely my new self was accepted or how much I sacrificed to keep my family housed and cared for, the irremediable sense of loss, of human frailty and superhuman failure, was always there. The most powerful creatures in our worlds, we were powerless to undo even the smallest fraction of the pain of those we loved. Clark's adoptive father died; Lex Luthor slid toward evil; Lana Lang tumbled from vampirism to drug addiction toward narrative irrelevance. My children were slipping through my fingers. My father found it harder and harder to walk as the poisons his failing kidneys couldn't filter built up in his bloodstream; my mother couldn't talk to me on the phone without crying. And now my children were so angry they couldn't bear to talk to me.

You have to stay alive so your children can reject you." So a therapist—covering for Susan, who was on vacation—had insisted at the beginning of the summer, when I called in the midst of a suicidal spiral. She wasn't trying to cheer me up. She was telling me the truth, reminding me that killing myself wouldn't free my children from the trauma of transition. She shouldn't have had to remind me. I had been told many times what suicide would do to my children. No matter how long they grieved or raged, shattered child-selves would huddle inside them for the rest of their lives, unable to grow up, unable to leave the scene of my crime, unable to prove their innocence of the blood I had left on their hands.

Of course, as mission statements go, staying alive so that my children could reject me left a lot to be desired. I needed more than my children's rejection—I needed their love. All parents need their children's love, but I needed it more than I should have, more than was good for them or, these days, for me. Among my lengthy list of lifelong emotional disabilities was an inability to feel others' love. For a long time I thought this meant that I was incapable of loving, that I could only go through the motions of affection and hope no one would notice the hollowness behind them. Even now I cringed during hugs and hand squeezes, terrified that my hugs and squeezes were too long or too short, too hard or too light, too clingy or too noncommittal, that my body would betray my inadequacy, revealing that I (am I the only one who finds that passage in *Alice in Wonderland* so painful?) was nothing but a pack of cards.

Even when I still lived with them, I found it hard to feel loved by my children. Now that they met me with sarcasm, sullenness, silence, my crumpled emotional antennae could detect no love at all. "They still love you," my friends assured me. One friend, whose parents had split when she was young, warned me that my need for my children to demonstrate their love for me was dangerous. If I insisted on it, I would turn them into emotional puppets who would eventually find it impossible to distinguish their feelings from my needs.

"You decided not to be their father anymore," my wife would tell me. Of course I protested that I was still and always would be their parent, but "parent," like "sibling," is a weak word, a psycho-social analysis rather than a blood-and-guts familial bond.

"Mother," "father," "sister," "brother"—these are the cardinal points on the family compass.

My children had no name for what I was becoming to them. They still called me "Daddy." Maybe they always would. But I was a Daddy who was often taken for a woman when we were out together, a Daddy who lived as a woman when they weren't there. Daddies could be child molesters, deadbeats, belt-wielding abusers, but, as long as they remained male, they were all more faithful, more "solid"—my son's term—than I would ever be.

I needed to stay alive so that my children could reject me. That was the easy part. The hard part was staying physically and emotionally present so that they could learn to face the void where their father had been—and recognize, beyond that void, the new kind of parent I was becoming. If I didn't stay within hurting range, they would forget that I was there, watching and waiting and loving, and forget that, no matter how great their anger, they were watching and waiting and loving, too, waiting to meet me anew, the way people who love are said to meet again in Heaven, on the far shore of rage.

Over the summer, my youngest daughter had started fighting with an imaginary friend she called Angryface. Angryface never tired of spoiling her fun, demanding her toys, grabbing her books, injecting the threat of loss into every game she played. "No, Angryface, no!" she would shout. I intervened as I did when she quarreled with her older siblings, calmly explaining to Angryface that this doll or that book was hers, that Angryface would have to wait his turn. I knew it was necessary, even healthy, for my daughter to express her fear and anger through play, but my heart broke whenever Angryface intruded on her happiness. That was me, I felt sure, that was my doing, that was what I had brought into the life that till now had seemed the least shadowed by my transition. Thanks to me, Angryface was a member of our family—and, unlike me, Angryface was always there.

My parental identity was confused, but my responsibility was clear: to restrain my need for demonstrations of their love and allow each of my children to define their distance from me. These days, that meant hugging and holding and feeding my youngest, who insisted that I prove that, even though I kept driving away and leaving her behind, I was still taking care of her. For my son, it meant acceptance of his pointed indifference to my comings and goings and willing participation in games he designed so that I could never win. For my older daughter, it meant following her through labyrinths of pain in which I would be forced to share the anguish I was inflicting on her.

It was already September, but summer, it seemed, would never end. Each day was brighter, hotter, more humid. The dense greens of leaves and lawn and rain-starved gardens seemed claustrophobic, grasping, hardened by their single-minded drive to grow. It was midafternoon, Sunday, and I had been with the kids—been acting like a man—for hours. I was sitting on the deck of the house I used to live in. My youngest was in my arms, my son was waving a thick, storm-shattered branch almost as tall as he, inviting me to "duel," and my older daughter was fussing with twigs in a wagon. She had her head down, peering into the rusty wagon, assembling impossibly delicate structures of twigs that fell to pieces at the slightest twitch. She was pointedly ignoring me, and I wanted nothing more than to be ignored, but I knew that, though she didn't want to want my attention, she would feel neglected if I didn't try to give it to her. I had a choice between being the parent who didn't notice how alone she was and the parent who wouldn't respect her obvious desire to be left that way. As usual, I chose the intrusive option. I still couldn't believe that a child who had always fought so fiercely for my attention really didn't want it.

"What are you doing?" I asked.

"I'm an old peddler woman selling my crafts," she answered, sarcasm giving an eerily aged quality to her seven-year-old voice.

"Oh, can I buy some?" I knew it was the wrong question—that kind of thing would work with my youngest, but the gates to my older daughter's fantasy worlds were much more heavily guarded.

"No," she snapped. "I'm finished with this village. I've been here for days, and no one has any money for my wares."

"Where are you going?" I asked, hoping she would give me a role to fall into.

"Nowhere that a peasant like you would know."

"Well," I said, "let me come with you. I'm tired of this village, and I want to see the world." I stood up with difficulty. My youngest's thirty pounds felt like one hundred.

"No," the old peddler woman sneered, turning her back and dragging the battered, clattering red wagon down the steep driveway toward the road. "It is not for the likes of you to come with me."

"But I want to," I said. "I'm an ignorant peasant, and I want to see the world with you."

"Your place is here. The road is home to me."

She was in the road now, heading away from the house. She wasn't looking back.

I couldn't let her walk off alone. It wasn't a busy road, but it twisted and turned, and cars roared down it at terrifying speeds. My daughter was deep into the role her rage had constructed, and I had no idea where that role would lead her—or how much attention it would allow her to pay to oncoming traffic.

My youngest clinging to my torso, I followed the old peddler woman down the road.

She whirled in fury. "What are *you* doing here? I told you I travel alone. I don't *want* you with me."

"I'm not with you," I said weakly. "The road is open to anyone. I'm just walking in the same direction."

"Don't!" she said, turning away again.

Swaying and staggering, I managed to match her pace. There was a right thing to do or say to get my daughter through what was clearly a crisis, but I didn't know what it was. Behind me, I could hear my son whacking concrete with the branch he'd selected for our battle. He needed me to come back so that he could vanquish me again.

It was much harder to play this game. My youngest was slipping through my arms, the house had receded behind a bend, and the road was dipping into a steep incline. Being an ignorant peasant wasn't helping me get closer to my daughter; it was only giving her a way to push me away. I decided that it was time for a show of force. Custer once made a similar decision.

"Stop," I shouted, in a bass rumble that made me want to throw up.

"What do *you* want?" the old peddler woman sneered. "I told you to go back to your village."

"Stop," I repeated, wanting nothing more now than to end this game and speak to my daughter again. "Come here *now*."

"No!" She twisted her lips into an ugly expression. "I told you, I'm a traveling peddler, and the road is my life. Now leave me alone."

"I told you to come here." My voice was harsh.

"Why should an old peddler woman come there? You are a peasant, and I'm done with your village."

I was furious now, shaking with rage and sick with fear that this game would never end, that my daughter was really gone, that we would never again speak to each other without anger and contempt.

"*Now*," I said, in a tone that had until recently held un-questioned authority in our family. "You are too young to walk down the road alone, and I'm not going to walk further with you." We both stopped, and she turned to face me. "You can be an old peddler woman on our property," I wheedled. "I promise I'll stay away if you want."

For a second, the peddler mask trembled on her face, and her muscles threatened to slip back into the expression of a seven-year-old girl. But only for a second. Then her face hardened, and, without deigning to look at the peasant who had forced her to return to his village where they were too stupid to appreciate her wares and too poor to afford them, the stoop-shouldered peddler woman dragged her wagon back toward the house.

"Thank you," I mumbled when we reached the driveway. My older daughter wouldn't even glance in my direction. She was too busy building intricate twig houses she knew would collapse the moment anything shifted in their rusty red world.

The next time I saw my older daughter, my wife had left on a day trip. We were at the family house. It was, I thought, a golden opportunity. With my wife gone, my daughter wouldn't feel torn between parents. She could express—and I would feel—her love again.

But, when I hugged her, her body stiffened. When I spoke to her with the old intimacy, she didn't answer. In every way she could, she was telling me that she wouldn't, couldn't meet me on the old terms of affection. In every way I could, I refused to acknowledge it. I praised her, I offered her treats, I tried to lavish attention on her. Every subterfuge of love failed.

Finally, I spoke with unforgivable directness. "I miss the way we used to talk. Do you remember how it was, a few weeks ago?"

She shrugged and tried to walk away. I kept pace beside her. "Mama and I both love you," I said. "You don't have to choose between us."

She stopped in her tracks and tilted her heart-shaped face up to meet my gaze. "As a matter of fact," she said, in a voice as hard and bright as her eyes, "I do."

Your children will come back to you," my trans friends promised. "It may take years, but they'll come back to you." It had only been a few weeks, but it already felt like years. The parts of my body that remembered my children best—my left side and hip where I always carried my youngest, the arm I would drape around my son's shoulders, the flat place above my breasts where my older daughter's head would rest when we hugged—ached as though pieces of them had been torn away. They are *my* children, I would think, swelling with the baffled rage of dispossession, like a cross-dressed Lear fulminating outside the gates of the castles his children had locked against him.

On days when I didn't see them, I would suddenly panic, wondering where they were and how I could have lost them. Then I'd come to myself and wonder where they were and how I could have lost them.

They had become a battlefield, the last front in the war over whether I, as a married, middle-aged father of three, had the right to become myself. I had won that war—whether or not I had the right, I was becoming—but I was losing them. I was no longer there when they woke or went to bed, I rarely fed them, I didn't help with or shout at them about homework. They never cuddled into me to watch movies anymore. Even when I was there, I was always about to leave. My youngest had taken a very practical approach to the uncertainty I had created. She had a list of activities that constituted being with Daddy, and she made sure that, no matter how short my visits, I fed her, held her, carried her, played with her—and that somehow enabled her to feel that the parent who so often wasn't there was still her parent. The older kids had more complicated definitions of Daddy. The flesh of our relationship, the daily activities of love, were gone, and the primary ways that I took care of them—financially supporting the household and sparing them the sight of what I was becoming—were abstract, intangible.

How could I fight for my children? Even if rage made me willing to say and do the unforgivable, my most effective weapons, the words that would most violently and effectively stake my claim, wouldn't only hurt my wife; they would scorch the earth where the children lived. And I didn't want to hurt my wife. She and I were suffering enough.

The only weapon I had to fight with was love. Of course, tactically speaking, love is a disaster. Love not only rules out aggression; it also rules out most defenses. Love requires unflinching vulnerability. No matter how often or how utterly my children rejected me, I had to keep coming back, to insist on acting as their parent, to show that my love for them was unaffected by their actions—that my love, if not my gender, was solid. Love wouldn't let me withdraw, or punish, or retaliate for rejection; it wouldn't even let me manipulate them by showing them how much they were hurting me.

But, though love demanded that I lose every battle, it would ensure that I won the war, because, from the perspective of love, there was no war, only five suffering people bound together, forever, by love. When our wounds healed, when our rage evaporated, love would still be there. And, though love demanded that I stay close enough to be hurt, it also conferred a kind of invulnerability. No matter how completely my family rejected me, they couldn't stop me from loving them. Even when gender dysphoria made me so sick that I couldn't stand my own skin, love gave me the strength I needed to care for them, proving, again and again, that no matter how weak I was, I was strong enough to act with love. Love offered no control over the present, but I was sure—am sure—that love owns the future and can even rewrite the past, transforming the most vicious incidents into symptoms of anguish, of fear, of—love. If I remained faithful to it, love would someday swallow the wreckage my transition had made of my family and—without, alas, erasing the pain—leave us, each of us, all of us, whole.

I'm in training to become a ninja. Summer has finally ended, and it's a cool September afternoon. My daughters are playing across the road, with a neighbor's children. For the first time in weeks, my son and I have time alone together. As usual, he knows exactly what he wants to do. He creates a ninja apprentice scroll on the computer, taking pains to select the right fonts from the hundreds he's loaded onto the hard drive, rolls it carefully, and ties it with a bit of ribbon. "Read it," he orders. "All of it." After a moment, he says, "Do you see what's written at the bottom?" I nod. "Well, then, memorize the rules."

My son needs to see me do what I'm told. He drills me, grading my mastery of the rules after each oral exam. When he's satisfied, he leads me outside for training in running and leaping. My heart sinks. I'm no superman. My balance is off, my landings clumsy, but I do as I'm told, leaping again and again onto a large rock, running as fast as I can onto a crumbling stone wall, grappling with my son, now almost as tall and heavy and strong as I am. I repeat each exercise silently, without complaint, waiting for the scathing criticism, the detailing of my failures, the recital of my inadequacy and incompetence. It never comes. My son is a stern but patient teacher. He corrects my errors, repeats his instructions, until my execution meets his approval. "You work hard," he says. "Always," I grunt, leaping, for the tenth time, onto the rock. He keeps staring at me, looking for signs of irony or subversion of his authority. There are none. It takes everything I have to do this; these minutes with him are worth it. When I'm done, he gives me a final exam.

"Not bad," he says, smiling kindly at his not-too-gifted pupil. "Pretty good, in fact."

There's a commotion behind us. The girls have returned. The youngest is in my arms again; my older daughter needs to be offered food that she will, as usual, refuse. The girls' needs and complaints fill the afternoon and evening. My son drifts away, to solitary concerns: reading, brooding, radiating dissatisfaction. I see him there, waiting for me, beyond the penumbra of his sisters' clamor, but I can't go to him. He isn't even interested in the movie we watch. He works on the computer instead, doing homework.

The movie is about a boy who responds to the loss of his mother by trying to become a saint. My older daughter murmurs, "He wants so much to be good."

I put my arm around her shoulders and whisper, "I want you to know that *you* are good, all good, no matter what you feel."

She turns to me with a puzzled expression. "Of course," she says. "Why would you need to tell me that?"

"Because when I was a child, I didn't know it," I say. "I tried so hard to be good, but I was angry and confused all the time, and I didn't talk to my parents about it."

She smiles. "That was stupid. You couldn't figure it out alone."

I give her an unreturned kiss goodnight and put my arms around my son from behind, steeling myself for the stiffening that has become his usual response to my gestures of affection. This time, to my surprise, he pulls me toward him. Hugs. "I had a good time today," he says. "So did I," I say. Tears fill my eyes. For the first time in months, I feel his love. For a few moments, I'm not for myself alone. I press my cheek hard against his head, until my skin takes the print of his bristly, sweet-smelling curls.

Part Three

The Door of Life

12

The Day
My Father Died

<u>*October 2, 2007*</u>

The day my father died—almost six months after my mother first saw me—I slept past dawn. My father had died in the darkness, around 5 a.m. I was dreaming. I wasn't dreaming of him.

The night had been as warm as day. "I have all the windows open," my mother had told me the night before. "He's so hot. I don't know how to cool him."

The day my father died, he had already died. He had fallen in the bathroom a couple of days before and never fully regained consciousness. He had been dying for months, since he refused dialysis. Decades before, he had refused to be my father. "He was so proud of you when you were young," my mother told me. "He thought you had such promise."

When I was a child I began imagining the day my father would die. That fantasy was a delicate operation, an autopsy on a heart—mine—that was still beating, a test that I always failed. I had gotten so good at suppressing my feelings, I feared I couldn't feel anymore. To see if I was still capable of feeling, I would imagine my father lying dead before me. I would imagine crying, but I couldn't cry. I couldn't feel anything at all. I performed this experiment in the dark, after I was tucked in and kissed goodnight. Sometimes, my father had been lying beside me, diagramming constellations with a flashlight, murmuring about distant galaxies and nearby stars. We lay on the edge of the universe together, a universe that was expanding and full of lights and smelled sweet and burnt like the tobacco of his pipe. But, sooner or later, the door would close. My father and his stars gone, I would imagine his death and fail to cry. You don't have feelings, I would say to myself. You wouldn't even cry if your father died. Your father is dead. He's lying there dead in front of you, and you aren't crying. You don't even know how to cry.

The day my father died, a father on the other side of the wall woke me by waking up his children. I was at Sarah Lawrence, the college I had attended as an undergraduate. When I was banned from returning to Stern, they gave me a class to teach and a room to sleep in the night before I taught it. I hadn't known about the father and sons on the other side of the wall. "Good morning, Mikey," the father cooed. I couldn't help comparing his good-morning coo with mine—that is, the coo that used to be mine, when I was a man waking up my children. His coo sounded a bit self-conscious. I wondered if mine had, too. Women do the good-morning coo much better, I thought. My eyes were still closed. As I dissolved my morning estrogen under my tongue, I could see him there, staring fondly into his sons' sleep-encrusted eyes. He was probably kissing his son's forehead, tasting the sweaty warmth, and his son was either smelling his aftershave or feeling the scratch of stubble or beard. I didn't think of it then—I was too busy envying him, aching for the morning kisses I had lost—but, later that day, I remembered waking to my father's stubble scratching my cheek in mid-winter darkness. "Where am I?" I mumbled, pretending that if I pretended to be talking in my sleep he would let me fall asleep again. "Timbuktu," he answered. I turned onto my side, away from him, and said, "Wake me up when we get to Timbuk-three." He had repeated my joke proudly to anyone who would listen. He was still my father, and I was still his son, and I had so much promise.

Thirty-five years later, I put my estrogen under my tongue and listened to the other father, the good father, the father who had stayed male, on the other side of the wall. Something was wrong with the way my body responded to estrogen; my hormone levels had quadrupled over the past three months. A healthy level was in the low two hundreds; I was in the mid-nine hundreds. The higher the level, the greater the risk of a blood clot. I used to take three pills; then I took two; now I had reduced it to one. It hardly felt like I was taking estrogen at all. The sweetness of the single dissolving tablet barely spread in my mouth.

On the other side of the wall, the sweet taste in the good father's mouth had soured. His sons were quarreling. His teasing greetings had been a mistake, igniting their feelings of inadequacy, each fearing that the other was supplanting him in the father's affections. The only thing that made them stop sniping at each other was turning on him. His cooing made them angry, his teasing made them angry, his anger made them angry, his vulnerability to their anger made them angry. Even his love—love I was certain they used to bask in—made them angry.

I threw my legs out of bed, pulled on the black sweater and wine-colored skirt I had planned for my class, shaved, rolled on some lipstick to make my face more credibly feminine, and stumbled out the door to do my half hour of voice exercises on the streets of what I hoped would still be a sleeping town. Walking was the last thing I wanted to do, but other people were staying in this house. I couldn't do my voice exercises here. I had just had my first voice lesson, and the initial benefit was losing my sense of how I should sound. I had a class to teach in a few hours; I needed to find a voice in which to teach it. The Bronxville streets were still deserted. Everyone at the college was asleep, and I had only to dodge a few unlucky commuters who were drifting toward the train. "Ayah, bah, cah, dah," I croaked, praying my voice, some voice, any passably feminine voice, would come back to me. Every week thus far, I had lost my voice; every week, I had called my friend Nancy right before class, begging her to help me remember it. Once I started walking, I didn't mind being out on the street. It was cloudy, and, instead of dawning, the light had merged with the humid air into a liquid luminosity. It was October, but lawns were still green; beds were still in flower. Nothing had died except my father, and, since I didn't yet know he was dead, to me he was still alive, still failing, still sinking deeper into the fever sleep my mother had tried so hard to cool.

I paused on the bridge above the highway that separated village from college to watch a flock of tiny sparrows settle on the pock-marked concrete. I stood right beside them, a foot or two away. For a moment, we seemed to have settled together. Then the illusion shattered. The flock startled, split into panicky wings. I was no longer a fellow creature, pausing on a bridge; I was death incarnate. One wing soared into the sky, the other skimmed along the ground. Both vanished. They were living too fast for me. Their hearts—something made it seem I could feel their hearts—were throbbing to a quicker rhythm than mine. To be alive this morning meant something different to them than to me, something I could never imagine.

The day my father died, something told me to turn around before I walked too far.

I was lucky that morning. When I returned from my walk, the single shower shared by the college's itinerant teachers was available when I needed it. I washed my hair in the sink in cold water, trying to prolong the student-beautician dye job, then took a quick, hot shower. More prayers—I had been so focused on my voice exercises that I had forgotten I was only halfway through my prayers. I had done the gratitude blessings—those were easy—and the affirmations of God's existence, but I hadn't even started the long and ever-lengthening list of those in need of healing. I was lucky that I still had time to pray, lucky that my hair was growing out so nicely. It had dried well the day before, and I was hopeful that I would look artlessly, artfully curly today, as well. There was a meeting of the writing faculty, and most of them were going to get their first look at their first transsexual colleague. I was lucky that I had planned such a good outfit, lucky that I had found time to bead a mauve and amethyst necklace that would go perfectly with the thrift-store skirt I had bought—how lucky I was—for fifty cents. I was so lucky that, when I was done with my shower, the father and boys and their terrible song of love was over, and I could dress in peace. I had plenty of time left to finish my prayers before teaching. Luckily, I had returned to my room in time to receive my mother's call.

When my cell phone rang, I was singing—well, murmuring—Hallel, the psalms of praise recited in honor of Sukkot, the harvest festival that commemorates, in the paradoxical Jewish way, both the abundance and the transience of life. It was only 8:03 a.m., and I knew it had to be my mother, and I knew my mother would call me at 8:03 a.m. only if she had to tell me my father was dead. "Did I wake you?" she asked me. "No," I said, suddenly confused about what day it was and how long I had been part of it. "No, I've been awake for hours." "Oh," she said, "I should have called you sooner. He died at 5 a.m." There was a little silent thud inside me, the first blow of the tiny hammer of death. It was just as I'd known it would be. My father was dead, and I wasn't even crying. "How are you?" I asked. A little sob rippled my mother's breath. "I'm okay," she said slowly, torn between truth and the eternal obligation not to worry her children. "It's a relief, in a way." "You told him he could let go," I said, "and he heard you. He let go." "Yes," she said hesitantly, as though we were lying, conspiring to cover the nameless crime of allowing her husband to slip through her hands. "Yes, he let go."

I wasn't crying. I had to decide if I was going to teach; I had to notify my students I'd canceled class; I had to pack. It took me a long time to figure out how my body would reflect my father's death. I was supposed to rip my clothing, but my clothing wouldn't rip. I didn't want it to. I took off the purple necklace I was so proud of. I took off the earrings that matched. I put away my makeup before I put any on. Death had stripped me. I had to look stripped. I had to walk the world with a face that reflected the ugliness of death. I had to bring my bags to my car; I had to get another cup of tea for the drive; I had to return the key to my room; I had to use the bathroom so that I wouldn't have to stop because, once I was driving, I knew I couldn't. I had to figure out how to do all these things when all these things seemed impossible to figure out. I seemed to linger for hours over each trivial task. I had to get home, I knew that, but home was not my home, and I had no particular reason to be there. Come to think of it, I thought, as I trudged up the steep hill to the administration building to return my key, I have no reason to be anywhere. I would have to drive, to eat, I would have to mourn, I would have to figure out how to mourn when I couldn't be with anyone who had known my father because the rest of my family didn't yet know I—the new me—existed, I would require innumerable phone conversations and expressions of sympathy as my luckless friends tended what I had become: a creature that didn't even cry when its father was dead.

I started crying on the Hutchinson River Parkway. I was crying for the loss of my home, the estrangement of my children, my skyrocketing estrogen levels, the indifference of my doctor, the end of my marriage, and, oh, yes, my father's death. When the tears that I had long ago believed would make me human came, they came at seventy miles per hour on a winding road. They came in gusts, they came in howls, they smeared the dotted white line across my field of vision, they swung the car back and forth like a slaloming skier. They came like colorless messengers from the dead father who had taught me when I was a child that life is nothing but the process of dying. Life, he used to tell me, puffing the pipe whose smell I loved, is a terminal illness. It was a mark of the promise he saw in me—you should do something important, he would tell me, like finding a cure for cancer—that he would share this truth with an eight-year-old still dewy-eyed, or so he believed, with the optimism of growth. Each day, I was growing bigger, stronger, smarter, but soon that would end, he told me, and then the decay that made up most of life would begin. The truth of life, the truth masked by the upward trajectory of childhood and the soft-minded sentimentality of maturity, was death. We all die, and that was what I was crying about, he told me angrily, as I hyperventilated on the floor of my room, eight years old, weeping hysterically over the death of a grandmother I had barely known, who had spoken little English, had spent most of her time in my presence playing solitaire, had made the sweetest latkes I ever tasted, had spent her last years silent and shrunken in the adult equivalent of a crib. You aren't crying for her, he told me. You are crying for yourself. You are crying for death.

I stopped sobbing as suddenly as I had started. I blinked until the road swam back into focus. I kept my car pointed straight along the darkness between the broken and solid lines. I slowed my breath. I wiped my nose. My air-conditioned tears cooled on my skin. I felt them disappear.

I didn't feel my father disappear. I should have. He had been relegated so long to the edge of my life, transparent, evaporating slowly, like a leftover tear, like the blue smoke rings he would blow when I sat at his feet—he in his recliner, I on the floor or on the footstool—after dinner. The rings left his lips in tight ovals, but the further they got from him, the larger and looser they became. The emptiness at their centers yawned. Their edges rounded and blurred. They framed his face, then disappeared into the larger haze of the living room.

The day my father died, I was surprised to feel that something had changed, that I had lost him again. It had taken me years to let him go, to realize that he would never speak to me again, that he would never explain how I had become something whose presence he couldn't bear. I had tried being angry; I had tried being sad; I had walked around repeating, "You are something even your father can't stand"; and I had tried, out of some twisted notion of loyalty and love, to follow that feeling into death. I was going to die anyway—he had taught me that—so I might as well die for him.

In my mid-twenties, I had even tried startling him into communication by appearing unannounced at the house where I had grown up. It was winter. He was alone in the house, as my mother had assured me he would be. I let myself in, and there he was, years older but still the man I had longed for and raged at across so many years of silence. His hair had receded into a steep widow's peak, and, though still black in the middle, it was shock-white on either side. He was wearing a bathrobe over pajamas, standing in the kitchen, when I burst in. "No," he said, or shouted—it sounded like a shout to me. He stared around wildly, looking for a way out. "Don't be afraid," I said. "I'm not going to hurt you. I only want to talk. I just want to ask you why—" "No, no, no," he said as he pushed past me and ran out in slippers into the ice and snow. I followed, but he had already reached his car. Curls of smoke were rising from the exhaust pipe, red and ghastly in his taillights' glow. I stood in the driveway shouting to him as he backed the car into me. He was moving slowly—he wasn't trying to hurt me—and it was easy, incredibly easy, to drop my hands from the rear of the car and step out of the way. I never saw him again. The therapists who couldn't help me understand my gender identity were very helpful when I told that story. His rejection had nothing to do with me, they said. My wish for death was a wish for his love; my anger at myself was anger at him. Hour after hour, week after week, I learned what I knew better than to say to them. His rejection of me was all I had left of him. That's why I kept it alive in my heart. My love and longing were a child's. I didn't want to survive without him.

The day my father died, a rabbi—I spoke to four that day, in a panicky effort to figure out how I could adapt Judaism's gendered, communal mourning rituals to my transsexual isolation—told me that mourning could be the beginning of a new relationship with my father. He had had a difficult relationship with his own father, who had died a couple of years before. "I finally realized," the rabbi said, "that what my father found so hard to accept in me was what he recognized of himself." But I didn't *want* a new relationship with my father. Years ago, I had become bored by him and his rejection, and, even now, in the first rush of the strange, new tenderness that had come with the news of his death, I didn't want to force on him a relationship he had so clearly rejected. "We don't believe the hand reaches that far from the grave," the rabbi told me. "Mourning is about the living, not the dead."

So, the day my father died, I became the custodian of whatever of him was in me. The relationship now was in my power, on my terms. I could summon or dismiss him, speak to his ghost or silence it, reject or embrace him. I could tell any story I wanted to about him, conjure regrets he had never voiced, phrase apologies he never delivered, weep as hysterically as I wanted to without fearing his rational sneer. I could proclaim to the world that I had survived his rejection. But what was most alive of him in me was the courage, the recklessness, with which he had embraced his losses. He, like me, had been determined to be himself at any cost. His estrangement from me was part of the price he had paid to be himself, just as my distance from my children was part of the price I was paying to become myself. How strange, when I had devoted so much of my life to being a different kind of father, that I, like him, would find myself standing stubbornly on the shore of myself, watching my children drift further and further away. Loss must have hurt him, too, but he had embraced it as the essence of a life he refused to live on any terms but his own. When his hearing went, he refused a hearing aid. Was that because there was nothing he cared enough to hear or because his sense of himself, his bodily integrity, would have been violated by having electronic equipment in his ear? When he refused dialysis, was it because he had given up on life, or was he affirming his dignity by embracing the downward trajectory of existence? He had paid for his refusal with months of increasing nausea, weakness, dizziness, failing breath, with the knowledge that every day he came closer to drowning in his own uncleansable waste. As far as I know, he never questioned his decision, never wavered in his conviction that this was the time and way to die, just as I knew that, even if taking estrogen meant that it was only a matter of time before my platelets fatally clotted, I would die rather than revert to what I had been.

My father's calm lived on in me. He and I both accepted the equations and inequalities of existence. We shared a humility that was hard to distinguish from humiliation. We had both wasted years in offices, aging under fluorescent lights, priding ourselves on intelligence that had little reflection in accomplishment, regarding life from the ironic shoals of despair, as though there were triumph in conscious desolation. "Settle down," he would say when I was upset about something, and I would settle down, watch the jagged shards of life fall into their usual painful configuration. Nothing, he taught me, could really happen; no matter what we did or didn't do, he and I and all of us would always be part of the colorless rainbow that arced from life to death. The day my father died, I realized that, even if my life was a failure, my new self a fiction, the losses it cost me permanent, I was still his son. I had inherited his nihilism, his capacity to confound blessing and curse, life and death, and to deny the choices they represented. But, when each of us faced the wasteland to which the refusal to choose life had led us, we turned in different directions. "No, no, no," he had said to the love that ran after him. But love was always there. Neither he, nor I, nor death itself, could change that.

13

The God Thing

Fall 2007

for Nancy

> Moses said to God, "When I come to the Israelites and say to
> them 'The God of your fathers has sent me to you,' and they
> ask me, 'What is His name?' what shall I say to them?" And
> God said to Moses, "I Will Be What I Will Be." He continued,
> "Thus shall you say to the Israelites, 'I Will Be' has sent me to
> you.'"
>
> Exodus 3:13–14

God comes after the worst nightmare I've ever had.

I'm at the family house, in the kitchen, at the end of a visit. My wife and children are leaving too, on their way to do something that involves boots and down vests. I'm curious. I'm always curious about their lives these days. My wife says little, and the older children consider it a betrayal of her to tell me where they've been or where they are going. My youngest is happy to tell me everything about anything but doesn't distinguish between memory, expectation, and fantasy. "Remember," she said to me once, "that night we were walking home and the dogs were barking at us and it was so terrible?" I didn't remember. I hadn't been there, and I was pretty sure she hadn't, either, but after I uh-huh-ed her through what I took to be a fantasy of externalized trauma, my older daughter filled me in. A night or two before, my family—minus me—had struggled through the dark surrounded by barking dogs.

My dream-self, dressed, like my waking self when I'm with my family, in a loose shirt that conceals my breasts, asks my wife what they are going to do. "Oh, a lot of things," she says vaguely, turning to usher her warmly dressed children out the door. "But what?" I ask. My voice has a note of pleading that I censor when I'm awake.

In the dream, my plea hangs in the suddenly emptied air. My wife and children are gone. I hear them outside on the deck, laughing, bumping into one another, murmuring about their plans.

In waking life, this moment happens on average four times a week; I don't even tear up anymore when the door to their lives closes behind me. My dream-self, though, hasn't learned to survive. It starts to cry. Not the stifled, make-sure-the-children-don't-hear sobs my wife and I perfected while I still lived in the house but full-blown, lung-emptying screams. In the dream, I want my children to hear me cry. Deeply asleep, choking on my own anguish, I nonetheless have the presence of mind to try to manipulate and punish them into love.

Their laughter recedes. They've started down the driveway, and I worry that my screaming isn't loud enough to reach them.

Then I realize what's going on. Dawn has broken. Light is leaking through the branches, nudging me awake. No, dawn is long over. The window is white with fog.

I start talking to God. You see how I feel, I say. You expect me to live through this?

God, as usual, responds with silence.

God's silence comes in many varieties. There's the testy "No comment" with which God responds to Holocaust theologians and others who try to reconcile human suffering with divine justice. There is the heavy Scandinavian muteness, like a blanket of icy snow, beloved of Ingmar Bergman. But God also speaks through intimate silences, like the moonlit silence that used to bathe my sleeping son when he was an infant. We had no curtains, so, when the moon was full, nothing interrupted the light pouring toward him, pooling on the pale, enormous cheeks that people would stop to touch on the street as though they were religious relics. I'm here, God seemed to say through that silence. Or, rather, God seemed to be that silence, gazing with me at the rise and fall of my son's chest. When he was three and a terrifying illness made it seem his life would end before it had begun, God's silence became both threat and promise. This was the silence of the God Thing, the inhuman God for whom love, as Job discovers, is compatible with torture, the God whose silent face is the only point left on the compass when existence becomes unendurable. I take life, God's silence said, and I give it, but, whatever I do to your son, I am and will be there.

Then there's the silence that constitutes God's contribution to my post-nightmare tête-à-tête.

"You see how I feel," I say to God, holding up my nightmare for inspection.

Silence. It sounds to me like assent.

"You expect me to live through this?"

Silence like a shrug. God, who doesn't live in time, is unable to expect. You are alive, the silence says. Life is this. Expectation is irrelevant. You live what is.

"I can't. I won't."

Another silence, slightly quizzical. You've been here before, the silence says. How is this time different? And what exactly do you mean: you can't, or you won't? You can live through this; you are; you have. You, like Me, will be what you will be. "Won't" is a different story—and here the silence clearly, infuriatingly, smiles, offering a glimpse of the God Thing's teeth, the pointed, inhuman acceptance of all that is.

A being who doesn't exist in time has no business smiling like that.

If you won't live through this, the silence says, you are making a decision—many decisions, in fact. You are deciding that this life is yours and that you can choose to end it. I have a different opinion, the silence says. But, even if life is yours to end, when did you decide that your pain is all that matters?

"You have no idea how it feels to have your children reject you."

The silence broadens into something like laughter.

"All right, you *do* know how it feels. Your children reject you all the time. I reject you all the time. Stop changing the subject. The question is . . ." I pause, realizing that the silence has managed to turn my assertions into a question and that asking a question has already moved me imperceptibly past my nightmare. "The question is, when your children reject you, how do *you* live through it?"

Silence. There's no answer, because there's no question. To love is to live.

God wins the argument again.

I know what my father would say. He loved to recount a cynical little experiment conducted at the dawn of the age of computers. Subjects were told that they were communicating with a therapist through a computer keyboard and screen. The therapist would ask them questions, and they were to respond. In fact, there was no therapist, only a computer program that used simple syntactical analysis to mimic listening. "How are you feeling?" the computer would ask, and if you answered, "Sad," the computer would say, "Why are you feeling sad?," building questions and affect-affirming "responses" around the algorithmically identifiable parts of speech in which the programmers expected "clients" to communicate their feelings. There was no artificial intelligence involved, simply patterns of ones and zeroes. Yet, people found themselves comforted, counseled, cured. According to my father, even those involved in the experiment, who knew what was going on, would sneak in after hours to "talk" to the program about their problems.

For my father, this demonstrated the absurdity of not only therapy but also communication. The sense of being understood was a purely mechanical response to purely mechanical statements. No training, no empathy, no consciousness, was required; all people needed was the illusion of a sympathetic presence to produce therapeutic effects.

God's silence, my father would say, is my version of the computer program, a fantasy of response that produces a fantasy of insight or, at best, enables me to recognize what I already know. But to me the computer experiment suggests the opposite: that our craving for presence contains in embryo the presence we crave.

Maybe my father was right to cut off communication; maybe we had nothing to say to each other. Maybe we could truly communicate only when silence was all we had.

I never have a good answer when my friend Nancy asks how I know that God exists. "Explain the God thing," she says, and I stumble through abstractions, intellectualizations, deeply felt mumbles that satisfy neither of us. Actually, she's the answer to her own question. Though she lives a thousand miles away and is overworked and underpaid, she has spoken and e-mailed me daily—often more than once a day—for months. The more I need her, the more she is there. Where, I want to ask her, could someone like you have come from if God doesn't exist?

Of course, she doesn't seem miraculous to herself, much less a proof of the existence of God. And, for me, no proof is called for. God exists, just as she does. It's as simple as that. For most of my life, I had no idea what the word "faith" meant. Even now, after being urged to have faith by so many friends, secular as well as religious, I'm a little shaky on the definition. Faith—I'm guessing here—is a sense that enables people to detect presence in absence.

When my wife and I were freshmen, arguing our way toward half a lifetime of love, a lot of what we argued about was God. "I don't *believe* in God," I would tell her, with a spiritual smugness life had not yet beaten out of me. "I don't believe in air, either. I just breathe." It wasn't quite that simple, but almost. God was something I had always felt, something that, despite its invisibility, shaped my life. In fact, as I told the girl I didn't yet know I would marry, God seemed a lot more real to me than I did. God was always there. I was something between a wish and prayer and rarely seemed to be anywhere other than the poems I was writing or the fantasies playing continuously in my head.

The contrast between the palpability of God's existence and the tenuousness of my own became clear to me when I was seven. Our family was on one of our summer camping trips in the

Berkshires. One day, we got up early, drove to the base of a not very high peak, and strolled up a winding trail to the top. It was a perfect summer day, the sun warm, the mountain air still cool. The peak was flat and fertile, a dense maze of trails lined with blueberry bushes. My parents had given me a pail and let me wander. There were berries everywhere. Wherever I stretched my hand, dusty blue globes tumbled forward to fill it. I reached into the damp labyrinths of bushy branches, feeling my way to lush clusters I could barely see. Bees buzzed around me, drawn by the same sweetness. I wasn't afraid. I knew they wouldn't hurt me. They settled awkwardly into tiny blossoms, banded abdomens gleaming. They were gathering; I was gathering. What they wanted, what I wanted, was right there, all around us. That was the way the world was, the way God intended us to see it. Wherever I stretched my hands, the world leaned forward to fill them. The perfect generosity of the world unfolded before me, a blooming, buzzing backdrop for the vast stupidity of humanity, of wars—it was 1968, and even my white middle-class childhood was reddened by the sense of distant slaughter—of starvation, of greed, of fear. There was nothing to fear, nothing to grasp at, no need that couldn't be met. The world was a maze of bushes bursting with blueberries, the air sang with sun and sweetness, God was there for the taking, a damp cluster dangling in dimness, a thudding abundance in a bottomless pail, a tart blue stain on my lips. It was all so clear, but no one seemed to know it. It was a secret, and it was my job to tell it, to tell the truth about the world we were living in, the God we were living with.

The sun rose higher, the air grew hotter. My pail was heavy now, but, everywhere I looked, there was more to gather. My parents called me. It was time to descend, and that, I knew, meant it was time for me to tell them the revelation God had entrusted to me. There they were, up ahead, chatting with other grown-ups, nodding down at me and smiling, exclaiming over the bulging blue dusk of my pail. I'll wait till they're finished talking, I thought. I'll wait till we're walking down the mountain. We walked down the mountain, and they kept talking. There were little silences, pauses for breath or laughter, and I kept thinking that I was about to tell them, kept opening my mouth and shutting it again. An enormous shyness enveloped me. They were grown-ups; I was a child. Whatever I said would sound as stupid to them as it had started to sound to me. We were almost at the end of the trail. I knew that if I didn't tell them on the mountain, I never would. It was my first job, my first responsibility to the world, and, step by step, silence by silence, I was failing. The path ended. The mountain was behind us now, we were heading toward the car, I was bickering with my sister, lunch was being planned, car doors opened. The vision of that perfect, abundant world had soured within me. It was the same vision, the same world, but now I knew it would always be stained with my failure to reveal it.

It was hard to imagine God as other than angry, disappointed, disgusted. I had seen so clearly that there was nothing to fear, and yet I was afraid. What was I so afraid of? Why was it so hard for me to tell the truth? The truth about God and the truth about me—I would never tell either to anyone. Entrusted with the great simple secret of life, and the small complicated secret of myself, I failed, failed daily, to deliver them.

God was there, beyond a doubt. But I was missing in action.

According to the Torah, God has a deep aversion to transgender behavior: "A woman must not put on man's apparel, nor shall a man wear women's clothing; for whoever does these things is abhorrent to the Lord your God" (Deut. 22:5). It's easy to contextualize the teeth out of this blunt expression of divine disgust. There is evidence that the law is aimed not at transgender people but at Canaanite religious practices that involved cross-dressing. Jewish law, even its most Orthodox forms, is evolving, not static; it takes account of post–Bronze Age advances in medicine and psychology. Non-Orthodox Jewish movements have already moved toward acceptance of transsexuals, though rabbinical assemblies still struggle with the complexities we raise. (For example, the Conservative movement distinguishes between pre- and postoperative transsexuals, equating gender with genitalia.)

But, though I have never followed more than a fraction of Jewish laws, I have been unable to rationalize, modernize, or ignore this verse since I first read it as a child. Perhaps it's because this is the only time the Torah seems to acknowledge the existence of people like me; perhaps it is because I, too, long for the clarity that the *yin* and *yang* of the gender binary seem to promise. If everyone is simply male or simply female, then perhaps every act is simply good or simply evil; every answer simply yes or simply no; every relationship simply loving or simply not; every life simply empty or simply full. A binary world, a world in which I couldn't exist, would be infinitely simpler. As long as men and women stayed on their own sides of the closet, God would not abhor us.

But I do exist, and so does the verse in Deuteronomy, and so neither the world nor my relationship with God can ever be as clear or simple as I long for them to be. Both God and I knew that, law or no law, I was sometimes going to wear female clothes, but, throughout my childhood, I tried to argue my way out of being abhorred. I was a child, not a man; perhaps the law didn't apply to children. But codes of masculinity and femininity were as strictly enforced in my family and school as in Moses' Bronze Age wilderness. My sister's wardrobe and mine had nothing in common; even on a dark night, my mother would never be mistaken for my father. God's abhorrence was not a factor in our almost entirely secular lives, but abhorrence of gender transgression was all around me, in the people I loved, in the air I breathed—in myself. I didn't *want* to transgress gender boundaries; I wanted to be a girl.

Perhaps that was how I could convince God not to abhor me for sneaking up to the attic and stuffing myself into my sister's outgrown skirts. I wasn't a man or a woman, a male or a female; I was a transsexual. Either I had no gender to transgress, because my female self and my male body canceled each other out, or the law was inoperative because I had no way not to transgress it. Whether I wore male clothing or female clothing, I was always cross-dressed.

That sounded right to me, but what were the chances that a God who abhorred cross-dressing would bother to go through the tedious and inconclusive exercise of sorting out my gender? God would abhor first and ask questions later. After all, that's what I did. I knew I shouldn't wear girl's clothing; it was wrong, it was stupid, and, no matter how much I wanted it to, it would never transform me into a girl.

And, yet, there I was, cross-dressing. I couldn't stop. That, perhaps, was the loophole I was looking for. Starving Jews are allowed to eat nonkosher food. I was starving to be a girl, and the nonkosher food of female clothing was the only way I knew to feed my malnourished self. Perhaps the law really meant, "God will abhor you for cross-dressing, unless you are dying to do it." That made sense in some ways—after all, God had made me a boy who was dying to be a girl. How could God abhor me for being what I was made to be?

Unfortunately, neither God nor I was comfortable with the idea that my desire to be female superseded the laws of the Torah. Perhaps I wasn't a basically good child doing an abhorrent thing; perhaps I myself was abhorrent. That was it. Like God, I would be what I would be. The law in Deuteronomy wasn't cutting me off from God; it was showing me that God and I had something in common. We could abhor me together.

Despite God's Deuteronomic disgust, when I lay in bed at night, stuffing my genitalia back into my body, it wasn't hard to convince myself that God was close, very close, to granting my prayers to become a girl. Like many transkids, I spent a lot of time bargaining with God, who was, after all, my only confidant. In exchange for becoming myself, I offered God—terrible things. Chunks of body, brain, soul. I offered to endure excruciating pain, to give my food to starving children, to do anything God wanted. I don't care, I whispered to the silence, whatever you want I'll give you—just let me wake up different.

If God keeps old prayers, there must be a special section for those of transsexual children. Strange prayers, awful prayers, prayers that precede overdoses of pills and crudely knotted nooses, prayers ravishing in their loneliness: *You made me what I am; You, at least, must understand.*

How could such prayers fail to evoke a response from God? It didn't seem like that much to ask. The only difference, after all, was a little bit of flesh between my legs. What was so hard about making that disappear? The world was full of girls—why shouldn't I be one of them? And sometimes I would sink into sleep with a tingling sensation bringing out gooseflesh on my arms and legs and something red and powerful stirring in my stomach, where I didn't yet know my womb should be, and I would go to sleep smiling, because I knew that, whatever it would cost me, I was finally going to change. I would wake up in the morning and immediately know that something was different. My hair would be longer, a tickling tumble over my shoulders, and I would stand up straighter, and I would open my door and pad in my new but oddly familiar flesh across the hall to show my parents what had happened—what I had become—who I had always been—and then my life would begin.

Except that it never did. The silence was answering my pleas, but I couldn't hear it yet. I knew only that I was trapped and that God, like a righteous or sadistic jailer, wouldn't set me free.

I don't know what would have happened if I had overcome my fear and told my parents what I was. It was still the sixties. Very little information about transsexuality was available. Trans children met with baffled, sometimes violent responses from family members. Some found their way to the few researchers and clinicians who accepted their crazy-sounding claims to be other than they seemed. Most kids who dared to say anything at all were kindly or brutally (some therapists used electric shocks to discourage attraction to cross-gender toys and activities) coerced to become "normal," to accept the clothing, attitudes, behaviors that went with their genitalia. Many were tossed out on the street.

I didn't know what other transkids were subjected to in the name of "curing" them; I hid because I was terrified of my parents' rejection. But, by concealing what I was, I was not only living out my worst fears of rejection but also proving myself a liar and a coward. Taken aback by my rage at my child-self, Susan, my therapist, once startled me by asking, "Did anyone ever teach you to be true to yourself?" No, I admitted. I was self-taught, and what I taught myself was that my family needed me to live in isolation, in terror, in hiding. If I spoke out, the world—my family's little

nuclear world, indistinguishable to me from the larger world—
would end, and no one could tell me what might rise from the
ashes, except, perhaps, for God, who wasn't talking.

Some people see transsexuality as a spiritual gift, a form of
chosenness. Following models from non-Western societies in which
transsexuality (or what seems to a Westerner like transsexuality) is
dignified with special religious responsibilities, they portray transsexuality as a capacity to stand beyond and to lead others beyond
the narrow confines of gender definitions toward more capacious
versions of humanness. I've always been skeptical of such claims.
And so, when a trans social group I briefly attended in the fall of
2007—cross-dressers, mostly, who seemed quite content with their
part-time female identities—invited a neo-pagan shaman to address
us on the spiritual functions of transgender people, I was, to put it
politely, dismayed.

The speaker was short, barrel chested, red bearded. His arms
were muscular and matted with red-gold curls. His eyes were quick,
and so was the deep laugh that rumbled in response to the murmurs
of the middle-aged man sitting next to him in wig and high heels.
I wondered what such a masculine man was doing here, in a room
full of guys in various states of feminization.

But he hadn't been born a man. For several decades, he had
been a sickly girl who became a sicker adolescent who grew into a
woman whose allergic and immune disorders produced a series of
hospitalizations and a coma she almost didn't survive. "I was
running from myself," the man told us, smiling, "but my self
hunted me down." I was listening closely now, my skepticism
suspended not just by his physical charisma but by the fact that
his gender, like mine, had led him into the maze between life and
death. I had been wandering there for months, looking for the
exit, but I still wasn't sure which exit I was looking for. His vitality
seemed to be pointing me toward life.

"Now I'm going to tell you something you won't believe," he
said. "You don't have to believe it, but this is the only way I can tell
my story." Uh-oh, I thought. Here it comes: the shift from ironic
self-awareness to black-and-white New Age dogma.

While the woman he had been lay dying on the floor of her apartment—so he said—she heard a voice, the voice of a goddess, an ancient Celtic goddess, summoning her back to life. But not to the same life: to life as a man dedicated to shamanic teaching and practice.

He was right: I didn't believe him, and I didn't have to. Despite the offense his story afforded my skeptical Jewish sensibilities, his vitality was all that mattered to me. This is what being fully alive looks like, I realized. This is what it looks like when someone is true to himself.

But he wasn't the point of the evening. He had spent years, he said, combing ancient mythologies for references to the spiritual functions of transpeople, our role in the spiritual life of our species. I had been fascinated by myths when I was a kid, particularly the few stories—Tiresias, Hermaphroditus, Caenus, the cross-dressed Thor—that seemed to reflect transformation fantasies like mine. But the myths were too fragmentary to be satisfying—they never explained, for example, why Tiresias wanted to become male again after discovering that sex is better for women—and it seemed unlikely that such time-bleared fragments could give meaning to my existence. The speaker seemed dangerously close to begging the question—he assumed that transpeople *did* have spiritual functions—but he had clearly done some serious research, and, if I accepted his claim to be a twenty-first-century transsexual shaman, his approach had a certain logic to it.

New Age hokum or not, the speaker had uncovered in me a deep yearning for a purpose to my transsexuality. I wanted it— me—to be *for* something, and, if talking to ancient Celtic deities and reading myths had enabled him to discover my purpose, I wanted to find out what it was.

The first two stories he told were disappointing, the myths familiar, their trans content minimal, his interpretations strained. Then he started telling a story about me. Technically, it wasn't a story about me—it was about Inanna, the Mesopotamian Queen of Heaven, a goddess of matchless power and beauty whose sister was the Queen of Hell. Inanna longed to see the dark realm her sister ruled. Her sister warned her not to visit. Beauty and power don't mean anything down here, her sister told her. Goddess or not, once you journey to me, you won't be coming back. But her sister's warnings only whetted Inanna's curiosity. Confident and radiant, she approached the gates to the underworld. They were guarded by eunuchs, male priests who had castrated themselves for spiritual reasons and dressed only in women's robes. The priests repeated her sister's warnings. Throw open the gates, Inanna commanded. They did as they were told and, when Inanna had passed through, slammed the gates shut behind her. As Inanna sank down through the darkness, she felt their hands upon her. They removed her halo of light, they tore off her gleaming robes, they tore her stays, they plucked off rings and pendants; by the time she arrived at her sister's throne, she was shivering in a nakedness she had never known. Her sister stripped Inanna's skin from her bones and nailed it to the darkness above her throne.

The Queen of Heaven was dead, and the world of life withered. Women miscarried; calves were still-born; crops blackened overnight.

One by one, gods appeared at the gates of Hell. Turn back, the priests warned them. The darkness that swallowed Inanna will swallow you.

One by one, the gods returned to the cold, still halls of Heaven.

Then the priests nodded toward one other. Silently they opened the gates; silently they descended, gathering Inanna's fallen garments as they slid through the darkness. Silently they stood before the Queen of Hell, and silently she glared at them as they pulled her sister's golden skin from the walls and brought it back to the upper world. Silently the gates of Hell swung open, and silently Inanna's bones reassembled themselves, and her skin, garments, and ornaments covered them once more.

You see, said the shaman, no one who was whole could descend to death and return again, not even the Queen of Heaven. But the transgender priests could. Transgender people move between life and death. That is our power, and that is our function. Because we die so often, death cannot hold us. We can follow souls into Hell and guide them back toward life.

He barely looked in my direction, but I knew he was talking to me.

For the shaman, the voice summoning him to life was that of his goddess. For me, the shaman's voice, including the hard-to-swallow stuff about his goddess, was an example of how a silent God communicates with us. The Hebrew word for angel, *malach*, also means "messenger." There is a Jewish teaching that we are all *m'lachim*, that we each carry messages from God to those around us, as though human lives were God's vocal cords. I had met such *m'lachim*. When I started college, I lost track of the Jewish holidays. Suddenly, in a crowded subway car, surrounded by ultra-Orthodox Jews, I realized it must be almost Rosh Hashanah. I could have asked any one of them when the holiday began, but I was embarrassed— a Jew shouldn't have to ask. But now I had to know, so I did something silly. I whistled. Loudly, passionately, I whistled every Jewish prayer I could remember. Halfway through my medley, the Hasid next to me touched my arm. "Rosh Hashanah is next week," he said gently. "It starts Tuesday, at sundown." He smiled and turned away. In Jewish tradition, each angel has one purpose, one mission, per manifestation. When the purpose is fulfilled, the angel disappears. The Hasid was once again a Hasid, utterly uninterested in the *kippah*-less, mushroom-haired college boy standing next to him.

Why would God, who had remained silent in the face of my most desperate imprecations, bother to let me know when Rosh Hashanah began? I have no idea. Or, rather, my only idea is that God usually answers us through one another. The Torah tells us that at Mount Sinai, when God spoke directly to the entire people, the Israelites couldn't wait for God to stop talking. Let God speak only to you, they said to Moses, lest we die. Every now and then, we long for the divine equivalent of room service, but for the most part we don't want to hear what God thinks of our thoughts, desires, actions, any more than children want to be followed around by nagging parents who are always right. So it makes an odd kind of sense that God would speak to us through the voices we do, desperately and constantly, want to hear: each others'.

I didn't want only to know when Rosh Hashanah was. I wanted a voice to reach out to me from the Jewish world, to recognize my disconnection, and to respond as the Hasid had, by telling me that, no matter how distant I felt, this was my holiday, too, that my people recognized me as one of them. "My people"—how dishonest that phrase sounds, given my discomfort with Hasidim, who look so different from the secular, Reconstructionist, Reform, Conservative, and Modern Orthodox Jews I have known personally. But, for a moment, there on that subway car, the Hasidim weren't strangers to me; they were home. God's voice from on high couldn't have made me feel connected to the Jewish people; the Hasid's Yiddish-inflected English did.

But sometimes God has answered me more directly. It happened the spring before I began living full-time as a woman, during the hard months between the time I came out to my son and the day I left home. My wife lived in our bedroom. I lived on the couch, in the living room. Most nights, after the girls were in bed, my son would tuck himself in with my wife and watch a DVD episode of one or another TV show. One night, when my wife refused to watch the *Star Trek: The Next Generation* DVD that had just arrived in the mail, he handed the unopened envelope to me.

I didn't feel like watching. But then—this is one of those goddess-calling-through-the-coma moments—I heard a little God-whisper telling me that if I watched with my son, something good would happen. I sighed and opened the red envelope, sliding the disk without looking into the mini-DVD player. The disk loaded, the introductory parade of heroic visages flashed by, and the first of the four episodes started.

I had seen every episode, but I didn't remember this one. It was about an alien race that had genetically eliminated gender, which they saw as the root of all social evils. The sane, stable androgyny in which they lived was disturbed by only one thing. Every now and then, one of their children was born with gender. Despite social programming and severe punishments, these offspring insisted on seeing themselves as male or female. So they were hunted down, convicted as criminals and then operated on to restore them to a healthy genderless state. One alien, who had spent her life hiding her female identity, came out to a human member of the *Star Trek* crew. She started by asking him what it was like to live in a society that had genders; she asked what the differences were between them; eventually, of course, she revealed that she was in love with him. By the end of the show, she had been arrested, tried, and convicted. In the last scene, the man she had been in love with visited her again. She'd had her operation and insisted that she felt so much better now that her femaleness was gone.

Needless to say, she was no longer in love with him. When her sense of gender was "corrected," she lost herself.

God was right—something good, astonishingly good, came of watching that episode. In the only form he could stomach, my son had just seen the story of my life and the terrible choices I faced between being loved and being myself.

It could be argued that this wasn't really a miracle. After all, don't good things always happen when fathers, even transsexual fathers, spend time with their sons? But Judaism rejects the idea that God becomes visible only when human action and choice have been scrupulously scraped away. Human beings, the rabbis tell us, were created to be God's partners: God left the world unfinished so that human beings could help complete it. By way of example, the rabbis point to circumcision, the ritual removal of the foreskin of the penis that, according to the Torah, is the most ancient sign of Jewish identity. The rabbis interpret circumcision as an operation that "perfects" the male sexual organ. God, they say, left a little extra skin on the penis so that Jewish men could remove it and turn their genitalia into a physical sign of their true identity.

From a trans perspective, this is a radical teaching. If an operation to alter genitalia is necessary to bring the male Jewish body into conformity with the Jewish soul, then God long ago acknowledged that medical intervention may be necessary for human beings to achieve their true identities. Transsexuals are embraced by the Torah after all, the seeds of our futures planted in Abraham's excision of the excess skin that prevented the males in his household from living as the Jews God wanted them to be.

Even when God is silent, that tradition speaks to me.

It would take more than one *Star Trek* episode to enable my son to speak to me about my gender. It took months before he found a way to tell me what he felt—and, when he did, it wasn't to cheer my decision to be true to myself. To him, that didn't matter. What mattered was knowing that I would do what it took to be his father. At first, when I still dressed as a man to see the kids, he told me when he thought my voice was becoming too high, my clothes too feminine. Later, he told me that he didn't mind if I wore a skirt but he didn't want to see me in a dress. Then he said that it didn't matter what I wore—he would never see me as a woman. Lately he's told me that he's bothered by the traces of masculinity—gestures, tones of voice—that clash with my female gender identity. While I welcome each sign of acceptance, everything he's said is a miracle—a sign that, no matter how we've changed, one thing hasn't: he will be there with me if I will be there with him.

In late October, a few weeks after my father died, I went back to the city I was born in. I hadn't been there in years. I had never seen my mother's new house. The art on the walls, the pictures on the refrigerator, and the furniture were entirely unfamiliar. Even the objects that I had known—"That's our old dining room table," my mother pointed out—meant nothing to me. I had always been focused on how little my parents knew me; now I realized how little I knew them.

My mother put me in my father's room. His desk, his computer, his papers—meticulously ordered before his death so that my mother would have no difficulty claiming her assets—a closet so full of his clothes that I barely had room to hang the few things I had brought. "I suppose you don't want any of these," my mother said, a little mournfully. I wouldn't have wanted any of it even if I were still a man. I've heard about people sniffing lost parents' clothing, using the power of scent—the olfactory center of the brain is located near the memory center—to bring back, for a moment, the dead. I didn't even want to touch my father's clothes. For twenty-five years, I had had no idea what he smelled like, and

I had no intention of finding out now. My mother gave me my father's watch to pass on to my son, who took it dubiously when I delivered it a few days later. "This belonged to the grandfather who didn't want to know me, right?" "It wasn't you he didn't want to know," I explained, trying to keep my tone upbeat. "It was me. He would have wanted to know you." I paused, wondering if I was telling the truth. "You can have him," I said finally, "even though he didn't have you."

Then my mother gave me a watch of her own. It was a smaller version of a man's style, androgynous in a way I would never have chosen, but even though I wasn't at home with it, it was at home on me.

My mother and I didn't talk about what was going on. We didn't mention that this was the first time I'd been welcome in her house, or how I felt about being in my father's room, or how she felt about having her son return as a woman. A claustrophobic sense of unreality settled over me like a second skin. There was nothing to say and no language in which to say it. I was home again.

I don't know whether what happened the next day was a miracle. It would be ridiculous to claim that, after coming out to my mother as a transsexual, I still needed divine intervention to tell her the truth.

It was all the hospice social worker's fault. After helping my mother through my father's death and my coming out, she had asked to meet the children—my sister and me—she had heard so much about. I planned to smile, shake hands, and keep my mouth shut. It would have been a very short visit if the social worker hadn't fallen in love with my family. "I really romanticize your family," she effused after we were all settled. "You care so much about each other."

For a moment, I panicked, wondered if I had wandered into someone else's counseling session. No—there was my mother, smiling proudly at her social worker. If this was the right room, I had the wrong memories.

"I don't romanticize my family," I said coldly, in a voice that, apart from its higher pitch, was identical to the distanced male voice I had worked so hard to leave behind. The social worker smiled. She was here to get to know me, not to project her feelings onto my life. I swallowed my anger and concentrated on answering her questions. I answered carefully, then not so carefully, then I was no longer waiting for questions, I was pouring out my long-hoarded history of self-hatred, suicide attempts, paternal rejection. I couldn't talk fast enough. Someone had finally joined me in the nightmare that had been my family; someone could finally see the agony I had endured.

So there I was, living out my fantasy of full familial disclosure, spilling my guts to a smiling, empathic woman I'd never met before. It wasn't until the session was winding down that I realized that I was in danger of entering the Guinness Book of World Records for shortest relationship with a mother. Telling her I was transsexual had started our relationship, and telling her about my childhood had probably ended it.

"Don't worry," the social worker assured me on the way out. "I've listened to your mother talk about you week after week. She really cares about you."

My mother had started out the hospice doors, past the lovely little garden adorned with flowers, benches, and an enormous statue of an eagle diving toward a kill. I caught up with her, and we walked together toward the car. She opened the door for me and moved slowly around to the driver's seat of the old gold Camry. The silence as she pulled on her seatbelt felt empty of God.

"Do you feel like going home?" I asked solicitously. "Or—we could go somewhere to talk. . . ." I was surprised, after my torrent of bitterness, to hear a note of uncomplicated tenderness in my voice.

"No," she said shortly, putting the key in the ignition. "I'm fine." She paused before turning the engine on. "It's just that—" Her voice started to break.

"It's just what?" I asked, dreading the answer.

"It's just that it was all a lie," she said, and I knew she was referring to the happy, caring family she had lived in until a few moments before.

I looked at her closely. She was staring fixedly out the windshield. "It wasn't all a lie," I said. "Some of it was a lie, some of it was true, and all of it was a long time ago. What matters now is what we make of now." My voice had a note of desperation. I was trying to sell my mother something I wasn't sure was possible—a life in which she and I really knew each other, in which love and honesty were not mutually exclusive.

She turned on the engine, moving on to the next item on our list of activities. How like me she is, I thought. Holding herself together by moving down her to-do list. No matter what happened, no matter how we felt, we were going to *do*. This was her answer to my revelations: to keep driving me, keep talking to me, keep moving with, if not toward, me. She wasn't my father; she hadn't cut me off.

We were entering my old neighborhood now. There was the park that had stood for freedom during my truncated adolescence, a wilderness at the edge of domesticity in which I could meet friends and experiment with drugs. I used to ride my bike there all alone, drifting along in a lazy haze of thoughts about doomed heroes, entropy, and emptiness.

The park was tiny, I could see that now, little more than a forested hill with some playing fields and a pond, but, when I was thirteen, fourteen, fifteen, it was the beginning of the rest of the world.

It was there, by the pond, during a chilly fall sunset, that I had fallen in love for the first time, with a boy with huge brown eyes and pale olive skin. It was a pure love, as thirteen-year-old loves go, for I had no body to express it. He couldn't even see me, couldn't see the girl who was loving him. He thought we were two boys, best friends, trying to impress each other with pseudo-intellectual, pseudo-mystical arguments. The pond was a blaze of gold behind his black-tressed head, and there were geese crying above us. I was cold, and, as a girl, I wanted him to notice and, as a boy, I didn't want to admit my weakness.

But now the park was already behind us. We were waiting at a busy intersection I half-remembered—it had been one border of my childhood world—and then we were turning down streets whose names I knew. "Does it look different?" my mother asked, as I gawked at porches and trees and cracks in sidewalks like a tourist from another world. "Yes and no," I murmured. The houses were different colors, the trees were taller, and there was a sense of vacancy, of meaninglessness. No one I knew lived in these houses; they weren't my lost past. They were ghosts, or I was a ghost—no, I wasn't a ghost, I was the future. I looked down at my skirt, my mother's watch on my wrist, the budding curve of my breasts. I had been a ghost when I haunted these streets with my adolescent yearnings and cataclysmic despairs. I was middle-aged now, but in some way the film had run backward. Then I felt that my existence was almost over; now I knew it had barely begun.

"It was so long," I muttered to my mother, "before I realized that all these streets were named for colleges." How pleased I had been when I learned that my street, Vassar, was named after a women's school. My block wasn't long, but we drove it slowly, my mother updating me on who now lived where. I was only half-listening. The grownups hadn't really mattered to me, and, besides, there I was, eight years old, walking home alone from a friend's house in a yellow raincoat in a pitch-black downpour, thunder booming, lightning flashing, as I let my pants drop to my ankles so that I could pretend the raincoat was a dress. "Please," I had prayed, knowing that in a few feet I would have to pull my pants up and surrender to boyhood again. "Please change me!" It had felt so right, the plasticized fabric brushing my bare, wet legs like a hem, as though for the first time my real body, slight and female, was being exposed to the elements. "Please," I repeated, clutching my trousers now, inching them upward. There was still time for God to turn me into a girl, there were still a few steps left. . . .

But there weren't. I was home again. There it was, the house I had grown up in. There was the place I had lain down in the snow—no snow now, in this preternaturally warm autumn—determined not to get up again. There was the scraggly little tree—it had been protected by a fence, my mother reminded me, because it was so small and delicate—that I had stared at through my window. In winter, the streetlight had shone above its slender branches like a frozen star. Now it was unfenced, massive. There was the lawn—I remembered lying face down there so that the grass and clover would look like a jungle. The house was a different, darker color now, and my memory of its structure was a little off. "I don't remember the porch being that large," I said. My mother laughed. "*That* hasn't changed," she said. There, above the porch, was my window, the one I had spent hours gazing through.

There *he* was. My God, he was still there.

"Do you mind if I get out?" I asked, voice shaking a little. My mother kept the motor running as I stood on the sidewalk, gazing up at him, the boy I had been. I could see him there, behind the window, hurting himself over and over. All these years, he had been there, hurting, waiting for me. "You can stop now," I whispered to him. "I told you I would come back to you, and I have."

My mother was waiting. I had to wipe away my tears, to return to that other kind of time, the only time that she and I could ever share. But . . . not yet. "Please," I whispered, praying not to God but to the child I had been. I could feel the boy unclench his fists, I felt him lift his head, and, as his hazel, time-blinded eyes turned in my direction, I heard the silence, the silence of God, smiling with satisfaction, laughing silently at our astonishment that both of us, the past and the future, the tortured boy and the woman he thought he would never be, had been answered by a single moment.

"You prayed for a miracle," the silence said. "Let's see what you make of it."

14

The Voice
of the Future

Some mornings I hear the voice of the future.
I wake early, dipping in and out of consciousness, muttering prayers that tangle with half-dreamt dreams. The trees behind my eyelids grow lighter, birds scream, and the paws of small animals rustle so loudly it sounds like they're foraging in my room. It's getting late, but for what? The sense of hurry that's dogged my life remains, but the rationales have faded. Life asleep and life awake—I know it is important to move from one to the other, but I'm not sure why, or to whom.

I wash and dress and step out of the latest in the series of inadvertently temporary shelters I've found since leaving the house that had been my home. It's summer, and there's a small waterfall next door. The sound of water, a hush that is somehow also a roar, is constant. The tangled white water-tresses remind me of the hair I never got to see on my dead father's head.

Morning is my time for walking. The area where I live is forest and water, with roads carved through and houses carved out of summer greenery. Unlike last summer, my first summer living as a woman, I'm not walking to be seen. This summer I'm walking to become visible to myself. I look down at the swirl of the hem of my skirt, the curves of my maturing breasts, the fish-belly flash of my legs. A piece of hair—my hair's grown down to my shoulders—falls over my right eye every step or two. I've repeated the gesture of brushing it back so many times that it has become natural to me, a feminine gesture that isn't a copy of what women do but something that I do naturally, because I need to.

I walk uphill as much as I can. Estrogen not only breaks down muscle and builds up fat; it also decreases oxygen absorption by the blood, which is why women tend to get winded faster than men. I need to feel winded and to ignore feeling winded. I need to feel my heart becoming equal to whatever road I'm on, no matter how steep.

After forty-seven years, I finally feel alive. It's a strange, almost terrifying feeling, amoral, self-justifying, triumphant. It's as though, on all the mornings before, I've never actually been awake. Never noticed the trees, the birds, the squirrels, the fat rabbit nibbling grass between worn train ties. In one pan of the scales is the shattering of my family, the pain of those who loved me as a man, the losses mounting behind me, and, in the other, there is only this: the feeling of being alive.

This, I know, is the voice of the future. If I listen, that future is mine.

Once I played the Voice of the Future. The future in question was a gymnasium stage, tricked out with shifting cardboard sets. The play was as ambitious as they come in grade school, a zero-budget account of human history from the invention of the wheel to the present day. The cast included cavemen, Roman soldiers, wagon-riding pioneers, refugees, and presidents. I was cast as the narrator, the Voice of the Future, whose booming, feedback-distorted function was to explain how the on-stage mayhem represented progress.

It was the perfect role for the nine-year-old me—bodiless, characterless, an invisible harbinger of things to come. The Voice of the Future had nothing to say about anything that might give meaning or shape to history. This had happened, this was happening now, soon something else would happen—and that was progress, because the present is inherently superior to the past, and the future is always better than both.

That, anyway, is what the Voice of the Future said, as empires crumbled and new empires crawled from the wombs of unacknowledged genocides.

"Do you ever regret what you're doing?" my best friend occasionally asks, meaning my transition. Her question reflects the moral logic of progress, which is a comic mode; as in romantic comedies, the happy ending moots all the car crashes and broken hearts that made it possible. Her question points the other way: if it hurts so much to be separated from my children, was the transition that caused the separation a mistake? If it's so hard to be a not-quite-woman without home, family, or identifiable future, wouldn't I have been better off living as the man who had all three?

But transition isn't progress; it's necessity. I didn't choose transition because I thought it would make me happy; I did it because I had to. When the siren song of real life—life as myself—began singing inside me, I couldn't turn away, no matter how painful real life promised to be. Newborns emerge from the birth canal covered in blood, faces bruised, genitals swollen, skulls misshapen; they are greeted by a cold, unpredictable world of harsh lights and strange sensations. Compared to the temperature-controlled, heartbeat-lulled environment of the womb, where everything exists to nurture, nourish, and protect, birth is hardly progress.

But you can't begin to live without it.

As I approached the first anniversary of moving out of my family home to live full-time as myself, I was in my third rented bedroom, a month or two away from having to move again. The past several months had included a car accident; being thrown, for no reason I could understand, out of a house I'd been invited to live in; being frisked by state police in front of my children in what used to be my kitchen; and having a court suspend my right to see my daughters without supervision until investigation could determine whether I was a danger to them. I had been invited to deliver a paper at a conference that was paying my way to Europe, but I would have to travel there with a passport and plane tickets that identified me as a man. Which, legally, I would remain, until I could provide a letter from a surgeon attesting to my having had the sex reassignment surgery that I had no prospect of ever affording.

When I returned from Europe, in addition to seeing attorneys about the divorce, I would be seeing my doctor to determine whether I had a tumor or other condition that made taking estrogen dangerous for me.

This was the price I had to pay for becoming myself, rather than remaining the mournful, hollowed-out simulacrum that I had been for so long. All of the things that constituted progress—family, love, career success, financial security—had receded beyond any foreseeable horizon. Each day was a blank; rather, each day I was a blank, a battered newborn peering from the birth canal into a world that had terrifyingly little to do with the life I'd left behind.

I needed a new Voice of the Future, a voice that spoke from and to the future into which I had been delivered, a future composed equally of tragic necessity and boundless possibility, a future that, though it had already had brought me more pain than I ever imagined, I couldn't regret.

There was a new voice in my future, but I had to make it from scratch.

Over the past two years, I'd heard my son's voice creak, crack, and finally plunge to a booming, gravelly bass that made him sound older than his fourteen years. My son was both shy and proud of his new voice, as he was of the suddenly adult-size body that he found himself inhabiting, the muscles bulking out his arms and shoulders, the fine curling hair making its way down his cheeks, across his lips, over his chin. Without any apparent effort, his body was becoming a man's.

Over the same two years, albeit with a great deal of effort, my body had been moving in the opposite direction. High-intensity lasers had burned out follicles my own male puberty had stimulated. My rough red-brown beard and mustache were gone, my chest and back hair almost eliminated, though I still had to shave my legs and arms every day or two. My upper body contours had become slimmer as testosterone-stimulated muscle broke down, my skin finer, softer—and more vulnerable to varicose veins and cellulite. Even in the androgynous, shape-concealing jeans and baggy shirts I wore with my children, strangers generally took me for a woman.

But, when I spoke to my children, it was in the voice they had always known—the deep Daddy voice, the voice of our shared past. As female-to-male transsexuals take testosterone, their vocal cords lengthen and their voice boxes expand, lowering pitch and shifting timbre to masculine ranges. But estrogen has no effect on a male-to-female transsexual's voice.

For most of my life, I believed that the same medical magic that would enable my breasts to grow would also change my voice. Of course, for most of my life, information about transsexuality was hard to come by. But, by the time I started to research transition in earnest, the world had changed. I typed "transsexual transition" into a search engine, clicked "Go," and there they were—websites offering transsexuals for sexual pleasure, websites offering hormones and prostheses to aid cross-dressing, discussions boards, true-life stories of transition, before and after pictures, "find the transsexual among the real women" games, dating services, advice on dressing like a woman, walking like a woman, shopping like a woman— and, here and there, nuts-and-bolts information.

According to these sources, transition was easy. All I had to do was suppress my testosterone level and elevate my estrogen level, and even my thick, hairy, middle-aged body would undergo a belated female puberty. My metabolism would slow, my endurance decrease, and fat cells would migrate from masculinity-defining sites like cheeks and belly to femininity-defining sites like breasts, buttocks, and hips. My center of gravity would shift downward from shoulders toward hips. My face would become thinner, my arms and shoulders more delicate. My erections would become infrequent, then incomplete, then more or less stop, as my testes underwent what the medical sites charmingly called "hormonal castration."

It would be slow—just like natural puberty, male-to-female puberty takes about six years in total—but, given a proper hormone replacement regimen, it would be inexorable, and, by the end of two years, my body should "read" as female.

It sounded like heaven to me.

But there were three holes in the heaven of medical feminization. Hormones wouldn't transform my genitals—as I'd known since childhood, only surgery could do that. Hormones wouldn't change my skeletal structure; my hips would always be too narrow and my shoulders too broad. And hormones wouldn't change my voice.

The first two were daunting but expected. The last was devastating.

My voice was the one male part of me I didn't loathe, the most important part of my persona as a teacher and a poet, the one means I'd found to touch other people without being touched. I had stopped exercising in my early twenties when I realized that muscle development emphasized the masculinity of my physique, but I kept working on my male voice, learning to exploit its depth (during my brief stint in a chorus, I was a bass) and resonance to sound honest, concerned, angry, soulful, playful, deadpan. I learned to fill it with love when talking to my children and to fill it with contrition when talking to God. I learned to sound crisp and authoritative on business calls and tender and vulnerable when murmuring in the dark to my wife. Most important, I learned to think of that voice as me.

To live as a woman, I had to start from scratch. Rather than developing my natural vocal qualities, I would have to learn to suppress and distort them. And, somehow, through that process, I would have to create a voice that was as supple, as expressive, as authentic—that would feel as much like mine—as the voice I'd been grooming since it first began to crack.

That seemed impossible. How could any other voice feel like mine?

I had always loved women's voices, but, in the fall of 2006, as I began, surreptitiously, so as not to scare my children or add to my wife's heartbreak, to fashion a new female self, I started to listen to women's voices in a new way. There were as many kinds as there were women—lilting and husky, light as butterfly wings and heavy as honey, brittle, broken, scratchy, maternal, sharp, sexual, ironic, naïve, yearning, trilling, breathy, breathless, cool, yearning. . . . In fact, there were more kinds of voices than there were women, because each woman had a repertoire at her disposal. I listened in awe as women shifted from a voice used in laughing conversation with a friend to the impatient tenderness of dealing with a needy child, the matter-of-fact superiority of telling a husband something he should have known, and back to the ease of friendship. Men's voices, I realized, hew close to a single pitch; women's roam up and down the scale, often in torrents of words in which I could hardly detect a breath. Some women's voices were so effortlessly gorgeous that they broke my heart; some sounded like the aural equivalent of a bad haircut; but all instantly identified their producers as women.

It was clearly time for another Internet search.

In 2.2 seconds, I had several thousand options. One detailed the mannerisms that distinguish male and female speech in our culture (women, according to this website, speak faster, use their hands more, and emphasize the ends rather than the beginnings of words). One urged me to sing along with deep-voiced women singers; one suggested I speak along with—and even act out—female roles in Hollywood movies. I started singing and speaking along, talking faster, reminding myself to do something with my hands occasionally (I wasn't sure what), and articulating final consonants. None of those changes seemed to move me significantly along the gender spectrum. Reluctantly, I turned to the technical websites. One pointed out that women use a lot more air when speaking than men do. Another told me to cut out the chest resonance that men typically use to amplify their voices and direct my airflow to the small cavities in my head. A third gave step-by-step instructions on how to nudge my pitch upward without breaking into falsetto and offered to sell me sound analysis software that would tell me exactly how many cycles per second I was from reaching femininity.

After a week or two, my growing list of things to remember to do and not do had turned speaking into an exhausting and humiliating exercise; the only thing I was sure I'd learned was that every sound that came out of my throat proved I wasn't a woman. I wasn't getting anywhere by imitating female NPR announcers, singing along with Sheryl Crow, or articulating the final "ng" of every gerund, and I didn't have the money for voice coaching or videos, so I turned to a free how-to manual called "Finding Your Female Voice" that I found on the website of Hollywood-based

Deep Stealth Productions, a company devoted to offering male-to-female transsexuals the skills they need to pass as women. The most encouraging part was the title: I loved the idea that I was "finding" a voice that was already female and already mine, rather than approximating others' voices. The successfully transitioned and assimilated transgirls at Deep Stealth had no doubt that if I did their exercises diligently, I would find a new, true, and definitively female voice. The least encouraging part was Deep Stealth's insistence that maintaining that voice would require extensive exercises every day for the rest of my life. The manual envisioned a monk-like daily regimen that involved warm-ups, herb tea with lemon, and a safe, quiet, private place to sit that would enable me to maintain the good posture necessary for an unobstructed airstream. Since I was still living with my family, I did most of my exercises on my daily walks. Rather than sitting calmly and breathing steadily, I did endless sequences of vocalizations ("Ayo, Bo, Ko, Do, Eyo . . .") while striding uphill and down, pausing occasionally to play myself back on the cheap handheld recorder that always told me the same thing: my voice sucked. Not only didn't I sound female; I barely sounded human.

But, as days of vocalizing turned into weeks and fifteen-minute practices turned into half hours, my voice started changing. I no longer had anything that could be called "my voice." The male voice I used with family and for teaching seemed rough, barbaric; the rasp and rumble of air in my chest felt like a foreign intrusion into my body. When I spoke, I was now conscious of the air moving in my throat, in my mouth, in the cavities of my head; I could shape it, direct it, increase and decrease amplitude, breathiness, resonance. The result was a new voice or, rather, a series of new voices that I practiced when talking to myself, on business calls, and with friends. These voices were strained and unreliable and required constant thought and effort; the unfamiliar buzz of air in the small cavities in my head gave me headaches. My pitch was too low, except when it was too high, my resonance either faux operatic or barely there at all. Even when I talked to my closest friends, I couldn't shake the sense that my voice was a caricature they listened to with pity.

But gradually, imperceptibly, my vocal gender was shifting. When I answered the phone at home, people often mistook me for my wife. When I made business calls, I was usually referred to as "ma'am." Though the tape recorder assured me that my voice in no way resembled that of a genetic woman, I had accumulated enough female markers that strangers "read" my voice as female, if only because it sounded nothing like a man's.

That, it seemed, was the voice of my future, a voice estranged from masculinity but not yet, perhaps not ever, the voice of the woman I was struggling to become.

That was the best I could do until, in spring 2008, a friend gave me something I was sure I could never afford—three lessons with a professional voice coach.

After the first five minutes of coaching, my teacher made it clear that I had done an amazing but completely wrong-headed job of remaking my voice. The voice I worked so hard to produce sounded artificial, pumped up with so much excess resonance it was hard to make out the words I was saying. The voice exercises to which I was devoting an hour a day weren't getting me closer to finding my female voice—they were wearing out my vocal cords. However, those exercises had given me so much control that I was instantly able to modulate airflow and resonance in response to my teacher's instructions. She adjusted my pitch downward, opened my air passages to increase breathiness, cut some of my head resonance, and added a trace of the chest resonance I had eliminated months before. The result was a voice that sounded and even felt easy and natural. She didn't want me to sound like "a woman." She wanted me to sound like me.

My life had always been defined by discomfort with myself. The steps I had taken to find my female voice had increased that discomfort, reminding me constantly of the difference between what I was and what I wanted to be. But, according to my voice teacher, the only way I could find my female voice was to realize that there was no difference between what I was and what I wanted to be. The voice of my future wasn't something to strive for, it was something to relax into, to accept in all its husky imperfection, not as progress, but as necessity.

To date, by trans standards, my transition had been relatively easy. I had been rejected by some of the people I loved most, but that was par for the course. Those rejections were emotionally devastating, but most of the people I came out to had been accepting, sympathetic, supportive—and some had become real friends. Like many transsexuals transitioning in middle age, I had lost home, family, best friend, and so on, but, surprisingly, I hadn't lost my job or my profession. My publisher, magazine editors, fellow scholars, and various other professional colleagues' responses had ranged from lack of interest to startling warmth and generosity, as when a Dickinson scholar I'd never met sent me several boxes of immaculately tailored and dry-cleaned clothes.

There were awkward moments, of course. I often had to introduce myself to people I had known for years. After giving a reading in Chicago from a book I had written in the voice of a female Holocaust survivor, a woman with a teenage daughter came up to tell me that she had been outraged that my publisher referred to me as a man—she had told her daughter that no man could have written the book. When she said she was going to write my publisher a letter of complaint, I explained that it wasn't his fault: when the book came out, I had been a man.

It was a dream come true.

Of course, dreams are a lot less complicated before they come true. I wasn't simply invited to return to teaching at Stern in September 2008; conditions of my return had to be negotiated. And, as usual when male-to-female transsexuals return to their former jobs after transition, those negotiations included a topic that hadn't for me been a subject of institutional interest since preschool: my use of the bathroom. Like most employers, mine wanted to reserve the women's rooms for genetically and anatomically correct women. Though I used women's rooms all the time without comment or incident, my anatomical maleness was a matter of public record. Not only was I about to make history as the first transsexual accepted by a modern Orthodox Jewish institution, I was also going to make history as its first tenured professor whose bathroom usage was a condition of employment.

My attorneys, whose careers had been dedicated to promoting the civil rights of gays, lesbians, and trans people, regretfully informed me that no U.S. court—none—had ever upheld trans employees' rights to use the bathroom of the gender with which they identify in the workplace. Other people—normal people, real people—were free to use the bathrooms designated for those of their gender. But, legally, I wasn't woman or, for that matter, a full human being. In fact, Congress had recently stripped a provision protecting transsexuals from a landmark anti-job-discrimination bill that would extend federal protection to sexual orientation; in my home state, Massachusetts, an uphill fight was being waged to pass human rights legislation that would protect transsexuals against discrimination. The rights that went with American citizenship didn't automatically extend to transsexuals; those rights were what the media call a "controversial issue."

"What about after surgery?" I asked my attorneys. "Can I use the women's room then?" "We can certainly raise that question," they said.

It wasn't only on the job that my rights were diminished by the conflict between my gender identity and my genitalia. When I applied for a new passport, I had to submit letters from my therapist and my endocrinologist explaining why I no longer resembled the man with the beard on my old one. The State Department granted the new passport but told me that it would be revoked after a year if I couldn't provide evidence that I had had sex reassignment surgery—and, furthermore, they listed my gender as male. That meant that I had to be listed as male on my plane tickets and on every other travel-related document—and, since I no longer looked even slightly male, that meant I would be outed in every official interaction. If any security person had qualms about the dissonance between my female appearance and my official gender, he or she could frisk me, go through my luggage, and hold me until satisfied that I wasn't a threat. My genitalia not only made me persona non grata in public restrooms; they were, potentially, a matter of national and even international security.

Of course, I had what in the trans world are called "walking papers"—a letter from my therapist "to whom it may concern" explaining my transsexuality and assuring whoever it might concern that I wasn't trying to perpetrate a fraud. I had several copies in different bags, though fortunately I had never had to use them. But, even if that letter kept me out of jail and off watch lists, it couldn't keep me from being humiliated or missing a plane.

Compared to the humiliation African Americans lived with under Jim Crow or the ongoing harassment engendered by racism, what I had to put up with was nothing. I didn't have to sit at the backs of buses, eat at separate counters, drink from separate water fountains. Since my transsexuality wasn't obvious to anyone who wasn't looking at my identity documentation, unlike many of my fellow transwomen, I wasn't a target for violence. All I had to do was use a separate bathroom.

And make sure that my children didn't see me dressed as a woman until their therapists said it was safe for them, which meant avoiding public places where they might be when I wasn't with them.

And hope that the guardian *ad litem* appointed by the divorce court to protect the best interests of my children didn't decide that my transsexuality was a threat to their well-being or that I had acted irresponsibly as a parent in any way in the course of my transition.

And pray that if I was ever stopped for a traffic ticket or was involved in an accident, the police wouldn't make an issue of the little "M" under gender on my driver's license.

And hope that none of my students, their parents, my colleagues (who included many Orthodox rabbis), university trustees, or donors decided that my transsexuality made me a threat to the university or to Judaism.

And accept that my insurance, which covers erectile dysfunction as a necessary medical expense, classes the surgery necessary for me to have functional genitalia as "elective and cosmetic."

And, if I ever scraped up the funds for surgery, send letters from my doctor attesting to the alteration in my genitalia to the bureaucrats—Social Security, my insurance providers, and so on—who have it in their power to change M's officially to F's.

And hope that then I could use the women's room at my job.

For millions of Americans, discrimination is a bitter given, an unavoidable concomitant of their pursuit of life, liberty, and happiness. But I had brought my otherness upon myself. Losing rights, opening myself to discrimination, negotiating with courts—it was all part of the process of becoming. Living as myself, without shame or hiding, meant living as a not-quite parent, citizen, person.

And, in this country, "not quite" represents progress. Things were much worse twenty years ago, and they are getting better all the time. The voice of the future assured me that I would get used to the social and legal disabilities of transsexuality, that they were as integral to my becoming as the heart-pounding thrill of feeling truly alive. But now, after years of living with these disabilities, I experience them as obstacles to self-realization, impalpable but well-aimed blows to my self-esteem delivered daily by a society whose members are mostly oblivious to the violence routinely directed at people like me. In so many ways, I have become myself, but, when I see that self reflected in newspaper articles about transsexuality, in congressional debates about whether it should be illegal to discriminate against transgender people, in the terms of the divorce agreement that severely limits my time with my children, my self seems twisted, hunched, misshapen. I am something ugly, something dangerous, an issue, a controversy, a claim, a problem, a discomfort that ripples through the room, a creature, a sight gag that always gets a laugh. Certainly not a woman.

It's July 4, 2008. I'm surrounded by people trying to find a voice. It's my first march—actually, it's the first Transgender Pride march in New England. Some trans people would arrive at a march like this and feel at home; I don't. After a lifetime of feeling alien, I never expected to feel a surge of oneness with my differently gendered brothers and sisters. I expected to feel lonely, to haunt the fringes while staring at everyone as though, if I looked hard enough, I would see what made us family. When I heard the weather report—a high in the nineties, with over 90 percent humidity—I expected to feel all this while dripping sweat down the front of a short sleeveless dress.

But, though I expected nothing but discomfort, I knew I had to be there. I had explained it to my son. As a relatively privileged trans person, I could tell myself that the violence and oppression most trans people face were not my problems, but that, I told him, was not the kind of person I was working so hard to become. To the person I was trying to become, privilege meant responsibility; precisely because I was relatively secure—for someone having to move every few months while fighting to maintain her rights as a parent—it was my responsibility to stand up and identify myself as trans. I found my speech quite inspiring. He just grunted.

The real reason I was at the march was that I wanted so much not to be. I didn't want to see myself in the damaged people who now surrounded me. I wanted to hide in my bedroom and write or to stroll in and out of stores where I would be identified as a woman, rather than as someone struggling to be one. I didn't want to be eyeing the police nervously, wondering if they were there to protect us from the rest of the world or the rest of the world from us. And I certainly didn't want to watch myself ruthlessly sizing up the gender performance of every female-presenting person (the males didn't interest me), winnowing the genetic women, and there were many, mothers and allies and girlfriends and sisters and grandmothers and political fellow travelers and sympathetic lesbians and earnest college girls, from—us. Most of all, I didn't want to be us. Many of us were obviously poor, wearing cheap, ill-fitting, or ill-chosen clothes. A few were in wheelchairs, a few were twitching uncontrollably; many had pain smeared like makeup across seamed, beaten faces. Some of us had been beaten. One said she was there because her daughter, who was getting married that day, wouldn't invite her to the wedding. Very few were people of color, but there were many shades of white. Some were young and radiant, delighting in transgressive self-invention, but most of us who were transsexuals—even at a march like this, transsexuals are a minority—looked like self-invention was an ongoing struggle. Some of us were chatting with friends, some were carrying banners, some shouting greetings to old comrades; all of us had come a long, long way to be there. Some fell within the range of genetic female appearance. Some had spent tens of thousands of dollars and were still marked for life as genetically male. My eye kept returning to a lissome young transwoman—she must've been in her early twenties—with supermodel legs, a dauntingly slender frame, fetching chestnut hair, and a face whose touch of androgyny only added to its beauty. She was alone, and her eyes were filled with pain. But she, too, was one of the lucky ones.

This was the real reason I had to go to the march—to learn to see myself as us, or, rather, to see my internalized transphobia, my own self-loathing for being trans, projected outside me, to stare it in the face, in all of our faces, and see whether I could see through it to the human beings behind our handmade masks of gender. If I couldn't see my trans sisters as human, I would never see myself as human. I might pass on the outside, but, on the inside, I would always be lesser, other, deformed. The deformity was there whenever I looked in the mirror. It was there when my hair was too wet for curls to soften the testosterone-warped bones of my face. It was there when I put on my pinkest, most feminine T-shirt and all I saw were hulking shoulders. It was there when I showered. It was there when a flicker of desire reminded me of the brutal truth of my anatomy. I wasn't there because I was proud; I was there because I was ashamed. I was there not because it was my responsibility to stand up for others but because only among those I didn't want to resemble—only among us—could I learn to stand upright.

I was milling behind a butch lesbian who was reminiscing to a young student wearing gauzy wings (her sign said something about "gender faeries") about how many times she'd been beaten up. Ten years ago, she said, I would look around for the community after a beating and there was nothing. I'm so proud, so proud to be here. It looked like she was going to cry.

It was time to march. One of the organizers warned us not to shout back at anyone no matter what abuse was hurled at us. The loose assembly shook itself into a line about twenty feet wide and jerkily moved into the street. A few cars honked as we headed toward the center of Northampton. There were more and more people on the sidewalk, some with cameras, some staring, some smiling, some waving. The police were there, all around us, keeping an eye out but somehow not looking at any of us. More cars honked; more people shouted. I softly added my voice to our chorus ("What do we want? Freedom. When do we want it? Now!"). I was among us, in the midst of us, indistinguishable from us. I glanced at the supermodel transgirl. Both of us were lonely, but neither of us was alone.

We were walking down the middle of a street that stood for the world that didn't know what to make of us. It had shunned us; it had hunted us; now, for a few minutes, it had no choice but to acknowledge us, if only by driving around us. We passed beneath a railroad bridge, our shouting growing louder, veterans of the longest war of all: the war to become human.

On the other side of the bridge, the streets were packed with men who had always been male and women who had always been female, some waving, some shouting, some staring. I didn't care. No one was looking at me; they were looking at us. I wondered what they saw, and then I stopped wondering, because I was too busy looking at them. There was something in their faces, excitement, anticipation, as though we were a horizon on which they glimpsed a speck that might just be a ship.

Our chant had grown louder, more coordinated, more confident. The people lining the streets began to clap, as though, in our willingness to walk as we were, without disguise or apology, shouting our determination to create a kind of freedom that had never yet existed, they heard the voice of their future. As though, for a moment, they were us.

15

Two Trips
to the Wailing Wall

March 2002 and October 2008

I t's 2002. I still have a family; I'm still a man and am sure I always will be. We're in Israel together, wandering through a Jerusalem emptied of tourists by a vicious cycle of suicide bombings and Israeli army reprisals. No one is in the souk, the Arab market, but the shopkeepers and us, a genteelly impoverished American family the shopkeepers can tell isn't likely to buy. They eye us sadly, half-heartedly calling out invitations to examine scarves and pots. Our son is eight, lively and curious and running ahead to touch everything he sees. Our middle daughter—our only daughter then—is two. She refuses to walk, and, since we don't have a stroller, when we're out she's always in my arms or on my shoulders, talking, laughing, crying. Carrying her for miles is exhausting and painful, or would be if dissociation from my body weren't my natural state of being. I take up space, move, eat, teach, but never actually feel that I'm there. The warm, squirming weight of my daughter in my arms merges with the blank weight of dissociation, turning my nonexistence into a form of love.

Here and there my wife stops to examine something—earrings, a skirt, a potential gift for friends back home. I want to look at those earrings and scarves, too, but that would undermine the wall I've built to shield the persona of husband and father from the inchoate craving to become a woman roiling behind it.

The souk seemed deserted, but, the moment we step across the line—it's quite visible—into the reconstructed *cardo* of the Jewish quarter, we realize how much life was represented by the dispirited Palestinian merchants. The excavated Roman shopping district is eerily empty, as still as the moment before an explosion. My wife and I hesitate; perhaps this *is* the moment before an explosion. But our children take the quiet as an invitation to make noise. Our son scampers off, darting between marble pillars, and our daughter startles me by demanding to be put down so that she can run after her big brother. My arms are aching, but I hate to let her go; without her warmth against me, I'm left with my own emptiness. Their game of tag echoes, laughter clattering among the ancient stones.

We gather the kids and climb from the *cardo* into the bright light and sharp angles of the Jewish quarter. For no reason at all, we feel safer. We're above ground, the sun is shining, and a few people are drifting through the clean-swept streets. We buy the kids ice cream and let them play while we rest in metal chairs on an open square studded with short pillars the Romans provided for the stabling of horses. It's a hot day, though it's only March, and our daughter's ice cream lathers her face and hands. We clean her up, I hoist her into my arms, and we climb through empty, shuttered shops and unvisited museums to a stairway ascending to a view that is one of the most famous in the world: the house- and grave-heaped hills, the great golden and silver mosques shimmering above paradise-blue mosaics, the broad open square, the Wall.

It's beautiful—no, it's beauty itself, human spirit transformed into stone and earth, color and form, for the sheer glory of God—a glory people can't stop killing and dying for.

Poor God. It must be hell to be glorified by creatures like us.

The kids ignore our oohs and aahs and play on the steps. I wish I could feel what my wife is feeling. The view seems to be entering her, filling her, intensifying her sense of the miracle of being alive. That's what I'm supposed to feel, but the beauty that fills my eyes and mind cannot reach my walled-off heart. Emotionally, spiritually, the view seems flat and far away, just another image projected on the blank white screen of my life, so distant that I fear I won't even remember it.

Indeed, it's already gone. We've moved on, herding the children past the guards, through the metal detectors, and into the view we were looking down upon. There, ahead of us, is the Wailing Wall, the last remnant of the ancient Temple, symbol of unimaginable suffering and inexplicable survival.

And there, at the Wall, is Gender.

As the most sacred space in Judaism, the Wall is under the zealous supervision of Orthodox Jews, which means that, like everything else in Orthodox Judaism, it is divided into a male part and a female part, with a physical divider—a *mechitza*—running down the middle. To approach the Wall, you have to know which side you belong on. That should be easy. I never let myself hesitate when I have to publicly identify myself as a man. I use men's rooms, fill in the "M" boxes on legal forms that I sign under penalty of perjury, dutifully make conversations with the male halves of couples with whom we socialize. So it shouldn't be this hard to hand over my daughter to my wife and make my way with my son to the men's side of the *mechitza* while my wife makes her way into the sea of black, long-sleeved blouses and ankle-length skirts that conceal the lowest stones of the women's side of the Wall.

As my son and I walk closer, I feel sicker and sicker. To approach the sacred, I have to erase what, despite all the repression and resolutions and lies to myself, I know and have always known I am.

I look down at my son. His face is glowing in the intense golden light. We are inches from the Wall, my arm around his shoulders. Twenty feet away, a bar mitzvah is being celebrated, and suddenly I realize that, in a few years, my son, too, will become a man. I hug him, hold him, try to feel him, to feel this moment. This is the Wailing Wall, and my eyes are brimming with joy, with pride, with decades of bitterness.

And now I'm worrying about my wife, my daughter—is my daughter fussing? is my wife feeling faint in the sun?—and now we are drifting back from the Wall, back through the space where boys become men, back to the bright blank secular square where tourists snap pictures without weeping or specifying their genders. My wife and daughter are there, my son's shoulders under my arm. My family is still whole, the wall between the man who sustains my family and the woman who will destroy it intact.

It's October 2008, the *Yamim Noraim*, the Days of Awe between Rosh Hashanah and Yom Kippur. I'm back in Jerusalem. In addition to the Wailing Wall and the wall that surrounds the Old City, the Jerusalem skyline now boasts a new wall: the hideous concrete security barrier that is intended to protect Israelis from Palestinians. It's working. There have been very few suicide bombings in the past year or two. Unfortunately, the builders decided that Israeli security requires the wall to cut into Palestinian territory, slicing through villages, cutting families in two and multiplying the already nightmarish maze of checkpoints and restricted areas that Palestinians have to negotiate in order to move through what is putatively "their" territory. The last time I was here, there were regular reports of Palestinian women in labor who were prevented by road closings and security procedures from reaching hospitals that were only a few miles away. Presumably, the number of babies delivered outside security checkpoints has grown considerably.

But the wall inside me has fallen. When I was last here, I thought I would spend my whole life as a man; now, I can barely remember living that way. The life that was always someone else's is mine now. The family that was mine is someone else's now.

I'm back in the Old City, on my own, sandals clattering on the cobbled streets. The ghosts of family past clamor around me, ghost-son running ahead of me in the souk, ghost-daughter melting in my emptied arms. Aside from the ghosts, I'm unencumbered, a brand-new woman without family, past, or obligation.

Merchants smile and call out as I walk by. It's early, the street is empty, and the woman I've become has a lot more commercial potential than the man I was the last time I was here. Then, I couldn't allow myself even to eye their wares. Now, I want something, anything, of the femininity that whispers to me from the scarves and skirts and lacy shawls.

I pause in front of a display of lushly colored scarves. I don't wear scarves, even in the bitter Massachusetts winter. But here I am, staring at scarves as though a scarf were something I'd been looking for all my life.

The moment I pause, the proprietor is there, easing me forward, guiding my eyes toward the richer, softer, lovelier scarves inside. Unlike most of the merchants I've passed, he's youngish, slim, with large, glistening black eyes set in a pale, smooth face. A handsome man, who looks—for professional reasons, I suspect— like he's got a very soft heart, the kind of man who can be moved by the sincere interest of a tourist to sell precious goods for far less than they are worth. He's smiling at me, and I'm smiling back, which is not what a hardened bargainer is supposed to do. I should be scowling, clucking my tongue, and muttering about his shoddy, overpriced wares. Instead, I'm trying to make him feel good, telling him how much I admire what he's showing me, shaking my head sadly when he tells me how much they cost. "Too much for me, I'm afraid," I murmur, imagining for a moment that I'm wringing his heart with pity for my underfunded Americanness.

"What can you afford?" he asks sympathetically. His glistening eyes say that he would hate for me to leave disappointed.

Now I'm in trouble. I don't want to insult him, nor do I want to cut short the play of his lips across white teeth and black eyelashes above his black eyes. If I tell him the truth—ten dollars—my episode of retail therapy is over. If I tell him what he clearly wants to hear—fifty dollars or more—my solvency as a tourist will be over. "Twenty-five dollars?" I murmur tentatively. Then, recollecting my position in this transaction, I hastily add, "And that's really more than I can afford."

"Ah," he says, shaking his head gently. He understands the pain I'm experiencing as I gaze at these fabulous scarves I cannot have. "Let me see," he says, reluctantly shelving his premium merchandise. He surveys his domain, looking for some way to make me happy. "Ah!" He lifts a pile of scarves, thinner but still gorgeous. He invites me to touch them. See, they're soft, not as soft, alas, as the scarves he first showed me, but still high quality. What's more, they are machine washable. Our fingers are very close now, separated only by the soft, sliding screen of woven fabric. The scarf in his hands is dyed in a pattern of deep forest greens and browns. The other scarves have disappeared, and our faces have drawn together over this one. This is it, and we both know it. This is what he will sell me.

"Really?" I mutter, my voice, suddenly hoarse, threatening to slip out of its carefully cultivated feminine register. "Machine washable?"

"Yes," he says proudly. "The dye won't run or fade."

"Wow," I murmur, overwhelmed by something I cannot name, some ancient emotion that flows at the root of buying and selling, the extraordinary intimacy of strangers exchanging bits of themselves before turning back to their separate worlds. It's a feeling that has something utopian in it, as though through this transaction, political differences, religious differences, gender differences, have been overcome, transformed into mutual sustenance and satisfaction. Our differences are still there, but here, in the protected space of the market, they are bringing us together, rather than hurling us apart.

"I think I could sell it to you for forty dollars," he says doubtfully.

I want to say "Yes," but it isn't time for that yet. "No, I'm afraid I can't afford that," I say sadly. A no or two later, I'm giving him thirty dollars—only three times more than I wanted to spend—and he is folding the scarf into a soft green lozenge.

"Thank you," he murmurs, reaching toward me. For an instant, we hug, and I'm still loosely holding one of his hands—soft hands, fine hands—as we pull apart.

When I look back, he's already looking away.

This time, the *cardo* isn't empty. More stores are open, and there's a group of tourists being led among the excavation points that reveal layers of construction from different eras in Jewish history. I pause at a display of T-shirts—American sports team names in Hebrew. If I can find the New England Patriots, my son will be happy. Though I've only walked a few yards, culturally, the souk is thousands of miles away. There's no shopkeeper in the doorway to engage me in conversation or flattery. A bored twenty-something is reading a magazine behind a counter, dwarfed by a wall of

T-shirts. I squint up along the rows but can't find the Patriots. I drift past shops of high-end handicrafts and find myself back on the street of Roman pillars. This time, it feels even more deserted. No children here to bring the stones to life.

I climb the steps to the streets of the Jewish quarter. It's hot, bright, and sparsely populated, just as it was six years ago. I pass the square where my daughter gave herself an ice-cream facial and wend my way past the same shops, the same falafel stands, the same memorials and museums, to the same extraordinary view of the Wall. The turquoise dream of the Mosque of Omar hovers above the desolation of graves, half-completed and bulldozed houses, gold-veined stone and burnt brown dirt, a world made, as my life has been made, out of death and life, bitterness and beauty, hope and rage.

According to Jewish tradition, the mount on which the Mosque of Omar is built includes the site at which Abraham bound his son Isaac to an altar of stones and put his knife to his son's throat. For once, at least, the human rage for God was arrested; an angel called from the underbrush, telling Abraham to stay his hand. It must have been deathly quiet on that mountain, but the angel had to call Abraham's name twice to stop the fatal fall of the knife. Mesmerized by the violence he was about to commit for the sake of God, Abraham wasn't listening for angels. He had given up on the idea that some other version of God might burst through the divine death mask that had ordered him to do the unimaginable. If God demanded blood, flames, and murder, Abraham, the faithful one, was determined to provide them.

According to both religious traditions, Jews and Muslims are children of Abraham.

I certainly am. I sacrificed my true self again and again for more than forty years, and for more than forty years I never heard a whisper of an angel telling me to stay my hand.

But that doesn't mean the angel wasn't calling.

They've upgraded the security booth since I was here last. I walk through plastic and glass, and then I'm there, in the wide, paved space that leads to the Wall. I stand still for a moment, dizzied by the collision of past and present, my own and my people's, trying to get my bearings among the deaths and deliverances, the violence endured and the violence committed, that have made us what we are. The Wall is straight ahead. There's the *mechitza*, still dividing the men from the women. If my son were here, I'd be in pants and a loose, shape-concealing shirt, walking with him toward the men's side. My arm would be reaching up around his shoulders—he's suddenly grown taller than I am—and my heart would be breaking with pride in his brand-new manhood and shame at the remnants of my own.

Our family isn't Orthodox, but a *mechitza* still runs down the middle. To have a place in our family, you have to be male or female, boy or girl, man or woman. I don't want to leave my son alone on the male side, and neither my wife nor my daughters can yet imagine welcoming me as a woman on the other, and so, to see my children, I have to disappear back into the man I was. I speak in his voice; when my children look at me, I see him reflected in their eyes.

The *mechitza* offers no possibility of change, no wiggle room or third choices, just as Abraham saw no third choice between betraying his God and killing his son. But somehow change is happening, has happened already. The man my children see when they look at me doesn't resemble the smiling dad in the old photographs, and yet they still embrace him, whine at him, joke with him, rage at him—even as they mourn him. At some level, they know he's gone, and so, at some level, they know that I—the real I, the I who loves, has always loved, and will always love them—is with them. That "I" is beyond gender, a third term, like the voice of the angel calling from the underbrush, the voice that dissolves the unbearable binaries of must and cannot be.

Though no one here knows it, my presence is also transforming the *mechitza* that separates the Wailing Wall into male and female portions. They wouldn't allow me on the men's side, not in my skirt and blouse and earrings and makeup, but, if the women knew what was behind my female presentation, they wouldn't allow me among them, either. For a moment, I'm not sure what to do. If I've learned anything from transition, it's that my need to be true to myself means that I have an absolute duty to acknowledge and respect the truths of others. For the women just ahead of me, the sacredness of this space depends on the strict distinction between genders. They don't mean to shame or exclude me; they probably don't even know that people like me exist. Their definition of sacred space is no more cruel or arbitrary than anyone else's; even though the psalms tell us that the world is overflowing with God, human beings have always constructed rules to bring God's presence into focus by restricting and sanctifying particular times and places. Those rules aren't comfortable for them, either. Wrapped head to foot in heavy black clothing that absorbs every ray of the intense sunlight, they spend hours and days in the sun, doing what they feel they must to be close to God. If I move among them, I will be violating their sacred space. If I back away, I will be cutting myself off from my people.

And then I realize I've already made my decision: when I committed myself to transition, I decided that I would no longer cut off pieces of myself to maintain walls between male and female. I belong to this place, this people, and they belong to me.

I pick my way through the guardians providing modest attire to underclad visitors, camera-snapping tourists, and women collecting charitable donations, into the throng of worshippers, most of whom seem to be middle-school girls. They are crammed twenty or thirty deep; if I want to get to the Wall, I have a long wait ahead of me. I wonder if I should bother. But then I see a distant black-clad woman press her face against the Wall, as though the rough stone were the cheek of a long-lost love, and I know that I have to be there, too, to feel the cool cheek of millennia of ruin against my own.

I close my eyes and start to pray. When I open them, the tide of schoolgirls has carried me a little closer. I peek into their prayer books and their faces, some blank, some pious, some furrowed with intense, unidentifiable emotion. I wish they were growing up somewhere else, somewhere where no one was dreaming of killing them, somewhere where they wouldn't drink in generations of hatred and fear along with their faith. Somewhere where it's easier to be human—wherever that is.

Now I'm only three layers away; only two. Despite my near-sightedness, I can see the furrows in the stone, the shadows of the lichen, an occasional flash of bird or lizard. Life clings to the crevices of the wall; far above the clefts Jews fill with notes to God, rain and wind have deposited bits of soil that seeds have rooted in, and where greenery is, so are bird and lizard. For them the Wall is neither relic nor ruin, not the seat of the Divine Presence nor the division between Judaism and Islam; it's simply where they live.

My eyes close again, and tears—the tears I haven't been able to cry since I arrived—are pouring down my cheeks. Sobs bubble up from my throat, from my chest, from holes and hollows I didn't know I had. I panic—how can I be crying in a public place?—but when I open my eyes I remember. This is the Wailing Wall. I notice another woman, two or three schoolgirls away, sobbing too, tears flashing on her cheeks; there are sobs behind me, sobs before me, sobs on either side. On the men's side, they are celebrating something. On the women's side, we weep.

Suddenly, I know, beyond argument or doubt: I am on the right side.

And now I'm there, at the Wall itself, though I can't see it through my tears. My pain, my loss, my rage pour like tributaries into a river of grief stretching backward and forward through the generations. The sorrow my wife and children are enduring, the sorrow of what feels like countless breakings of my heart, merge with the grief that these children and all children of Abraham have suffered, are suffering, will suffer. I'm barely a ripple in that river. God, I sob, save Your children from ourselves. And now I'm sobbing for the One I'm praying to, because I see the mouth of that river of grief, and the ocean into which it empties is God.

Suddenly, I've cried myself out. I lean my cheek against the Wall, conscious of nothing but the light that warms me and the stone that holds me up. I lift my head and smile at another woman, much older, whose cheeks are also streaming. She smiles back. We have nothing in common but the broken hearts that brought us here. For a moment, that's the only gender that matters.

I back away slowly, keeping my face to the Wall until I reach the first camera-snapping tourist, give coins to a woman collecting *tzedekah*, receive a blessing in return.

Orthodox Judaism assigns men and women different daily blessings for the miracle of being. Men say, "Blessed are You, O Lord, who has not made me a woman"; women euphemistically acknowledge getting the short end of the gender stick by saying, "Blessed are You, O Lord, who has made me according to Your will." Jewish feminists justly despise this separate-and-unequal system, but women get the better blessing. The male version is defensive, as though male privilege might collapse if men forget to look down on women for a day. The female version is an affirmation that who and what we are reflects God's will—that we are what we should be, what we need to be, that our existence is a blessing.

You made me, God, I say when I say those words. I belong in this world, just the way I am.

I've turned my back on the Wall, toward the hot, bright, empty square. No sorrow now, no rage, no bitterness. Only gratitude for who and what I am, calling out to me, like the angel to Abraham: *Blessed be You, O Lord our God, Ruler of the universe, who has made me according to Your will.* I've whispered that blessing to myself for years, echoing a voice I thought I could never follow. Now I say it aloud and add the blessing—this is part of the daily ritual, too—that follows:

Blessed be You, O Lord our God, Ruler of the universe, who has made me a daughter of freedom.

16
Teaching Naked

I wish I could ask Rachel, the young woman sitting two feet away from me, passionately explicating a poem: "Do you know that I used to be a man?"

Rachel's eyes are glowing, kindled, as they always are, by the friction of sound and meaning. Her eyes bounce between the poem and my face, her smile—she is one of the few people I've met who can speak at breakneck speed while smiling—intimating her delight that she and I are on the same page, excited by the same words, scenting the same insights in the thickets of thought. This is the intimacy that first drew me to teaching, the rub of mind against mind that seemed to moot the question of gender. Reading texts with students was a kind of ecstasy, though one I paid for before and after, when I had to shrink back into the man they saw, the mask of masculinity that belied the truth we sought and made together.

But now, three semesters after the end of my "involuntary research leave," the mask is off. Rachel and my other Stern students see me as I am—or do they?

In September 2008, the *New York Post* turned me into America's most famous publicly Jewish, publicly transsexual professor. But my students don't seem aware of the talks I've given or the essays I've published. The convoys of hushed undergraduates that used to hover in sight of my open office door have ceased, the students who knew me as a man have graduated, and, unlike former students, the current students don't ask me respectful questions about transition. (The hardest question my old students asked me after my return to Stern: "Has living as a woman changed the way you read?") My class registration has been down—my composition class only has five students this semester—but that could be the result of my reputation as a tough grader. In any case, I no longer know what my students know about me. I'm teaching naked, projecting femininity into a void, without denial or confirmation: my male mask is gone, but I can't tell whether my students see me as a woman, a man, or something stranger.

Rachel's reading of the poem is branching, as her study of poetry always does, into reflections on God and Judaism. For her, secular studies illuminate rather than undermine her faith. Poetry always leads us to God—for both of us, it's a natural progression—and, as our focus shifts, so do our roles. Now she is the teacher, connecting the poem to passages of Talmud, biblical commentaries, and books of Jewish theology she knows (I'm quick to admit it) I haven't read. She shifts fluently among Hebrew, Aramaic, and English, talking so fast that it often seems as though she, like a page of Talmud, were giving text, commentary, and translation simultaneously. Both as teacher and as student, my job is to slow her down, interrupt her flood of words so that she can reflect on her stream of thought and the mind and soul mirrored in it. As my children know, I'm good at breaking the natural flow.

During the summer 2008 negotiations that preceded my return to teaching, Yeshiva's attorneys said that I would be expected to abide by the school policy that prohibits teachers from talking about their lives to students. That was absurd, as I told my lawyers: teacher-student relationships are so intimate at Stern that, when professors are sick, students often include us in daily prayers for healing. Though discussion ended when my attorneys asked for written evidence that there was such a policy, I now find myself bound by the same concerns that prompted Yeshiva to try to limit me to academic intercourse: the fear that my students will be harmed if I speak about my life, that sharing what I've learned about gender and identity (constant subjects in our literary discussions) will distract, distress, or alienate them.

When I was a man, I made a point of relating my readings of literature to my life. I wasn't trying to be confessional; I wanted to shatter the margins around the texts, to show students that, for all the wonky academic discourse that seems to elevate "literature" beyond lived experience, poems and stories speak from and to the struggles we all face in being human. But now I steer clear of personal anecdotes. It's too hard to figure out what to say and not to say, how to translate memories I lived as a man into gender-neutral terms that are neither dishonest nor insistent about my identity.

In a way that is painfully reminiscent of my relationships with my children, standing before my students as myself rather than as a male persona has increased the distance between us.

But who and what am I to them?

Sometimes it seems clear that my students see me as a woman. When I was a man, preclass chatter used to stop dead when I entered the room. Now they keep talking about dates and clothes and weddings and so on as though I weren't there—I often have to bang the desk or whistle to get class started. They don't even mind if I join the conversation, as I did when I walked in on an exchange of dating survival tips. The subject was the worst foods to eat on a date. As someone new to the dating game, I thought they seemed like a panel of experts, and I was desperate for tips that might reduce the awkwardness of looking for love as a middle-aged, divorce-impoverished woman who, as a moment's Googling would reveal, used to be a man. They were happy to help. No long pasta, they told me, no sushi, and nothing that involves large leaves of lettuce. Then they turned back to one another.

It's hard enough to talk about literature, which is, of course, chock-full of ideas about what it means to be men and women, without referring to my own gender experience and perspective. It's almost impossible to have a heart-to-heart about men and their discontents without even nodding to the fact that I used to be one. In fact, one of the few unqualified benefits of transition is that I can see the friction between men and women from both sides. My heterosexual friends assure me that I could have a glorious career as a marriage counselor. That's what Rachel is asking me for now. Keats's insistence on pursuing thoughts and feelings has led us to reflect on Jewish injunctions to pursue truth through Torah study, and that, naturally—since, like most Stern students, Rachel is part of a culture that expects her to marry by the time she graduates—has led her to describe her recent date with a nice Jewish boy bewildered by her insatiable craving for intellectual and spiritual conversation. "Do you think you'll be this way after marriage, too?" the dazed fellow asked at the end of the meal. "Oh, yes," Rachel tells me she told him. "This is the way I am."

Whether Rachel sees me as a man or a woman, she certainly sees me as a mentor. She is telling me this story because she wants my help in juggling the contradictory values that guide her life: the Orthodox culture that will judge her a failure if she isn't engaged soon even if she graduates with highest honors, and the secular academic culture that will judge her a failure, even if she marries the Messiah, if she doesn't realize her enormous intellectual potential.

I have a professional duty to offer her whatever wisdom I can about this archetypal collision between Jewish tradition and modernity—wisdom that includes what I've learned from my own navigation of the contradictions between being true to myself and being true to those I love, as well as the maze of gender. I also have a professional duty not to endanger the relationship that allows her to trust me with this story by dropping what would be the bombshell of my transsexuality if she doesn't already see me as trans.

If only I could ask her.

Being a transsexual professor at Stern who couldn't refer to being transsexual was an infinite improvement over the permanent exile I had expected—a fear the dean had confirmed after I informed her of my transition in June 2007.

Her summer was off to a rough start. Shortly after I informed her of my intention to return to Stern in the fall as a woman, one of my colleagues in our small English department died in an accident.

Under these circumstances, I wasn't surprised at hearing nothing for several weeks in response to my coming-out letter. What was surprising was that the response, when it came, wasn't a certified letter from Yeshiva's attorneys but a series of informal e-mails from the dean. The first, a brief apology for the weeks of silence, came with neither greeting nor farewell—the parts of a letter that would force her to name me and define our relationship. In the next e-mail, she invited me to lunch, omitting the greeting—no "Jay" or "Joy" or "Professor Ladin"—but signing her name. I accepted her invitation, adding that I would be meeting her as myself rather than as the man she had known. That, I thought, would be the end of this strangely cordial process. The dean would take my self-assertion as an act of aggression, a way of forcing her, an Orthodox woman, into contact with something her tradition considered *treyf,* unkosher, contaminating and contaminated. My wife, my best friend, and my children couldn't bear to look at me; why should the dean, when a few letters between lawyers were all that the situation demanded?

The dean replied by suggesting a time and place for our meeting; for the first time, she addressed me as "Dear Joy."

The embodiment, to me, of both the university and modern Orthodox Judaism was going to see me as myself.

If Stern had an official school restaurant, Mendy's, the closest sit-down kosher fleischig place in the neighborhood, would be it. It was July, but there was still every likelihood that someone who knew us—or, rather, someone who knew me as a man—would see us.

I wish I knew what the dean told the waiters. Two converged on me as I walked up the steps that separated Mendy's informal nosheria from the formal restaurant. "You're here to meet the dean?" one asked. "Yes," I croaked, and he led me between largely empty tables into the kosher dusk. Outside, it was almost painfully bright; here, the light was as murky as the brine puddled around the pickles that appeared on the table the moment I was seated.

The dean's face, as always, was frank and focused. She rose, smiling, and offered me her hand. "You look lovely," she said. "I wasn't sure what to expect."

"I know," I murmured sympathetically. At that point in transition, I pitied those enduring the shock of meeting the new me.

She asked about my family and then got down to business. She began by assuring me that I wouldn't lose my salary, benefits, or connection to the university. "Your family doesn't have to worry," she assured me. "You are still a valued part of the university community." I nodded hesitantly, waiting for the axe to fall. "But . . ." She paused, and then, as though reciting mechanically from a cue card, she said, "It is the policy of the university that no physically male person may appear on campus in female clothing."

That was it: the end of my relationships with my students, my newly tenured career, my life as a teacher.

"What does 'physically male' mean exactly?" I asked desperately.

In a life that now seemed to consist of painful self-revelation, this was a new low: as the dean knew, I was talking about my genitalia.

"We can't discuss that now," she said tactfully. "Maybe at some later point."

"So I might be able to teach at Stern again?"

"No," she said gently. There were tears in both our eyes. "We'll be happy to help you find a position at another institution, but Stern students and parents just won't be able to accept you at this point."

"At this point?"

"For the foreseeable future," she said firmly. "Maybe in a generation or two. . . ."

I finished my falafel. It wasn't easy to swallow, but I was determined not to cry, not to beg, not to make a scene. I talked, instead, as a member of the faculty, offering advice about the Writing Center I had, till then, directed, asking about the impact of my colleague's death on the department. In the world outside the murk of Mendy's, the world beyond Stern College and Yeshiva University and Modern Orthodoxy, trans activists were marching in the streets, risking beatings and humiliation to fight for their rights as human beings. I was fighting to smile and swallow the mash of crushed chickpeas, rage, grief, and abject gratitude for being told so respectfully that I was no longer considered fit to be seen on campus.

I was sure that my LGBT-activist attorneys from Lambda Legal would be disgusted with me when I told them, but they thought the meeting had gone well. "Most organizations tell trans employees to go away for a year after transition," they said. "Give Yeshiva time to get used to the idea. Then we'll see what happens."

They were right. The dean's decision to meet with me one on one, her insistence on treating me with kindness, her acceptance of my transformed appearance, and her affirmation of my continued worth as a person and professional were the first signs that I would, in fact, be able to teach again at Stern. The Modern Orthodox tradition that made my transition so problematic from a religious perspective also made it hard for my dean or my students to disdain me. Whatever they felt about my gender, they lived up to the religious law that demanded that I be treated with the consideration due to a human being created in God's image.

The dean asked me not to communicate with students or colleagues about my transition during fall 2007, the first semester of my "involuntary research leave." While I bounced from bedroom to bedroom in western Massachusetts, Stern students debated whether it was me or one of my children who was wrestling with a fatal illness.

Meanwhile, the Internet did its mysterious work of connection and revelation. By mid–October, I had started receiving e-mails from students and former students who had heard about my transition. One told me how proud she, an Orthodox woman trained to accept male superiority, was that I had chosen to join "her team." Another began by telling me that, though she was "politically very right-wing," she was outraged that I wasn't allowed on campus; I later heard that she had met with the dean to protest. Some students were angry that I had misleadingly presented myself as a man. All of them, even the most supportive, were confused.

A group of students who missed studying poetry with me asked me to meet them off campus. They found a cavernous café several blocks west of campus and set a date. Ensconced in the Orthodox bubble of Stern, which operates almost exclusively on the Jewish calendar, they didn't realize that we were meeting on Christmas.

None of us knew the etiquette for this kind of encounter, and none of us was prepared for how quickly we relaxed with one another. I was relieved that I wasn't hiding from them anymore;

they were relieved that the gender divide between us had vanished. Orthodox Judaism's insistence on gender segregation meant that they had lived most of their lives in a world of girls and women. Because I didn't *look* transgender, they responded to me as they responded to other women.

There was something they just had to ask me, they said, when we were all settled around the table. One young woman looked hesitantly at another, and finally one of them said it: "Are men *really* as bad as they seem on dates?" That question dispelled all the fantasies of rejection I had imagined since I'd been hired by Yeshiva. Contrary to what I had feared and my dean believed, contrary to all my stereotypes of Orthodox Jews, and contrary, I think, to what many Orthodox Jews believed about one another, my devout, sheltered students could talk, laugh, and learn with a woman they knew had once been a man.

And so it was that, after a year of "involuntary research leave," in September 2008, I returned. Between the *New York Post* and the Stern College *Observer*, which responded to my return with a groundbreaking issue on "Transsexuality and Judaism" that brought together interviews with Orthodox rabbis and interviews with trans Jews living in hiding in the Orthodox world, it felt like a spotlight shone on me as I walked the hallways, ensuring that everyone who saw me would notice the peculiar spectacle of my gender. But, other than one frank discussion with the Writing Center tutors—I was once more their director—and a few heartfelt one on ones with current and former students, I spoke very little about my transition. Those disquieted by my presence—I hear there were some heated cafeteria conversations about whether a transsexual should be teaching at an Orthodox Jewish school— kept their feelings out of my range of hearing. The convoys of curious students maintained a respectful distance from my open door. Some colleagues, particularly male colleagues, looked queasy when their eyes happened across my face. But, between secular conventions of political correctness and Jewish conventions of *derech eretz*, respect for others, the school turned out to be a surprisingly safe place to be out as a transsexual. Like other tenured professors, I was given committee assignments, invited to meetings, kept in the loop; when I applied for early promotion to full professor, I received it.

I was myself, I was safe, free to be myself without fear of comment from those around me. But my gender was the elephant in the room that none of us, including me, knew how to acknowledge. Now that I was officially kosher, I couldn't bring my transition up without making others uncomfortable, and my colleagues couldn't bring it up without making me uncomfortable, so we tried to ignore my obvious differences from my former self.

Of course, for most people at Stern, my transition was a minor event, and the discomfort it occasioned was fleeting. But what about my students? They had to look at my face and listen to my intermittently fraying voice twice a week for months at a time. What difference did my difference—did they know I was different?— make to them? How were the limits on what we could and could not say—did they feel them, too?—affecting our classroom and one-on-one discussions? Kate Bornstein writes eloquently about the sacrifices most of us, trans and non-trans alike, make for the sake of gender, the joys we forgo, the evils we endure, the pieces of ourselves we cut off and the prostheses we stick on in order to be seen as men or women. I had thought of transition as a rejection of this sort of bondage, a statement that I could now, without shame or compromise, be exactly who I was. Somehow my transition had become a verbal straitjacket, a zone of silence constraining me and everyone around me. Somehow, I was back to hiding, worrying that referring to the deep, dark, but widely publicized secret of my transsexuality would hurt, was hurting, my students.

When my students looked at me, what did they see? I ached, every class, to ask them.

Rachel is back, talking poetry again. Our weekly tutorial is almost over. As usual, my office is a mess. My fantasies that living as a woman would unlock some secret wellspring of tidiness were just that—fantasies. I still didn't know how to make a space my own. Whether because of decades of feeling that no space, even that of my own body, belonged to me, or because of some other disconnection between psyche and soma, I rarely noticed my surroundings. Now and then I realized that after six years of teaching at Stern, there still wasn't anything on my walls: no decorations, no posters, no diplomas, not even a calendar. My desk was strewn with papers, but there were no pictures of my children, nothing, other than the mess, to mark the space as mine. When I returned from involuntary leave, I found that my office had been used to store old computer equipment. The equipment was still there; I kept forgetting to ask that it be removed.

I hate the ugliness of my office, but I rarely think about it until I hear a knock on the door. Rachel is knocking now. As I invite her to sit down, I glimpse the room through her eyes: the half-crushed cereal on the floor, the stacks of papers and boxes, the stripped white walls. But, as embarrassing as it is to imagine how she sees my office, it's worse to be unable to imagine how she sees me. Though I always plan my wardrobe with care—I've learned from experience how uncomfortable it is to feel underdressed among Stern's throngs of long-skirted, long-sleeved, high-necklined women—when Rachel's eyes fall on me, I feel naked. Does she notice what I'm wearing? Do my clothes, like hers, define me as a woman, or are they mooted by my body's journey between genders? Even after a year and a half of public appearances as a trans advocate, I can't help wondering if I look like an imitation of a woman or if, in Rachel's eyes, I'm real.

Over the past two semesters, between tutorials and classes, we've probably spent forty-eight solid hours in each other's presence. I want, I need, to know how she sees me. No—I want to know *if* she sees me, whether, in all our intimate conversation about poetry and God, I have really been there.

"What do you want to read for our next session?" I ask, flipping, as I have every week, through the table of contents of our massive anthology of British and American poetry.

"Actually," she says, "I'd like to read some of your poems, if that's okay with you."

I color. It's been years since a student asked to talk about my poetry with me. "Of course," I say, trying to show her—is she still young and naïve enough to believe this?—that we can read my poems as frankly as we've read the others, without regard for my flattered, fluttering ego. "That would be fun. What do you want to read?"

"I'd like to read your latest book, *Transmigration*. That's my favorite." She's smiling, her dark eyes, as always, shining; I'm too startled to smile back. Until now, I didn't know she'd read any of my poetry, so I didn't know if she had encountered the bibliographic peculiarity I explain in the author's note to *Transmigration*: the fact that each of my first three books of poetry appeared under a different first name—Jay, J., and, finally, on *Transmigration*, Joy.

Rachel knows—knew—probably has always known—that I'm trans. When she's talked about poetry, God, dating, she was talking to me, the real me, the transsexual me, the woman she knows was a man.

She sees, has seen, has perhaps always seen, me.

Bare walls, discarded computer equipment, crushed cereal, love of poetry, love of God, and all.

17

The Door of Life

March 2010

The day before the day on which I had decided to die, I met the love of my life.

It's hard to explain why, but, as winter 2010 was ending, I realized that the life I'd fought so hard to create was unlivable. Mostly, it was the pain. Life hurt, and it seemed it would always hurt.

The hurt came from all directions. It hurt to live apart from my children; it hurt to wake up and go to sleep without them; and often, too often, it hurt to see them or, rather, to see the chasms that yawned between us. It always hurt when, after a few short hours, I had to say goodbye.

The divorce hurt, too. Not just the bruising legal process, which began in 2008 with my wife's accusations that I was a danger to my children and concluded with a settlement that left me little time with my children and so little money that I had to spend my commuting nights in New York City on ex-students' floors and as the overnight volunteer in a men's homeless shelter, but the death of a quarter-century of love that the divorce process represented. I re-enacted that death nightly in my dreams; the fact of it stunned me anew with every chilly e-mail exchange.

I had loved my now ex-wife for more than half my life. The hole the death of that love had left would always be filled with pain.

It isn't easy to "meet someone," as they say, in middle age. It's harder when the answer to a bland icebreaker like "What have you been doing lately?" includes getting divorced, sleeping in a homeless shelter, and dealing with the publicity surrounding transsexual transition.

Not that I hadn't tried. Shortly after moving out, in June 2007, in a frenzy of jealousy over my ex's suddenly public relationship with another man, I had registered with eHarmony. I was jealous not of the boyfriend—even in my dreams, I couldn't imagine rekindling my marriage—but of my wife's apparent ease in turning from loving me to loving someone else. According to eHarmony's newsletters, finding true love requires being "the real you"; now that I was the real me, it seemed only fair that true love should find me.

But, in order to find each other, true love and I were going to have to weed through the desperately lonely throngs I found as I flipped through hundreds of ungrammatical profiles. At first, I found this process exhilarating. Simply by registering with dating sites—eHarmony was only the first of several—I had leapt from the bottom to the top of the romantic food chain. Scores of hopefuls were lined up before me, sorted and sifted according to my personal preferences. According to their profiles, they couldn't wait to meet me, but I—I didn't want them. I was an English professor; they were semiliterate. I was sane; they might not be. I wrote poetry; they kayaked. I was a practicing Jew; they were vaguely spiritual. I was ironic; their clichés were full of heart.

The euphoria of rejecting dozens of potential lovers per minute soon turned to nausea. I wasn't actually looking at other people; I was looking at myself, and, instead of true love, I had found a nasty, superficial, stuck-up snob, to whom physical beauty, well-formed sentences, and proximity to western Massachusetts mattered more than any quality of character. Grammatically, physically, and geographically, most of the human race wasn't good enough for me; morally, I wasn't good enough for them.

I decided to stop looking at dating sites. Even if I did stumble upon the infinitesimal percentage of middle-aged singles who were close enough, educated enough, attractive enough, articulate enough, literary enough and so on, what were the odds that they would want me—the real me, the broke, broken-hearted transsexual behind the woman bubbling vaguely over coming to life I presented in my profile?

And then, of course, there was the question of sex. My true self had never even romantically clasped someone else's hand. I didn't know what kind of sex I wanted, whether I wanted a woman or a man, or even whether I wanted sex. I found the thought of touching another body scary; the thought of being touched was downright terrifying. It was hard to imagine anyone, male or female, regarding my body with anything other than disgust. When I gave talks about being trans, I tried to project the comfort with myself that I had gained through transition. But transition hadn't yet touched my primal sense of ugliness, my lifelong belief that, as a transsexual, I was a monster.

I knew I wasn't the only person who felt ashamed of my body. I knew that part of the thrill of mutual desire is the terror of being seen. But I couldn't be comforted by the knowledge that I was surrounded by people who hated their bodies because my search for love wasn't about other people: I couldn't separate my search for love from my search for the self I was becoming.

I swung like a bell clapper between hope and despair, renouncing and returning to my Internet searches every couple of weeks. One October night in 2008, hope clanged so insistently that I stayed up late, going through the profile of every woman—I decided I would look for women because the thought of getting physical with a man terrified me—within a hundred miles. I found one, Emily, a dark-haired, dark-eyed Jew about my age whose sentences included both subjects and objects and whose face was shadowed by a sadness that I found incredibly attractive. I didn't want to be with someone who was depressed, but I did want someone who understood sorrow and wouldn't be scared off by my pain.

Emily did understand sorrow and wasn't scared off by pain. A few e-mails later, the attraction generated by our still photos and brief profiles blossomed into an exchange of intimacies; she accepted my transsexuality, I accepted her struggles with a traumatizing childhood, and by the time we met—it was only a week or two after we had made e-mail contact—we were both ready to find true love through each other. We met in downtown Northampton. She looked different from her photo—don't we all?—but the most important difference to me was that she was flesh and blood, rather than pixels and words, and that she was smiling into my eyes, rather than turning away in disgust. Overcome by gratitude and desire, I seized her hand. It too was real, firm and warm, squeezing mine as I squeezed hers. My search was over. True love and I had found each other.

Emily lived about an hour away, in Connecticut, off the highway I took when commuting to New York. Despite the distance that separated us, Emily, an unemployed social worker, had a lot of time for communication. We talked on the phone many times a day. We talked when we were going somewhere, we talked when we were done, we talked first thing in the morning and last thing at night, we talked around noon, and we talked before and after. When we weren't talking, we e-mailed. We saw each other in the flesh about three times a week, when my job and schedule with the kids allowed; I would drive to her apartment on Monday nights, after dropping off the kids, and leave before dawn the next morning to go to Stern. We never took off our clothes—Emily had issues with her body, too, and probably with mine—but we hugged and kissed and held hands and passionately rubbed our fully clothed torsos.

I liked the body contact—for years, I had been starved for touch—but, for people who spoke a couple of hundred minutes a day, according to my cell phone bill, we didn't have much to talk about. There were other problems, too. Neither of us liked the fact that we lived in different states; Emily didn't like the fact that I spent more time with my kids than with her; I found it hard to keep up my phone regimen with Emily while working full time. When I started getting trans speaking gigs that cut into our scant weekend time together, Emily dumped me, and I was happy to be dumped.

But I wasn't happy to be alone. I had discovered that I liked being touched, and it was depressing to think that I had lost the one person who wanted to touch me.

I had also become very sick, inexplicably—it is still unexplained—and with a wide and ever-varying range of symptoms. Emily had dumped me in April; by the time the spring 2009 semester was over, it was getting harder and harder to leave the house. When I could sit up, I cruised dating websites; occasionally, I communicated with someone promising, but, though I was ready to look for love as a transsexual, I wasn't ready to come out about my illness. Some days, I struggled through a few hours with my children; most days I spent completely alone. That gave me plenty of time to reflect on the failure of my attempt to create a life as the real me. The real me could write, see her children a few times a week, and, if not too sick, drive back and forth to New York City to teach. That was about it. Every other aspect of life seemed to be out of reach.

I got sicker. I would spend all day in bed or, when I was feeling frisky, on the couch, writing poems—two, three, four a day. By 5 p.m., even my friskiest days were over. I would eat a little cold food and then crawl into the bath—I called it my "gratitude bath"—for my nightly date with God.

The hot water burned pleasurably, easing my knotted muscles. Pain lifted off me like steam. Even if I hadn't felt grateful for a moment of the day, I felt grateful for this moment. "Thank you, God," I would murmur, stretching out my legs, sinking in suddenly luxurious exhaustion into the dark viscous warmth that buoyed my body. For one grateful moment, the scales of self-pity and despair would slip from my eyes, and I would tell God how lucky I felt to have a bath and a body that could enjoy it, to have windows that looked out onto forest, to have made it through the day, to feel myself surrounded by a love as quiet and palpable as the water in which I lay. "You have been with me," I would whisper, "but I haven't been with You."

Then God and I would talk over my life. God would listen as I poured out my bitterness, silently reflecting it back to me, breaking it down into its component angers and frustrations and then peeling those back to reveal the hidden wish behind them, my first infant wish for love, total love, the love my parents hadn't and, I saw now, couldn't have given me no matter how hard they tried, because no human being can love another so utterly. For a few heartbeats, I would see that my circumstances, hard as they were, didn't matter. Ill or well, I would always long for that love; ill or well, I was always bathed in it, if only I would acknowledge the God who was always there, loving me into existence.

Then the water would feel too hot or too cold, the walls would spin, pain would shoot through a limb. As the water drained from the tub, my soul would drain back into my suffering. The tub was empty, the porcelain cool and hard and quiet. I would lie there a long time, until I could sit up, climb out, and make my way to bed and another night of nightmares.

Apart from the bath, I spent most of my waking hours that summer meditating not on gratitude but on failure. I had become a real person, with real, albeit not very pleasant, feelings, but I had failed to make a real life. The stupidity of destroying my family to become someone who had no idea how to live made me so angry that I came, daily, to the same conclusion: I had had my chance to live; now it was time to die.

Then a strange thing happened. In early August, my symptoms, which for weeks had been steadily growing worse, began to fade. My exhaustion was no longer constant; sometimes I even felt spurts of energy. I began to sit up without dizziness, walk without pain. It seemed ridiculous to kill myself when I was getting better, but illness, I realized, wasn't the problem: I didn't know how to make a life any more than I knew how to decorate my office. Life would have to teach me how to live it.

A new semester beckoned; the shofar, the ram's horn blown to awaken souls from sin and slumber each day of Elul, the month leading up to the Jewish New Year, sounded in synagogues. I promised myself that, for the next six months, I would stop thinking about suicide and accept every invitation and opportunity life sent my way. No matter what the question, my answer would be "yes."

The first yesses I gave I gave to God.

It was Annie's idea. She told me that if I was going to live, I couldn't spend every day wrestling with my fears and frustrations.

"Make a list," she told me, and, as I had since I first came out to her over the phone while walking in the forest behind the family house three summers before, I did what she said, boiling my doubts, despairs, and desolation down to five questions that I would ask myself and answer each day in the presence of God. Because God was listening, I had to listen, too, and that transformed my simple yesses into commitments whose difficulty—I was hesitant and sometimes downright scared to make them—forced me to recognize my real problem: not what life had withheld from me but what I was withholding from life.

"Okay, God," I would murmur every morning, "it's time for the Five Questions."

Will You enable me to do what I need to do today?
Yes.
Will I make it through the day without killing myself?
Yes.
Do I want to learn what You are teaching me today?
Yes.
Do I want to live with an open heart?
Yes.
Do I want to learn to live with a broken heart and with absolute uncertainty?
Yes.

Every day my answers were the same, and every day they surprised me. Every day, even when I was sick, I believed that God would enable me to do what I needed to do. Every day, even when I was in despair, I would make it through. Every day, no matter how much the lessons hurt, I wanted to learn what God was teaching me. Every day, no matter how hardened I was by bitterness and pain, I wanted to open my heart; and even though my heart would always be broken and my life, as illness and transition had taught me, would always be subject to change without notice, I wanted to learn to live.

But I still couldn't get a date. I dutifully answered every wink and message, no matter how improbable the writer seemed. One woman urged me to read to read the self-help book that had taught her to be happy even though she had lost her job and her friends and was living in her car. Sunrise was still beautiful, she said. Another, a twenty-one-year-old aspiring rocker recently arrived from Germany, wanted me to show her around the New York music scene; our correspondence petered out before I could tell her that my New York nightlife consisted of sleeping on former students' floors. The attractive, literate, poetry-loving single mother who lived in the next town couldn't find time to answer my e-mails. Neither could the male former professor, a master of sardonic sentences, who thought that, despite my stated proclivity for women, we might bond in mutual contempt for other users of the site. Another man, a worldly, relatively young retiree, was on the verge of asking me for a date until, in response to his questions, I came out as trans.

Rosh Hashanah came and went, the leaves flushed and blazed and faded and fell, the days got shorter and the nights got colder. Yes, I said fiercely to myself, whenever the question of whether I would keep my promise to myself came up. Yes, I said to each of my five questions. Yes, I said, whenever I had a chance to get a little extra time with my children. Yes, I said, when my new attorney asked me whether I wanted to settle with my wife, rather than fight it out in court. Yes, I said, when I wondered whether I could get through a semester of commuting and teaching without knowing where I would sleep from week to week. Yes, I said, when I was invited to give talks and readings. Yes.

Yes, I said, and kept saying, to Sofia, a South American émi-grée who was looking forward to quitting her high-level executive position someday and devoting her life to making and teaching art. We began exchanging messages in September, but, at Sofia's prompting, we soon moved from the cumbersome dating-website communication system to long e-mails and longer, endearment-sprinkled phone calls. "Okay, my love," she would say, and I would try to respond in kind while avoiding the "l" word. Sophia's endearments had a pointedly perfunctory quality that combined affection with reminders that, as she often told me, she wasn't sure whether she wanted a relationship with me. Sophia was looking for someone *positive*, someone who felt that life was good and was always getting better. Yes, I said, and did my best to talk positively about the circumstances of my life. I explained how *good* it was that I would be sleeping one night a week in New York at a homeless shelter so I had to find only one couch or floor to sleep on. It was *good* that, although divorce settlement negotiations were going badly—my first attorney had been disbarred late in the summer, setting the whole acrimonious process back by months and thousands of dollars, though my new attorney, as I told Sofia, was *great*—the divorce would soon be over.

We talked for hours on the phone and exchanged innumerable e-mails, but we met only three times. On our first date, Sofia was skittish, simultaneously flirtatious and distant, demanding and uninterested. On the second, she drove me to the airport for an October presentation in Washington, DC, and we made out passionately in the parking garage, twisting toward and around one another across the huge front seat of her SUV. On the third, she did her best not to look at me while she drove me back from the airport, and I knew—as her e-mail later confirmed—that whatever I had been saying "yes" to with Sofia was over.

That, I decided, was it. I would keep my promise: for the next few months, I would correspond with anyone who wanted to correspond with me and date anyone (though there wasn't anyone) who wanted to date me. But Sofia had taught me two invaluable lessons: I didn't want to be with someone who didn't want to be with me, and I wasn't ready to settle for someone I didn't truly want to be with. I wanted an attractive, educated, verbally dexterous, laughter-, poetry-, Judaism- and God-loving, gainfully employed woman my age, who, though emotionally mature and self-aware, would be crazy about me, the real me, transsexuality, children, poverty, divorce, commuting, illness, and all. If I couldn't find her, I wanted to be alone.

The Isabella Freedman Retreat Center, like the rest of New England that March, was chilly, muddy, and scabbed with patches of dirty, melting snow. I didn't know what I was doing there. By that point—my six months of saying "yes" was up—I didn't know what I was doing anywhere, but I really didn't know what I was doing at the Nehirim Queer Jewish Women's retreat.

For one thing, since transition, I had avoided women-only events as scrupulously as I had when I was a man. Janice Raymond wasn't the only woman who didn't accept the validity of male-to-female transition; at a Sukkot gathering of queer congregants at my local synagogue, one lesbian told me frankly that, after her history of abuse by men, she felt violated when she found trans-women in women-only spaces. Of course, I had been invited to the Nehirim retreat—but the fact that I was invited to help participants learn about transsexuality suggested that some queer Jewish women didn't know what to make of people like me. For the next three days and nights, I would be living among the hundred or so women who had signed up for the weekend. If anyone's definition of woman-hood didn't include me, I was probably going to hear about it.

I was also uncomfortable identifying myself as "queer." Apart from a shared legacy of social oppression, gay and trans people don't have much in common. Sexual orientation is unrelated to gender identity, and, thanks to the gay rights movement, gay people have less and less oppression to share with us. In LGBT settings—the acronym referred to a list of distinct sexual preferences and gender identities—my differentness was implicitly acknowledged. "Queer" was something else again, an umbrella term designed to make a single "us" out of a variety of "thems."

My older daughter understood my discomfort. We were in the car, driving the country highway that connected my apartment with the gas station whose convenience store offered the Subway sandwiches that were the only food she would eat when she was with me. As she unwrapped her six-inch tuna and cheddar sub, I told her about Nehirim.

"Why do they call it a 'queer' women's retreat?" she asked.

"'Lots of people use 'queer' to refer to LGBT people in general."

She frowned and wiped a shred of tuna off her upper lip. "I understand why they would call *you* queer, Daddy, but the only thing queer about gay people is that some people don't accept them."

"I agree, darling," I said. "But—don't tell any gay people that they aren't queer, okay?"

I had never thought of myself as queer—"weird" was the term I used—and, like my daughter, I found it unlikely that, during all these years of feeling "other," I had actually been part of an "us." "LGBT" envisioned community as an alphabet soup of differences; those differences dissolved—or were supposed to dissolve—in the term "queer." But would the lesbians who didn't understand or accept transsexuality in LGBT settings magically feel connected to me at a queer retreat? And, even if they did, was I ready to include myself in the community that queer identity seemed to offer, to give up feeling other and alone?

I didn't know. All I knew was that I felt as uncomfortable presenting myself as queer as I felt presenting myself as a woman. Thank God I was sure I was Jewish.

I was sure of something else, too. Despite months of evidence that I would always be single, I was hoping to find someone at this retreat. Don't be an idiot, I told myself. Every woman at Nehirim, I was sure, would have short hair, jeans, boots that were perfect for hiking in New England in March; most would be coupled, and the few who weren't would be seeking, as every lesbian singles ad announced, soft, medium rare, or well-done butches, rather than a mascara-ed, skirted, formerly male femme.

But femme or butch, they would certainly be looking for a lesbian. I had never lived as a lesbian. No one, not even my lesbian friends, saw me as lesbian; if the occasional public handholding I'd done with Emily and Sofia qualified as a lesbian lifestyle, Stern College would be 100 percent gay.

"Yes, yes," a little voice kept whispering inside me, "but maybe someone will kiss you."

Yes, I muttered. Yes.

The retreat started Friday afternoon. After parent-teacher conferences at my daughters' school, I drove to Smith College to pick up a student who needed a lift to Nehirim and headed south toward Isabella Freedman. It was a raw, changeable March day. Blinding sunshine alternated with clouds and spitting rain. I didn't feel much like talking, so I kept feeding my passenger questions about herself, which she seemed happy to answer.

There were still a couple of hours of daylight left when we pulled into the muddy parking lot and followed the signs to registration. I was dismayed. "Retreat Center" had conjured visions of hot baths and wireless Internet connections; the parking lot put those visions to rest, and, since I lived in western Massachusetts, I wasn't mollified by the rustic mountain charm. I was tired; I was lonely; I was ridiculously dressed for so much mud; I wanted to go home.

The registration line moved quickly. A bright-eyed, short-haired woman startled me by greeting me by name. She flashed an enormous smile, handed me a folder of materials, and told me how to find my room. Things were looking up. I had a room to myself.

I hauled my skirt- and blouse-stuffed suitcase through mud and puddles to my room. I felt as if I had arrived at the wrong sleep-away camp. All around me, women were arriving in SUVs and late-model sedans—real women, real lesbians, all of whom seemed to know or be partnered with other women. My room, though, was clean and quiet and had a private bathroom and shower. There was a bright wood floor, inviting blankets, and two twin beds. I locked the door, hung up my clothes, and plugged in my laptop. Nope—no Internet connection. I sighed, closed my computer, took a deep breath, and reluctantly stepped outside. I didn't want to be late for orientation.

The meeting was in the synagogue, a single large room with a soaring ceiling, clean lines, and a huge window-wall that looked out onto a black, half-iced-over lake surrounded by wooded hills. Ducks skidded into the water and took off in frenzies of flaps and squawks. I was early. Good. Whether or not I was really a woman or really queer, I could help set up chairs.

Orientation was brief and painless. As we were filing out, one of the organizers asked me to read a poem at the Shabbat service that would start in a couple of hours. I said "yes," as usual, hurried back to the safety of my room, lay down on the bed, opened my laptop, and did something I never do during the day: I fell sound asleep.

When I woke, it was dark. Too dark. Shabbat, and Shabbat services, begin at sundown, and it was pitch-black. I hurled myself out of bed and stumbled down the rutted road to the synagogue. I could hear joyous voices in the distance. They were singing the closing prayers. I'd missed the service, blown off my first official duty at the retreat, broken my promise to take whatever life gave me. Now I had to face the community—I had two readings that night—not only as a transsexual but as a transsexual screw-up. "I'm so sorry, Holy One," I muttered over and over, forcing myself to step into the bright, crowded light of the synagogue, trying to smile to everyone while looking for someone to apologize to. I found the woman who had asked me to read as the other women—the women who hadn't screwed up—were streaming out toward dinner. "I'm so sorry," I said. "I never do this. I fell asleep. . . ." "Never mind," she said, smiling. "I bet you needed that sleep."

She was right, but at the moment it seemed that sleep was the worst thing that had ever happened to me, proof—I hadn't even realized I was being tested—that I was unfit to be here, unfit, as I had so often felt, to be anywhere. I wanted to run back to my room and hide, but I had to keep smiling and nodding at the women I had failed. Women smiled back, sorting themselves into conversational clusters, welcoming one another to rapidly filling tables. "I'm so sorry," I kept murmuring to myself, looking futilely for a corner where I could nurse my failure in private.

Elaine, a woman I had met earlier when she had recognized me as a fellow contributor to *Keep Your Wives from Them*, an anthology of Jewish lesbian writings, invited me to join her, her ex-girlfriend Miryam, the editor, and another ex-girlfriend Liz, who had copyedited some of the essays. My heart sank, but I said yes.

Elaine and Miryam sat down across the wide round table, too far for conversation over the dining room din. On one side of me, a woman had strapped a baby into a high chair; she was completely occupied trying to fill the baby's plate with food and retrieve the falling and flying silverware. On the other side of me sat Liz. She was small, trim, natty, and boyish in trousers and button-down shirt. Dark blonde hair, sprinkled with gray; spots of color on her pale cheeks; light blue eyes sharp as a bird's behind blue-templed glasses. I hadn't noticed them when we were introduced—I was too busy feeling like a failure—but, as I settled into the realization that no one else was within conversational distance, her eyes drew mine in; like the blue distances of summer mountains, they seemed to simultaneously blur and point to ranges beyond them.

But there was nothing distant about her gaze. She was not only looking in my direction; she was seeing me.

Some previously dormant muscle twitched, just once, somewhere between stomach and heart.

"I went to Sarah Lawrence, too," I heard myself answering. Liz had arrived the semester after my ex and I had graduated, and had, as eHarmony would say, a lot in common with me. She too had taught at Yeshiva, though uptown, at the boys' college; she had a PhD in literature, loved poetry, and was a writer, finishing her first novel; and, after explaining that she had curated a Romanticism collection at the New York Public Library, she mentioned that she was an overnight volunteer at a synagogue's homeless shelter.

"Really?" I said incredulously. "I am, too!"

"Which one?" she asked.

"Ansche Chesed," I answered.

"Me, too!" We were playing a spectacularly successful round of her favorite game, Jewish geography. Sleeping at a homeless shelter hadn't been on eHarmony's list of ways to meet that special someone. In fact, it was one of the many things in my life that seemed to disqualify me as a romantic partner. But it didn't feel like I was meeting Liz so much as recognizing her, as though she was someone I'd known but somehow forgotten.

"Did you go to NYU for graduate school?" she asked, as eager as I was to add to our list of things in common. I shook my head. "Then I guess we aren't really the same person," she said. Though it was a joke, she sounded disappointed.

Oh, well, I thought, almost regretting that I'd gone to Princeton. But, truth be told, I wasn't sure that I wanted to have a serious relationship—somehow, after fifteen minutes, I was assuming

that this conversation was about having a serious relationship—
with someone who was looking for someone exactly like herself.

Too bad. Liz met so many of my romantic criteria that I had
stopped keeping track, distracted by the kindness of her face, the
openness of her gaze, the witty complications of her syntax. "So,"
I said, as I always do when I meet someone who writes, "tell me
about your book."

She hadn't been working on it much lately, she said. She'd
devoted herself to writing essays about another writer's work. "I'm
obsessed with her," she confessed.

I tried to smile encouragingly, but, even apart from my disappointment and jealousy—I wanted Liz to be obsessing about
me—something felt wrong. "I wonder if writing about her work
is a way of thinking about yours," I said, and then—since we were
speaking PhD to PhD—I quoted Emerson: "'In every work of
genius we recognize our own rejected thoughts: they come back to
us with a certain alienated majesty.'"

The elevator in my stomach lurched upward. Liz was blushing,
looking down and away. She had felt it, too: Emerson's words
entering her, moving inside her, shifting the way she saw herself
and her life. Suddenly, I felt certain that everything I said to Liz
would be the perfect thing to say.

"I'm sorry," I said, though I wasn't sorry in the least. "That
seems to have upset you." But I knew my words hadn't upset her;
they had stirred her, as the intensity of her listening had stirred
me. "I'd like to hear some of the novel, if you feel comfortable
sharing it."

"You didn't upset me," she said, lifting her bright blue eyes to
mine. "I'm just thinking about what you said. Would you really
like to hear some of the novel?"

"Yes," I said. In all the yessing of the past six months, I'd never
said it with such complete conviction.

Dinner was ending; it would soon be time for me to start
presenting and reading. Liz remembers it differently—no doubt
she's right—but I remember standing up together and, following
that strange certainty that had possessed me during our conversation, taking her into my arms. *Yes*, my body said, *this is the one*.

For a moment, my life seemed settled. I could see them all, the decades of love we would share. You're crazy, I told myself, but I knew I wasn't. And then, as we reached the door, it turned out that I was.

"We'll have to get together in New York sometime so you can see the novel," Liz was saying, as though our souls and futures hadn't just fused into a deliriously happy future. She wasn't feeling what I was feeling; the absolute certainty I had felt for the first time in my life had been absolutely wrong.

Okay, I said to myself, and to God. Somehow, when it came to Liz, I couldn't do anything other than say "yes." A moment ago, I had given myself completely to her; now I gave myself just as completely to life without her, because that was the life she wanted. And, yet, though it had been proven utterly false, that strange certainty still filled me. As though my life hadn't just blossomed and died between bussing our trays and walking to the door, I gazed into the blue distance of her eyes. Liz's cheeks—did I see it or feel it?—flushed, and I knew as clearly as though I were reading her thoughts on a teleprompter that her body, like mine, had said "yes."

She came to both of the events I participated in that night. Before I realized that I was thirsty, she brought me a glass of water, and, after the Q&A about transsexuality and poetry, she told me to stop by her room around 4:30 on Shabbat afternoon.

For me, that was a very long wait.

I went to bed dazzled and dazed by two utterly contradictory visions of my life. In one, Liz and I were already living happily ever after. That, I knew, was nuts. The other vision, the suicidal abyss of failure and despair, had been ripening inside me for decades. That was the life that made sense, and, when the Shabbat sun woke me the next morning, that was the life into which I woke. The other vision nagged at me: "What about Liz?" it whispered. But the whisper stilled when Liz wasn't at breakfast—I had been so sure I'd find her there—and, though she was more observant than I was, she wasn't at services, either. The abyss smiled and yawned: it seemed my *bashert*, my divinely ordained true love, wasn't in any hurry to see me again.

The soaring synagogue was filled with women; the hymns of gratitude for the glory of God's creation echoed the glory of the sun on the lake and the flight of ducks and hawks. I wasn't accustomed to congas in shul, but it was one of the most beautiful services I'd ever experienced.

I closed my eyes to the glory and talked to God. I saw it now: my pain was a part, a natural part, of the glorious Creation we were hymning. God's creation was whole and perfect now, and it would be just as whole and perhaps even more perfect once I wasn't here to *kvetch* about it. My six months was over: I was going to kill myself soon, this week, on Wednesday.

I couldn't stop crying. My sweater was soggy, my tissues soaked. At least, thank God, it was over.

That was when I heard the voice of the angel.

Okay, maybe it wasn't an angel. I'd never met an angel before, except for the Hasid on the subway, so I had no basis for comparison, and maybe the voice, despite its otherworldly calm, compassion, and humor—its speech was a kind of laughter—was just another unknown part of me coming to life as I was dying. In any case, I heard it as the voice of an angel, and, as it spoke, I glimpsed a broad-backed presence.

"So you're going to die," the angel said.

"Yes," I said, worried that the angel had come to take my one certainty, the certainty of death, away from me.

"Don't worry," the angel said. "You can die if you want to. Death is your birthright; no one can take it from you. Look, the door of death is right over there. I'll even walk you through it when you're ready. But . . ."

"But?" Naturally, there was a catch. God couldn't be making suicide this easy.

"The door of death is open," the angel assured me. "But right next to it—see?—is the door of life. You've never opened that door, have you?"

"No," I admitted. It was true. Transition had brought me to the door of life, but, no matter how hard I tried, I hadn't managed to open it.

"It's open now," the angel said. "The door of life is open, and, if you want to see what's on the other side, I will lead you through it. I promise that, if you step through that door, you will find something that makes it worth your while on the other side. Don't worry," the angel said gently. "Your precious pain will still be there; so will the door of death. But, if you're going to die anyway— Wednesday, is it?—you might want to take a peek at what you are leaving behind."

I could see them now, ajar before me, the door of death and the door of life. I could walk through either one, and, no matter which I chose, God would be with me. I wouldn't walk alone.

Have I always been so scared to live? I wondered.

"Okay," I said. It was the bravest thing I'd done in almost five decades of existence. "Open the door of life."

On March 13, 2010, shortly before noon, I followed the angel into life. The abyss closed the lips it was licking and sank back into my depths. The angel had told the truth: even now, my pain was still there, my fear, my despair. But something had changed. I wasn't a stranger anymore. This world of sun and mountains, ducks and women, was mine, and I belonged to and in it. No matter how lonely I felt, I no longer walked alone.

Liz didn't know any of that when I appeared at her room at 4:30 to listen to her novel. She didn't see the angel smiling as we awkwardly faced one another.

Then my awkwardness fell away, as the confidence that I couldn't do or say anything wrong filled me again, and the strange knowledge of this stranger—I seemed to hear her thoughts, to know what she was about to do and say, as though we had played out this meeting, our first moments alone together, many times before—unfurled inside me like angel's wings. I wanted to laugh out loud. It seemed so silly that we had to act as though we didn't know each other inside and out, as though neither of us could hear our deeps calling and answering one another.

We thumped down on the narrow camp bed, and I waited for her to say what I knew she would say. "I'm very attracted to you, you know." She blushed.

"I know," I smiled. "I'm very attracted to you, too." Like eighth-graders', our hands groped toward each other, and, as our fingers intertwined, I felt it again, the sense that some part of me was inside her, that our souls were tangled like our fingers. *Yes*, my body kept saying—really, it was quite annoying—*yes*, and I had to swallow to keep that *yes* from rising into an audible *mmmm*, and I turned my back pointedly on the angel, who stood in the shadows, deepening the dark grain of the wood.

And then we kissed, and I couldn't stop the *mmmm*, because, unlike every other kiss in my life, during this one, my tongue and lips and teeth knew exactly what to do.

There, we'd done it—reached, finally, after all these silly years, the moment when our lives would join together. What my soul seemed to have known all my life, what my body had known since I had taken her into my arms the night before, had now officially happened. We sank back awkwardly into separate angles on the bed and did the next thing I knew we would do: Liz read me a chapter of her novel, and I listened, and it was very, very good: her writing, and her mind, and her fingers, and her lips, and the body that was soon pressed against mine, and the body I pressed against hers, and the intertwined souls I could no longer distinguish, and the laughter of the angel, and every blessed particle of the world I touched and tasted in the light-filled darkness on the other side of the door marked "Life."

18
Try

Why did you have to be a girl?" my youngest asks. It's spring
2010, almost three years since I moved out. She's naked
and glistening in a bath whose bubbles are disappearing, surrounded
by a flotilla of toys—plastic animals, a large submarine, a battered
Barbie, an empty vitamin bottle—she alternately buries and resur-
rects from the fragrant white foam. She doesn't realize it, but I look
up to her: unlike me, she's utterly, unapologetically delighted with
herself. She doesn't seem to measure herself against larger, faster,
stronger, defter peers. Her delight in herself is part and parcel of her
boundless delight in existence.

She's grown up a lot since I left my family. She's no longer
an inarticulate, uncritically loving three-year-old; at six, she has
found words for what she's lost. Whenever I see her—now it's only
twice a week—she grills me about the motives and morality of my
transition.

The subject first came up between us when she was five; we
were at the tiny local public library, and we both needed to use the
bathroom. "Why do you use the girls' bathroom, Daddy?" she
asked me. I hesitated. Most parents dread the moment their kids
first ask them about sex; for me, the scariest subject was gender. I
took a deep breath and did the only thing I could think of: I told
her the truth.

"I use the girls' bathroom because, to other people, I look like a girl," I said.

"But why do you look like a girl, Daddy?"

"Well," I said, retreating into the talking-to-a-five-year-old version of my professorial manner, "most boys have boy brains, and most girls have girl brains, but some people, like me, have girl brains in boy bodies or boy brains in girl bodies. It got too hard for me to have a girl brain in a boy body, so now I look like a girl."

She cocked her head critically. "I don't see why people think you look like a girl. Your hair isn't even long." She giggled, and that was the end of our discussion.

But lately she had started to question my identity again, because she had learned something about her own: that she was a child of divorce. Other kids got to live with both their mom and their dad; she could live with only one and occasionally see the other. When she asked me why her mother and I were separated, I explained that, because of my girl brain, I hadn't been able to keep living as a man, and Mama hadn't wanted to live with me if I looked like a woman. Suddenly she understood: the twin cataclysms that had shaped her brief life were connected. After that, each time she saw me, she asked me the questions that would re-enact this discovery and force me to admit my responsibility for her pain.

She spills water from the vitamin bottle into a heap of bubbles, creating a clear space in which I glimpse her skinny legs. "Why did you have to be a girl?" she asks, with a grin that seems wider than her round, curl-topped face. I start to repeat my well-oiled lines about girl brains in boy bodies, but she interrupts. "But *why* did you have to have a girl brain in a boy body?" she demands.

"I don't know," I say. "That's the way God made me."

"Didn't God tell you why?" Her face is still bright with water and suds, but the smile has turned serious. We've veered off script, beyond the ritual accusation and admission of guilt, into the wilderness of life—her life—whose meaning, she is starting to see, is strangely unreadable.

"No," I answer slowly, "God didn't tell me. Or maybe God did, but I didn't understand what God was saying."

"Let's listen," she says. "Listen to what God is saying."

She scrunches her eyes closed and listens. I close my eyes, too, and hear the usual silence. It isn't an answer, because I'm not asking this question. God made me what I am, and what I am, the person who could have come into existence only through the awful birth canal of transsexuality, is what I have always wanted to be. That's been true through the whole agonizing process of transition; it was true during the decades when I pretended there was nothing and no one I wanted to be; it was true when I was my daughter's age, playing in a bubble-filled bath, telling myself that, when the bubbles cleared, my body would miraculously be mine.

I'm asking God a different question: why can't being myself make my children happy the way their being themselves makes me happy? Because, as the silence reminds me, that's not what it means to be a parent. Being a parent means working to turn whatever I am, however hard for me or for them, into an expression of love.

"What did God say?" my daughter demands.

"I can't tell," I say, half-truthfully, knowing she will think I mean that I couldn't tell what God was saying, when I really mean that I can't tell her what the silence said.

She frowns. "You have to listen harder," she says reproachfully, squinting into suds from which she retrieves a small plastic figure: Diego, the animal rescuer. "I rescued Diego," she announces.

"Good work," I say, wondering if love's inquisition is finished for today.

It isn't.

"Why did you have to be a girl when you knew it would be bad for me? Why did you have to leave?"

"I wish I didn't have to be a girl," I say slowly, "when it's so bad for you. Parents aren't supposed to do things they know are bad for their children, but I did—I became a girl even though I knew that you needed me to stay a boy. I knew it would be bad for you and I did it anyway and you are right to be angry because that's not what parents are supposed to do."

Her huge hazel eyes are fixed on mine. Diego, the rescued rescuer, floats forgotten in the little lagoon created by her knees. "So why did you do it, Daddy?" she asks softly. "Why did you leave me?"

"I was so sick," I begin, and then I realize that's not what she's asking. She knows, in a way that my older children can't, that this self is the real me, the me I had to be. She's asking how I could have destroyed her family when I knew how much she would suffer, how I could have given up all the hours and days and years with her, all the meals and bedtime songs and wake-up stories and silly games, the whole lost life, the life of her growing up, we should have lived together.

"I didn't want to leave you," I say, pushing each word out with a thickening tongue. "I hated to leave you, and I hate that I don't live with you anymore, and I wish that I had never left you because it hurts every single day."

"Look, Daddy, Diego is going to rescue the dog," she exclaims. She's smiling now into the wet bubbly world in which everything lost is rescued, in which everything that's drowned will be revealed as the waters drain away. She's gotten what she needed today—proof that, even though our bodies live in separate houses, our hearts are still floating together, in a shining bubble of love and pain.

So now you're happy," my older daughter says, the day after my youngest and I asked God our different questions. It's an accusation, and a fear, and a release from the fear that she will always see my face, as she has for years, splashed with agony. To get some privacy, we're sitting in my latest used car in the latest driveway of the latest of my living spaces. Our lives have improved in the three years since I moved out. The living space isn't a rented bedroom, it's a studio apartment, with a private entrance that opens onto forest and farmland and the quiet gurgle of a creek just visible through the trees. There's no yard, but she loves to clamber down the fallen, moss-slicked trunks and dip her bare feet into the always icy stream.

The divorce was finalized in February, and the kids have gotten used to shuttling among the family house and the house—horse farm, really, with a lovely apple orchard—of my ex's boyfriend and my studio apartment. The divorce settlement left the kids and me with far too little time together each week, but now at least there's a framework to our lives, a patch of not-quite-scorched earth on which we can rebuild our new four-person family. The kids still call me "Daddy," but we're done with the baggy shirts and pants and deep male voice. I no longer hide myself from them, and they have reluctantly become accustomed to—me. Though my son assures me he will never see me as a woman, he's become an LGBT ally at his high school. My older daughter says that, even though she doesn't see me as a woman—"It's confusing," she says, "after all, *Mama* is our mother"—she no longer sees me as a man. My youngest proudly introduces me at school—I've been volunteering weekly in her classroom to get an extra non-court-mandated hour or two in her presence—by saying, "This is my Dad. I know he looks like a girl, but he's my daddy; isn't that funny?"

The kids are still angry, but the shunning is over. My youngest begs for more time with me—"Why can't you live with us again?" she asks, over and over, raw longing ripping open the usual sheen of joy on her face.

My son, almost sixteen and much taller than I am now, tells me little about his life, but he jealously insists on our time together. Whenever we're alone—that's Fridays, mostly, the one day I see him without the girls—he whirls me into his ever-ramifying imaginative realms, parallel universes we roam together, free of the strictures of his life and mine. When the weather is good, he leads me through meadow and forest, training me in the use of elemental powers—he wields fire, I wield water—teaching me to hunt astral creatures and gorge myself on their flesh. Like him, I am immortal, but he is much older, remembering scenes from previous lives that stretch back to Ice Age caves. The pain he experiences daily as he struggles to piece together the jagged jigsaw of his family is barely a whisper in the deep well of lives echoing inside him. The meta-phorical deaths he mourns—the man who was his father, the family that fit together—pale beside the physical deaths of previous bodies that lived through infinitely harder times.

The worst, I told myself, is over, the violent outbursts behind us. We've reached the more or less normal waters of family turmoil, fights about limits and communication and junk food and home-work. We're no longer fighting about what I was and what I am.

But today I know I was wrong. My daughter and I are not only sitting in the car; we're sitting in the aftermath of an emotional earthquake that came close to leveling the life I thought we'd made. It was Monday, and, according to schedule, I picked up the girls at their charter school and drove with them to pick up my son at his charter school. The girls' school is forty-five minutes away from me, my son's a half hour from theirs, and then it's twenty minutes more to return to my place—and I have them for only four hours, door to door. Usually, the drives are pleasant enough, but that day the kids were quarreling, and, when I tried to stop them from screaming at one another, they started screaming at me. The screaming grew louder and louder, the substance of the argument smaller and smaller, until we were screaming at one another about screaming at one another.

"Let me out," my son demanded when we were a mile or so away from my apartment. "I'll take the bus home."

"No," I said. "This is my time with you."

My older daughter leapt to my son's defense. "He's old enough to go home alone. He takes the bus all the time."

My youngest was sobbing loudly; none of us would listen to what she was saying. I tried to comfort her while fighting with my son, telling my older daughter to mind her own business, and guiding the car along the twisting country road. It's hard to be comforting when you have to scream to be heard, and, now that I no longer used my lower registers, I wasn't very good at screaming. The car shook with sobs and shrieks and my son's deep rumbles of rage.

When I pulled into the driveway, I thought the crisis would be over: the kids would jump out, and rage and pain would disappear into fresh air, sunshine, and the lure of afternoon snacks and TV. Instead, things got much, much worse. My son stalked off down the driveway. "Where are you going?" I demanded. "To the bus stop," he threw back over his shoulder. "I'm going home, and you can't stop me." My youngest's howls grew louder, and my older daughter stopped defending my son's right to leave me and started wailing, "He's leaving me alone. . . . He's leaving me. . . ."

Her words disintegrated into gusts of tears. The youngest was clearly terrified: her hyperverbal sister couldn't speak, her big brother had left her behind. The twin pillars that supported her world, regardless of where she found herself in the bitter no-man's-land between her parents, had collapsed. She sobbed as though someone were taking a hammer to her heart.

Pieces of the family I thought I'd finally cobbled back together were flying in all directions; we were losing one another again. I tried to act like a parent, speaking softly but firmly to my youngest until her wails quieted, then turning my attention to my older daughter, whose tears had devolved into animal howls of loss. "He's not gone," I said. "We're going to bring him back."

I backed out of the driveway and drove toward my son. He had covered a surprising amount of the mile and a half that separated him from the bus stop, walking with a crook-backed fury I'd never seen in him before. He didn't turn when I honked and called. "I have to go get him," I told my sobbing daughters. "But we'll both be back soon." "He's left me," my older daughter wailed. "He's—"

I closed the car door on my daughters' anguish and ran to catch up with my son. "Stop," I shouted, as scared as I was angry. I'd spent plenty of time on the other side of father-son power struggles, but I'd never fought with my son before, and my father's example wasn't much to build on.

"I don't have to stop," he said. "You don't have authority over me." He had turned to face me, glowering down in rage. I looked up at him, conscious of how much stronger and heavier he was. If he was determined to leave, I couldn't physically stop him. "I don't consider you my parent anymore," he said flatly.

"Do you still consider Mama your parent?"

"Yes."

"Okay," I said as evenly as I could. "But, however you feel, legally you are still a minor, and I am still your parent. If I called them, the police would bring you back."

"Are you going to call the police on me?" he challenged.

"There's a more important question," I said. "Look at your sisters. They think that you've left them. You may want to walk away from me, but they need you to come back."

His eyes swerved from me to the girls howling—their screams were audible twenty feet away—in the car, and his face twisted as love wrestled with rage. As always with him, love won. "I'm not going back to you," he said stiffly. "I'm going back to them." He opened the car door and slid in beside my youngest. "Look," I said to my daughters, "he's come back to you." Their sobs slowly quieted as I drove the half-mile home.

Stiffly, silently, we settled into a shattered semblance of the routines we'd developed for Monday afternoons. I gave the girls food as they stared at the TV. My son set up his laptop and turned his back on us all, then closed the lid and summoned me outside. We faced each other warily on the narrow walk that separated my apartment from the forest. I steeled myself for the next round of rage and rejection. After all, as that therapist had told me long ago, that was my raison d'être: I had to stay alive so that my children could reject me.

My son looked down at me sadly, with a maturity I'd never seen in his face before. "I think there are a lot of unspoken feelings between us," he said after a long silence. A new feeling pushed its way through the crowd inside me: pride. I could never have said something like that to my father. "I can't trust you," my son continued. "I still don't know who you really are or what you might be hiding."

So much for my fantasies that we'd put my transition behind us. For him, it seemed, the shock was as fresh as the day I'd moved out. For all the hours we'd spent running through forests together, I was still an unpredictable stranger, someone who might at any moment turn out to be someone other than the father he knew and loved. But, even if his feelings about my transition hadn't changed, he had: as he fought his way through love and rage, he had grown into a man strong enough and sure enough to tell me that, even though he neither trusted nor knew me, he wouldn't walk away.

So now you're happy," my older daughter says as we sit in the driveway, questioning and accusing and hopeful that, for me, all this pain has been worth it. We're side by side in the front seat of the car, watching a bird fly in and out of a nest built above a metal eagle that decorates the landlady's garage door. It's quiet here, away from the constant three-way fight for my attention that will resume the minute we return to the apartment. Life seems simpler, safer, seen through the windshield: a garage, a nest, and a bird that, for all her fluttering, isn't going anywhere.

"No," I say, though when I'm with Liz—we've seen each other only a few times since the women's retreat—I've begun to feel that I am. "I'm not happy."

"But isn't that why you left us? So you could be happy?" There's no edge to her voice now, none of the sarcasm that cuts us both so deeply. She really believes that I left them to be happy: that's the story they tell themselves to explain the inexplicable tragedy of my transition. It isn't true, but I've been reluctant to challenge it, because I know that story restores some of the clarity, the certainty, that my transition destroyed, channeling the anger that threatens to overwhelm them, reducing complicated, painful questions about my motivations and choices to a single, simple sentence: I left my children to be happy. My happiness mattered more to me than their misery. I don't need them; I don't want them; I can be happy without them.

As angry as the happiness she imagined made her, my daughter also found it comforting: she wanted her tormented, tormenting father to be happy, because, for all the pain my fecklessness had caused her, she couldn't help loving me. And, because she couldn't help loving me, my happiness made her sad, because the life she thought made me happy didn't seem to include her.

I'd first glimpsed that tangle of love and sadness last summer. The violence of her rage had abated, and I began acclimating her to the sight of me dressed as a woman by showing her pictures on my computer. My son had glanced at them and grunted, "Not as bad as I thought." My daughter, though, stared in silence, tears welling in her wide brown eyes and spilling down her freckled cheeks.

"Why are you crying?" I asked her.

"Because I've never seen that light on your face," she murmured. "Even when you look at us."

"Yes," I answered. "That's one reason I want you to see me as myself—to share that light with you."

But whatever light I'd shared with my children hadn't been enough to steer us clear of Monday's maelstrom.

Neither had the story that I left them to be happy. But how could a ten-year-old understand that the happiness—and it was happiness—of living with my children as a shell of a man was harder to bear than the agony of living as a woman without them? It was bad enough for my daughter to think that I would leave her to be happy; wouldn't it be worse for her to realize that I had left her even though I knew that leaving meant misery?

It didn't make sense, even to me. But it was the truth.

"I didn't transition to be happy," I tell her. "I knew that I couldn't be happy without you."

"Then why did you transition?" she asks quietly.

"I transitioned because when I was living as a man, I couldn't be really alive."

We're clinging to one another now across the emergency brake that separates our seats.

"And are you now?" she whispers, as though afraid to hear the answer. "Are you really alive?"

She's squeezing my hand so hard it hurts.

"Yes," I tell her, releasing a breath I've held for two and a half years. "Now I'm really alive."

We're all crammed into the car now, older daughter ensconced beside me in the front, son stuffed into the back beside the youngest's booster seat. Our lives, as usual, are changing. My son has discovered a passion for the law. When school is out, the girls will go to Venice for six weeks with their mother; my son has decided to stay with me. I don't know it yet, but we'll have to move shortly after he arrives. All of us are graduating, getting bigger, moving on.

It's a late spring evening, the sun gone but the sky still glowing along the darkened humps of the mountains that ring this valley. Where it's darkest, you can just see Venus. It might be the same day I told my older daughter I hadn't transitioned to be happy, but it might be another Monday evening when the sadness of parting— I'm driving them back to the house, their house, Mama's house, home—is suffused with the setting sun of pleasure in one another.

My son didn't complain when my older daughter took the front seat; he and I exchanged the kind of look, bemused and resigned and tender, that my wife and I used to exchange when surrendering to the implacable will of one of the children. My youngest clambered happily into her booster seat and is leaning affectionately toward her brother, turning the pages of a book she suddenly knows how to read. And my older daughter hasn't plugged into her MP3 player or started blasting the car radio or snarling at her siblings or at me. The rage that often possesses her when it's time for us to leave has given way this time to a twilight penumbra of sorrow, acceptance.

We back out of the driveway into the wide suburban street and slide slowly toward the gilded mountains in the distance. As she often does on evenings like this, my older daughter puts on Sheryl Crow's greatest hits, forwards to Crow's cover of "The First Cut Is the Deepest," and commands us to sing. My youngest calls this song "Try," because, whenever we sing along with it, I muff the bridge to the first chorus, yowling the word "try" after the line "Try to love again" even though Crow doesn't. I doubt that it occurs to any of us that this song is the anthem of our fledgling family, that our fitful sense of home, a home without permanent structure, is built on hearts that someone—me, their mother, God, gender—has torn apart, that, for all the love that fills the car, every time we see one another, we have to try to love again.

Tr—i—i—I yodel, right on or, rather, off cue, and they all join in and shout me down: "Daddy!" This is the play-therapy version of the times, like that Monday, when their separate rages fuse and they close ranks against me, attacking from all sides in a desperate attempt to defend their family from my stubborn, stupid need to be really alive. Now, they joyfully shout me down, knowing I will make the same mistake again, knowing that, even when I come in at the right time, my screechy voice will make it seem like the wrong time, knowing that this time the discord I sow and their screams of disapproval will bring us closer, rather than driving us apart, knowing that they are telling me that I am, we are, family. I'm the someone who's torn their hearts apart, and I'm the one they still want by their sides, drying their tears, the one whom, if I want—and they know I want this more than I want anything—they will try to love again.

*Tr—i—i—*Now we are all coming in together at the wrong time, and that makes it the right time. This is *our* anthem, after all, of failed first love and love that cannot fail because, as we have all been forced to learn amid the wreckage and resurrection of our family, there is no difference between trying to love and loving. The love that binds our lives together cannot be frayed by happiness or pain: even when we are torn apart, love goes on, forever.

LIVING OUT

Gay and Lesbian Autobiographies

David Bergman, Joan Larkin, and Raphael Kadushin
SERIES EDITORS

Two Novels: "Development" and "Two Selves"
Bryher

The Hurry-Up Song: A Memoir of Losing My Brother
Clifford Chase

In My Father's Arms: A True Story of Incest
Walter A. de Milly III

Midlife Queer: Autobiography of a Decade, 1971–1981
Martin Duberman

*The Man Who Would Marry Susan Sontag: And Other Intimate Literary
    Portraits of the Bohemian Era*
Edward Field

Body, Remember: A Memoir
Kenny Fries

Travels in a Gay Nation: Portraits of LGBTQ Americans
Philip Gambone

Widescreen Dreams: Growing Up Gay at the Movies
Patrick E. Horrigan

The End of Being Known: A Memoir
Michael Klein

Through the Door of Life: A Jewish Journey between Genders
Joy Ladin

*The Last Deployment: How a Gay, Hammer-Swinging Twentysomething
    Survived a Year in Iraq*
Bronson Lemer

Eminent Maricones: Arenas, Lorca, Puig, and Me
Jaime Manrique

Body Blows: Six Performances
Tim Miller

1001 Beds: Performances, Essays, and Travels
Tim Miller

Cleopatra's Wedding Present: Travels through Syria
Robert Tewdwr Moss

Taboo
Boyer Rickel

Secret Places: My Life in New York and New Guinea
Tobias Schneebaum

Wild Man
Tobias Schneebaum

Sex Talks to Girls: A Memoir
Maureen Seaton

Outbound: Finding a Man, Sailing an Ocean
William Storandt

CPSIA information can be obtained
at www.ICGtesting.com
Printed in the USA
BVHW040214240222
630000BV00013B/428